THE
ULTIMATE
QUIZ
BOOK

Also by Norman G. Hickman

The Quintessential Quiz Book
The Quintessential Quiz Book 2
(with Minnie Hickman)
Quizzes for Whizzes
(with Minnie Hickman)

THE
ULTIMATE
QUIZ
BOOK

by
Norman G. Hickman

E.P. Dutton, Inc. / New York

Published in the United States by E.P. Dutton, Inc.
2 Park Avenue, New York, N.Y. 10016

Library of Congress Cataloging in Publication Data

Hickman, Norman G.
  The ultimate quiz book.

  Summary: Ten questions each, with answers, on 143
different topics including automobiles, British cooking,
curious derivations, television, U.S. presidents, and
World War II.
  1. Questions and answers. [1. Questions and answers]
I. Title.
AG195.H53 1984   031'.02   84-10173

ISBN: 0-525-24277-5
Published simultaneously in Canada by Fitzhenry & Whiteside, Ltd.,
Toronto.

COBE

10 9 8 7 6 5 4 3 2 1

To Minnie, best of wives

I am most grateful to Arthur Prager, who helped with the overall form of the book, and to Timothy Dickinson for his keen editorial eye and expertise in recondite lore.

Other friends and authorities in various fields who have made invaluable suggestions include Morgan P. Ames, Father John Andrew, William E. Appleyard, Roy Bartolomei, Anthony Montague Browne, Dudley F. Cates, Pamela W. Combemale, Robert B. Cooke, Chandler Cowles, Wilbur L. Cross III, Ormonde de Kay, W. Allston Flagg, Jr., J. Russell Forgan, Judy Frank, Mary C. James, R. Campbell James, Benigna Kirsten, Alexander McIlvaine, Coleman W. Morton, David M. Norman, Sir Ronald L. Prain, Lucy Randolph, Dr. Edgar A. Riley, R. Stockton Rush, Jr., Richard L. Russell, William R. Salomon, Toby Shaw, John Train, Mimi C. J. Verine and Sue Younghusband.

I also wish to acknowledge the assistance provided by the Library of the Academy of Motion Picture Arts and Sciences, the American Museum of Natural History, the Smithsonian Institution, the Royal Oak Foundation, and especially the Telephone Information Services of the New York Public Library.

To Elizabeth Ferris, who so ably and cheerfully coped with the typescript, I owe my deepest appreciation.

The reader should be advised that any errors or typos found in this book have been put there intentionally as a public service for those who enjoy finding fault with something.

Lasciate ogni speranza voi ch'entrate!
(Abandon all hope you who enter!)

—*Dante*

All is grist that comes to his mill.

—*Folk Saying*

Writing a long and substantial book is like having a friend and companion at your side to whom you can always turn for comfort and whose society becomes more attractive as a new and widening field of interest is lighted in the mind.

—*Winston S. Churchill*

There is no sin but ignorance.

—*Christopher Marlowe*

For all knowledge and wonder (which is the seed of knowledge) is an impression of pleasure itself.

—*Francis Bacon*

As a general rule, the most successful man in life is the man who has the best information.

—*Benjamin Disraeli*

A book may be amusing with numerous errors, or it may be very dull without a single absurdity.

—*Oliver Goldsmith*

Every man has a right to his own opinion, but no man has a right to be wrong in his facts.

—*Bernard M. Baruch*

Informed people make wise decisions.

—*Wendell Willkie*

Make him [the reader] laugh and he will think you a trivial fellow, but bore him in the right way and your reputation is assured.

—*W. Somerset Maugham*

Never pursue literature as a trade.

—*Samuel Taylor Coleridge*

CATEGORIES

"IN THE BEGINNING"

1. According to the Gospel of St. John, what was "in the beginning"?

2. When asked how to start in Lewis Carroll's *Alice's Adventures in Wonderland*, how did the King of Hearts respond?

3. Who was referred to as the First Gentlemen of Europe, and why was he so styled?

4. Why does this verse logically appear here?

   > Sumer is icumen in,
   > Lhude sing cuccu!
   > Groweth sed, and bloweth med,
   > And springeth the wude nu—
   > Sing cuccu!

5. This notice appears as preface to what famous novel: "Persons attempting to find a motive in this narrative will be prosecuted; persons attempting to find a moral in it will be banished; persons attempting to find a plot in it will be shot"?

6. What did the words "The Eagle has landed" signify?

7. For what is Earl Winfield Spencer most remembered?

8. Which former bank clerk and cousin of historian Samuel Eliot Morison wrote the following?

   > And so each venture
   > Is a new beginning, a raid on the inarticulate
   > With shabby equipment always deteriorating
   > In the general mess of imprecision of feeling,
   > Undisciplined squads of emotion.

9. Why did Louise Brown hit the world's headlines in July 1978?

10. Which former best-selling novel ends with Dr. Spielvogel saying, "Now vee may perhaps to begin. Yes?"?

"IN THE BEGINNING"

1. "In the beginning was The Word, and The Word was with God, and The Word was God" (John 1:1).

2. "'Begin at the beginning,' the King said gravely, 'and go on till you come to the end: then stop.'"

3. The Prince Regent, later George IV of England, because of his gracious manner and deportment in public.

4. The "Cuckoo Song" was recorded around 1250 by John Foster, a monk of Reading Abbey, and is the first surviving poem written in English understandable today.

5. *Huckleberry Finn,* by Mark Twain.

6. They constitute the first message sent from the moon. When Apollo II reached the moon in July 1969, Neil Alden Armstrong reported from the lunar module: "Houston, Tranquility Base here. The Eagle has landed."

7. A U.S. naval officer, he was the first husband of Bessie Wallis Warfield, who eventually caused the abdication of Edward VIII and became the Duchess of Windsor.

8. T.S. Eliot, in "East Coker," one of his *Four Quartets*.

9. English-born Louise Brown was the world's first test-tube baby.

10. *Portnoy's Complaint,* by Philip Roth.

AIRBORNE

1. When the Montgolfier brothers' paper-and-linen balloon first took off in the summer of 1783 from Annonay, France, who were the first passengers?

2. Two classic planes from World War I—the Spad XIII and the Fokker Triplane DR-1—were immortalized by whom?

3. Explain the significance of the sinking of the American cruiser *Frankfort* and the former German battleship *Ostfriesland* off the Virginia coast in July 1921.

4. To fliers, what is a stuffed cloud?

5. For what purpose are VTOL and STOL aircraft designed? Explain the meaning of these terms.

6. According to Gilbert Keith Chesterton, why can angels fly?

7. In airplane construction, what is meant by redundancy?

8. The Nightingale is a special airplane of the U.S. Air Force. For what purpose is it used?

9. In 1983 a French "château" flew over Washington, D.C., to celebrate 200 years of balloon flight and inaugurate a new series of postage stamps honoring the anniversary of the first balloon flight. Who flew the "château"?

10. Which fictional anti-hero flew a second-hand, single-engined Bresthaven Dragonfly III monoplane all the way around the world without stopping, carrying with him only a gallon of bootleg gin and six pounds of salami, and placing full reliance upon floating auxiliary gas tanks invented by a mad New Hampshire professor of astronomy?

1. A rooster, a duck and a sheep were the first passengers. The sheep broke a leg in the landing.

2. The opposing aces Eddie Rickenbacker and the Red Baron, Manfred von Richthofen.

3. The exercise showed the vulnerability of capital ships to aerial bombardment. The dramatic show of air power was led by Brigadier General Billy Mitchell in a flight of open-cockpit DH-4 planes. He was later court-martialed for publicly criticizing military leaders for their neglect of air power.

4. A cloud with a mountain inside it.

5. These aircraft are used for short-haul traffic between small airports that require planes capable of operating from minimum length runways. VTOL stands for Vertical Take-Off and Landing; STOL means Short Take-Off and Landing.

6. "Angels fly because they take themselves lightly."

7. Redundancy means that, for safety's sake, if one system fails another takes over.

8. A Nightingale is a C-9, called a Medevac (Medical Evacuation), a hospital plane with a red cross painted on its tail. It is named for Florence Nightingale, the heroic British nurse in the Crimean War.

9. The publisher Malcolm Forbes, an avid balloonist and sportsman, flew the 105-foot-wide "Château de Balleroy," a hot-air balloon built in 1982 as a scale replica of his 350-year-old French mansion, which serves as a museum of ballooning.

10. Jack ("Pal") Smurch, an erstwhile mechanic's helper in a small garage in Westfield, Iowa. According to James Thurber's "The Greatest Man in the World," Smurch was "a congenital hooligan mentally and morally unequipped to cope with his own prodigious fame." To save the country from inevitable embarrassment, Smurch was pushed out of a window with the assent of the President.

ALL THINGS LARGE AND SMALL

1. Which of the United States contains a state park that is larger than any of the national parks?

2. What are the two smallest things mentioned in the Bible?

3. "Imprisoned in every fat man a thin one is wildly signaling to be let out" was an observation made by which English writer?

4. Name the smallest, yet historically notable, dependent territory in the British Commonwealth.

5. Who was forced to hold up a particularly heavy load and gave his name to both a range of mountains and an often consulted reference book?

6. Can you name the largest hotel in the world?

7. In a novel by Charles Dickens, whose father had the misfortune to be responsible for an uncompleted contract with the government's Circumlocution Office, and as a result had been so long in Southwark's Marshalsea Prison for debtors that he became known as the "Father of the Marshalsea"?

8. What is the largest lake in Europe?

9. William Howard Taft was the stoutest of U.S. Presidents, weighing at one time as much as 354 pounds. At a dinner the orator and politician Chauncey Depew glanced significantly at Taft's girth and blandly inquired what he intended to call the child when it was born. How did Taft reply to this gibe at his portliness?

10. Corn Off The Cob, a Thoroughbred owned by the Miami sportsman Ted Gary, was retired to stud and sired a colt within a year. Then the question was what to name the yearling. How was this solved?

ALL THINGS LARGE AND SMALL

1. New York, whose Adirondack Park, with forests on all horizons, will be kept "forever wild."

2. The widow's mite and the wicked flea. "And there came a certain poor widow, and she threw in two mites, which made a farthing" (Mark 12:42), and "The wicked flee where no man pursueth: but the righteous are as bold as a lion" (Proverbs 12:1).

3. The rather portly Cyril Connolly in *The Unquiet Grave*, paraphrasing his schoolmate, the gaunt George Orwell, who in *Coming Up for Air* wrote: "I'm fat, but I'm thin inside. Has it ever struck you that there's a thin man inside every fat man, just as they say there's a statue inside every block of stone?"

4. Pitcairn Island, a dot in the South Pacific between Tahiti and Easter Island, which was settled in 1790 by mutineers from H.M.S. *Bounty* and their Tahitian women.

5. The Titan Atlas, who, when the Titans were defeated by the Olympians, was condemned to hold the sky on his shoulders for all eternity—a mythical explanation of why the sky does not fall. The word atlas comes from his representations on 16th-century books of maps.

6. The Hotel Rossiya in Moscow, which has accommodations for 5,350 guests.

7. The father of Amy Dorrit, or "Little Dorrit," who was born in the Marshalsea and whose diminutive status is compensated by greatness of heart.

8. Not the Lake of Geneva (or Lac Léman), but Lake Ladoga in Karelia, northeast of Leningrad. It is 130 miles long and 80 miles wide.

9. "If it's a girl, I shall name her for my wife. If it's a boy, I shall call him Junior. But if it is, as I suspect, just gas, I will call it Chauncey Depew."

10. The name Niblets was approved by all concerned.

ANCIENT TIMES

1. The anthropologist Mary Leakey discovered hominid footprints that she estimates to be 3.6 million years old. Evidently made by two bipeds on a stroll, the prints were preserved in a tract of hardened volcanic ash. Which lines of Henry Wadsworth Longfellow come to mind?

2. Why was Rameses II long considered by Egyptologists to have been a very great pharaoh?

3. A Pyrrhic victory is one won at ruinous cost. Who "won" the first one?

4. What had Julius Caesar just done in 49 B.C. when, according to Plutarch, he quoted the proverb "Alea iacta est" ("The die is cast"), why did he send this terse message and what did it start?

5. Where would one have to go to find the remnants of the Roman Empire's principal northern boundary?

6. Of whom was it said, "When they make a wilderness, they call it peace"?

7. What was the strange and melancholy coincidence in the two names of the last Roman Emperor of the West?

8. The speeches of Aeschines and Demosthenes had different effects on people. When Aeschines had finished speaking, the people said, "How well he spoke." But when Demosthenes had finished, what did the people say?

9. Which barbarian was called "the scourge of God," and over whom did he rule?

10. Who parodied Percy Bysshe Shelley's celebrated poem "Ozymandias" as follows?

> And on the pedestal these words appear:
> "My name is Ozymandias, King of Kings!
> Look on my works, ye Mighty, and despair!"
> Also the names of Emory P. Gray,
> Mr. and Mrs. Dukes and Oscar Baer
> Of 17 West 4th Street, Oyster Bay.

1. This verse from Longfellow's "A Psalm of Life":

   > Lives of great man all remind us
   > We can make our lives sublime.
   > And, departing, leave behind us
   > Footprints in the sands of time.

2. He substituted his name for that of the real builder on an enormous number of structures and monuments.

3. The term derives from Pyrrhus, King of Epirus, who, after defeating the Romans at the Battle of Asculum in Apulia in 279 B.C., declared, "One more such victory and I am lost."

4. He had crossed the Rubicon River in northern Italy, which marked the boundary between Cisalpine Gaul, of which he was governor, and ancient Italy, which was controlled by his enemies. Rome had bidden him to stop sending long-winded accounts of his military activities. This precipitated a civil war from which Caesar emerged victorious.

5. To the northern part of England, just below the Scottish border, where Hadrian's Wall, built from A.D. 122 to 126, extends some 73 miles from Solway Firth to Wallsend on the river Tyne. It is one of the most significant remains of the Roman domination of the island.

6. The Romans. The historian Tacitus reported a British leader, Calgacus, saying this to the Caledonians before the Battle of Mons Graupius in Scotland in A.D. 83.

7. His name was Romulus Augustulus. Thus he bore the names of both the first Roman king and the first Roman emperor (diminutive form).

8. "Let us march."

9. Attila, the king of the Huns, who were Asian nomads. Owing their successes to small, rapid horses, they overran a large part of Eurasia in the 5th century.

10. Morris Bishop, in "Ozymandias Revisited," from his book *Paramount Poems*.

AND SO FORTH

1. Name the two countries separated by the Denmark Strait.

2. In the making of champagne, what are meant by the terms *crus* and *cuvée*?

3. Which book, written by a woman, has a woman's name as its title and is told in the first person by a woman whose Christian name is never revealed?

4. Can you identify a royal princess who became an archduchess and then an empress of a country not in Europe?

5. Why is this old English nursery rhyme indeed remarkable?

> Lucy Locket lost her pocket.
> Kitty Fisher found it;
> There was not a penny in it,
> But a ribbon round it.

6. What three characteristics do the people of Charleston, South Carolina, share with the Chinese?

7. An embarrassing event overtook the flagship of Henry VIII's navy, the *Mary Rose,* named after the king's sister, in 1545 when she sailed to meet the French fleet. Can you describe what happened?

8. In which group of Greek islands would you find Andros, Melos, Naxos and Tenos?

9. The Iditarod, a canine event, takes place in Alaska. What is it?

10. A philtrum and a tittle are common things seen every day, but you would only see a thole if you went boating. What are they?

AND SO FORTH

1. Iceland and Kalaatdlit Nunaat (Land of the People), the new name for the island nation of Greenland. Both countries are former Danish possessions.

2. *Crus* refers to the different wines to be used in the blend, and *cuvée* to the actual blending.

3. *Rebecca,* by Daphne du Maurier. The story is narrated by a woman known simply as the "second Mrs. de Winter."

4. Carlotta, the daughter of Leopold I of the Belgians, married the Archduke Maximilian of Austria, who later became Emperor Maximilian of Mexico.

5. The two ladies, celebrated courtesans in the time of the lascivious Charles II, are the only two prostitutes to appear in a nursery rhyme. Lucy Locket was the inspiration for Lucy Lockit in John Gay's *The Beggar's Opera.* The song "Kitty Fisher's Locket" provided British troops with the music for "Yankee Doodle Dandy."

6. They eat rice, speak a foreign language and worship their ancestors.

7. The *Mary Rose* foundered in full view of the king at Southsea Castle. Part of her hull was raised in 1982 and is now being restored at Portsmouth, where she will become the world's oldest complete warship to be seen.

8. The Cyclades, a name originally used to indicate that these islands, among others, formed a rough circle around Delos, the seat of the treasury of the Delian League.

9. The Iditarod is the most grueling sled-dog race in the world, covering 1,100 miles from Anchorage to Nome and lasting about twelve days. The sleds and drivers are pulled by teams of specially bred dogs, half husky and half Labrador.

10. A philtrum is the cleft on your upper lip under your nose and a tittle is the dot over the letter i. A thole is another name for an oarlock, the fulcrum holding an oar in place while rowing.

ANIMAL KINGDOM

1. According to John Milton in *Paradise Lost,* how did the elephant amuse Adam and Eve?

2. The name of which animal derives from the Malay name for "man of the forest"?

3. Which is the fastest land animal over a short distance? Over a sustained distance?

4. What is the difference between a dormouse and a titmouse, and how did their names come about?

5. Who offered this opinion of the Arabian camel?

   > The Dromedary is a cheerful bird:
   > I cannot say the same about the Kurd.

6. What did Hamlet of Dublin have in common with this statement: "Mr. Speaker, I smell a rat; I see him forming in the air and darkening the sky; but I'll nip him in the bud"?

7. Which animal had a name that means simply, "Look!"?

8. Which animal, other than man, can you easily teach to stand on its head?

9. Which famous writer observed, "It was like feasting with panthers; the danger was half the excitement," and to whom was he referring?

10. With what animal did Prime Minister Churchill compare his successor Clement Attlee?

1. In *Paradise Lost,* Milton wrote:

    . . . th' unwieldy elephant
    To make them mirth us'd all his might, and
        wreathed
    His lithe proboscis.

2. The orangutan, or *Pongo pygmaeus,* of Borneo and Sumatra.

3. The cheetah, with a probable maximum speed of over 60 m.p.h. The pronghorn antelope of the western United States can average 55 m.p.h. for half a mile and 35 m.p.h. for four miles.

4. The dormouse is a small rodent which, being nocturnal and hibernatory, is often found sleeping—hence its name, from the French *dormir,* to sleep. The titmouse is a small bird of mouse-gray plumage, tit being dialect for small.

5. Hilaire Belloc, in *The Bad Child's Book of Beasts*.

6. They are the two most famous Irish bulls. Hamlet of Dublin is famous for siring 75,000 calves by artificial insemination. The quotation, an Irish bull in the sense of a manifest contradiction or ludicrous inconsistency unperceived by the speaker, is attributed to Sir Boyle Roche. In the words of Oscar Wilde, "The Irish bull was always pregnant."

7. The indri, a large lemur of the Malagasy Republic, formerly Madagascar, having silky fur and a short tail. When the natives cried *Indri!* (Look!) after sighting the lemur, the French naturalist Pierre Sonnerat mistakenly assumed this to be the animal's name.

8. The elephant can be taught to stand on its head. In putting words to Camille Saint-Saëns' *Carnival of the Animals,* which the composer called a "grand zoological fantasy," Ogden Nash wrote:

    If you think the elephant preposterous
    You've probably never seen a rhinosterous.

9. Oscar Wilde, whose homosexual association with "common lads," as he called them, led to his imprisonment in Reading Gaol.

10. "A sheep in sheep's clothing."

ASK ME ANOTHER

1. What was Thomas Jefferson's rather bitter comment on government officeholders?

2. How did Canon Spooner, dean and later warden of New College, Oxford, announce a hymn in the college chapel?

3. Name the only game in which the defensive team always has possession of the ball, the offensive team can score without even having touched the ball, and the game itself is timeless.

4. Can you explain what powers an extraordinary airplane that has neither fuel, batteries nor human propulsion?

5. An actor once boasted to Oliver Herford, "I'm a smash hit. Why, yesterday I had them glued to their seats." What was Herford's comment?

6. How did Ambrose Bierce cynically define marriage in *The Devil's Dictionary*?

7. It literally dropped like manna from heaven, making which small nation the richest on earth on a per capita basis?

8. What was Woody Allen's observation about mortality, and how did an estate lawyer define it?

9. The celebrated Oxford scholar A.L. Rowse recently claimed that Shakespeare's "dark lady of the sonnets" was the fascinating half-Italian Emilia Lanier (née Bassano), who was married to one of the queen's musicians. Name two famous American writers who are descendants of this union.

10. What did the man say when he heard the commandment about adultery read in church?

ASK ME ANOTHER

1. "Few die and none resign."

2. "Kinquering Kongs Their Titles Take" instead of "Conquering Kings Their Titles Take." Spooner was famous for the unintentional transposition of (usually initial) word sounds that gave rise to the term Spooner-ism. He once referred to the "assissination of Sassero" in a Roman history lecture.

3. Baseball.

4. The sun. The plane, called the Solar Challenger, is powered by wing and tail panels of photo-voltaic cells and designed by the same man, Paul McCready, who built the first man-powered plane, the Gossamer Con-dor, and the Gossamer Albatross, which flew across the English channel with human propulsion.

5. "How clever of you to think of it."

6. "Marriage—a master, a mistress and two slaves, making in all, two." Bierce also penned these lines:

   They stood before the altar and supplied
   The fire themselves with which their fat was fried.

7. Nauru, a small island state in the southwestern Pacific, whose phosphate deposits, resulting from birds' guano, has annual sales of $125 million, or about $25,000 for each of the Nauran citizens. Oil sheikdoms do not do as well per capita.

8. Woody Allen said, "It's not death I'm afraid of. I just don't want to be there when it happens." The estate lawyer defined death as "the penultimate commercial transaction consummated by probate."

9. The poet Sidney Lanier and the playwright Tennessee (Thomas Lanier) Williams.

10. "*Now* I remember where I left my umbrella."

AUTOMOBILES

1. What was the first automobile company in the United States?

2. The first competitive event for motorcars was held in France in 1894, a time trial rather than a true race. Between which two cities was it run, and who was the winner?

3. Which piece of equipment, now a standard part of any car, was offered as an option up until 1909?

4. A limousine is now generally thought of as a large sedan with a glass partition between the driver and passengers. What was it originally, and how did its name derive?

5. Charles Stewart and Frederick Henry were the Christian names of which two early car manufacturers? How did the cars they built serve with distinction in one particular theater of war from 1916 to 1918?

6. How does this verse, sung by a celebrated early motorist, end?

    > The motorcar went Poop, poop, poop,
    >   As it raced along the road,
    > Who was it steered it into the pond?

7. Why was it alleged that Charles E. ("Engine Charlie") Wilson, former Chairman of General Motors, developed the automatic transmission?

8. Which refulgent fictional villain drove a primrose yellow Rolls-Royce with the license plate AU-1, and what children's book about a car did his creator write?

9. The United States has adopted the international system for traffic signs, which uses both different shapes and colors. What does a red circle with a diagonal red line through it indicate?

10. When a man was ticketed for parking beside a sign that said: "No Stoping," how did he prove his innocence?

AUTOMOBILES

1. The Duryea Motor Wagon Company. Founded in 1895, it survived until 1918.

2. From Paris to Rouen. The winner was the Comte de Dion, in a steam-powered car that covered the 79 miles at an average speed of 11.6 miles per hour.

3. The windshield, which did not seem necessary because of the automobile's slow speed. The Oakland became the first car to have it as standard equipment.

4. A limousine was a large motorcar with an enclosed passenger compartment and an open driver's section. The name comes from a flowing mantle or coat, to keep the driver warm, that was popularized in Limousin, a region of central France.

5. Rolls and Royce, respectively. A fleet of nine armored Rolls-Royces and two Rolls-Royce tenders afforded T.E. Lawrence great mobility in his desert campaign against the Turks. As he was to write, "A Rolls in the desert is worth more than rubies."

6. Ingenious Mr. Toad!

   The verse is, of course, from Kenneth Grahame's *The Wind in the Willows*.

7. So that Mr. Wilson, later a maladroit Secretary of Defense under Eisenhower, could have one foot free to put in his mouth. Wilson is remembered for saying, "What is good for the country is good for General Motors, and vice versa."

8. Auric Goldfinger, in Ian Fleming's *Goldfinger*. (Au is the chemical symbol for gold, from the Latin *aurum*.) Fleming also wrote *Chitty-Chitty Bang-Bang,* about two children, a nutty inventor and his girl in an automobile that flies and floats in 1908 Britain.

9. A red circle with a diagonal red line through it prohibits movement. For example, it is used to prohibit entry by trucks or bicycles, and such movements as U-turns, right turns and left turns.

10. He produced a dictionary, which defined "stoping" as "mining ore by a series of steplike excavations."

BAFFLEGAB AND DOUBLESPEAK

Having a common language in America helped unite the country. In recent years a new language, or rather a patois that parodies language, has emerged, wherein people are "impacted," matters "prioritized" and procedures "effectuated."

Not content with emasculating the mother tongue with verbalization, academicians, professionals and bureaucrats have gleefully seized on simple, readily understandable terms and transformed them into miasmas of obfuscation.

Can you make any sense of the following gobbledygook? If so, put the phrases into plain English.

1. Social expression products

2. Environmental control specialist

3. Multiphasic health screen

4. Empirically validated learning package

5. National species of special interest

6. Paradigmatic behavioral parameters

7. Audio-visually qualified person

8. Ethnically pluralistic national societal communities

9. Terminated with extreme prejudice

10. Combatwise, the time frame is upcoming.

BAFFLEGAB AND DOUBLESPEAK

1. Greeting cards
2. Garbage man
3. Physical checkup
4. Textbook
5. Endangered species you can kill legally
6. Normal conduct
7. Teacher who can operate a movie projector
8. Integrated housing
9. Murdered
10. I have not yet begun to fight.

BASEBALL AND FOOTBALL

1. Can you name the first major league manager to be ejected from both games of a doubleheader?

2. Who was the first football player to have his jersey retired?

3. Describe a Baltimore Chop.

4. Which two college teams met in the most one-sided football game in the annals of the sport?

5. When he retired in 1980, Sadaharu Oh—in Japanese Oh means king—was the highest-paid athlete in Asia, with an estimated career income of $7.5 million. For what world's record is he most remembered?

6. Name the only college to have two Heisman Trophy winners in consecutive years. Who were they?

7. To his chagrin, Willie Wilson of the Kansas City Royals broke a World Series record in 1980. What was his dubious distinction?

8. Which great baseball player derived one of his nicknames from a play on the title and refrain of one of the *Nonsense Poems* by Edward Lear?

9. In baseball, what is meant by the expression "Around the Horn," and how did it originate?

10. What telling criticisms did Yogi Berra, manager of the New York Yankees, make of baseball strategy?

BASEBALL AND FOOTBALL

1. Not Leo Durocher, Earl Weaver or Billy Martin, but the Giants manager Mel Ott, in two games between the Pittsburgh Pirates and the New York Giants in June 1946.

2. Harold "Red" Grange, the "Galloping Ghost" of the University of Illinois, who made the number 77 famous.

3. A Baltimore Chop is a high-bounding hit ball that usually goes through the infield for a base hit.

4. In October 1916 Cumberland University of Lebanon, Tennessee, lost to Georgia Tech by a score of 222–0. In a futile effort to lessen· the carnage, Cumberland elected to kick off after every Tech touchdown; as the Cumberland coach later explained, this "forced them to run the whole distance of the field for the next touchdown instead of from the place where we fumbled."

5. Honored bearer of uniform No. 1 for Tokyo's Yomiuri Giants, Sadaharu hit 868 home runs in 21 years as a professional, surpassing Babe Ruth's 714 and Hank Aaron's 755.

6. Yale. The 1937 and 1938 football captains, Larry Kelley and Clint Frank, both won the Heisman Trophy.

7. Wilson struck out 12 times in the 1980 Series against the Philadelphia Phillies.

8. George Herman "Babe" Ruth, called "the Sultan of Swat" in tribute to his prowess as a hitter, got his sobriquet from Edward Lear's enquiring about a Himalayan holy man:

   Who, or why, or which, or what,
   Is the Akond of Swat?
   Does he wear a turban, a fez, or a hat?
   Does he sleep on a mattress, a bed, or a mat?
   Or a cot?—The Akond of Swat?

9. "Around the Horn" means throwing the ball from third to second to first. The expression refers to the long sea voyage around South America via Cape Horn.

10. "Arghh! How can you t'ink and play ball at de same time?" and "Ninety percent of this game is half mental."

BATHROOM AND BOUDOIR

1. In the Old Testament, who "painted her face, and tied her hair, and looked out a window" prior to being devoured by dogs, and who was the first man to shave?

2. To which famous English poet are these lines attributed?

   > Oh, Cloacina, goddess of this place,
   > Look on thy supplicants with smiling face,
   > Soft, yet cohesive, let their offerings flow
   > Nor rashly swift nor insolently slow.

3. According to Edmund Clerihew Bentley, why did this occur?

   > Geoffrey Chaucer
   > Took a bath in a saucer.

4. Dorothy Parker and a friend went into their hostess' bathroom one weekend and espied a particularly frazzled toothbrush. When the friend wondered what she used it for, what did Miss Parker opine?

5. What are pomanders, and why were they used so extensively by our forebears?

6. The only facial hair that H.M. Guardsmen in Britain are allowed to wear are moustaches and tufts of hair on the cheeks. How are the latter generally referred to?

7. What was Sir John Harington's contribution to bathroom efficiency, and why is Ajax such a suitable name for a bathroom cleanser?

8. Explain the connection between linen and a toilet.

9. Who penned the following on archaic British bathrooms?

   > Tho' the pipes that supply the bathroom burst
   > And the lavat'ry makes you fear the worst
   > It was used by Charles the First
   > Quite informally,
   > And later by George the Fourth
   > On a journey North.

10. When he was Prime Minister, Clement Attlee got in the habit of following Churchill into the men's room of the House of Commons and watching him as he peed. What was Churchill's reaction?

BATHROOM AND BOUDOIR

1. Jezebel (II Kings 9:30), and Joseph (Genesis 41:14): "Then Pharaoh called Joseph and they brought him hastily out of the dungeon: and he shaved *himself*, and changed his raiment, and came in unto Pharaoh."

2. George Gordon, Lord Byron. Cloacina does not appear to be a bona fide goddess, but *cloaca* is synonymous with sewer or latrine.

3.   In consequence of certain hints
    Dropped by the Black Prince.

4. "I think she rides it on Halloween."

5. Pomanders—literally and originally, apples of amber—were gold and silver balls containing aromatic substances. Ostensibly they were worn to ward off infection, but their practical purpose was to alleviate the ripe aromas emanating from practically everyone in those unhygenic days.

6. Bugger's grips.

7. Harington invented the flush lavatory, installing one for Elizabeth I in her palace at Richmond, Surrey. Known for his indelicate humor, he wrote the Rabelaisian *Metamorphosis of Ajax*, using ornate style and classical allusions to discuss at length the construction of an Elizabethan privy. The name Ajax might be construed as a play on the word jakes, which came into rather common usage around 1530 as a synonym for privy.

8. The word toilet derives from the French *toilette*, a dressing table, which itself is a diminutive of *toile*, the linen fabric covering the table.

9. Noël Coward, in "The Stately Homes of England," from his 1938 production *Operette*.

10. "I wish you would stop looking at me. Every time you see something large and operating well, you want to nationalize it."

BELOW STAIRS

1. Name the "illiterate loiterer" and clownish servant of Valentine in Shakespeare's *Two Gentlemen of Verona*.

2. What group of servants are, in an etymological sense, judges?

3. Who is the "servant of the servants of God"?

4. The great Elizabethan poet Sir Fulke Greville, first Baron Brooke, met a tragic end at the hands of one of his servants. Why?

5. At the Court of St. James's there is a very high functionary called the Groom of the Stole. What were his original duties?

6. Which noted playwright made this observation: "When domestic staff are treated as human beings, it is not worthwhile to keep them"?

7. If you had been dining out in Edinburgh in the 19th century, you might have encountered a butler named Valentine. What made his such a strange story?

8. A certain fictitious family lived at the equally fictitious address of 165 Eaton Place, London. Can you name the family and the butler who headed their staff?

9. Can you remember the housekeepers at these fictional great houses: Bly, Manderley and Thornfield?

10. What was the "reference" occasionally given to unsatisfactory servants in India in the days of the British Raj?

BELOW STAIRS

1. Speed.

2. Lackeys. The word derives from the Spanish *alcalde,* meaning mayor, in turn from the Arabic *al-qadi,* a judicial official; its meaning has gone downhill steadily as it moved north.

3. The Pope.

4. His servant Haywood, who was asked to witness the signing of his will, believed himself to be denied a legacy, and as a consequence, murdered Brooke.

5. "Stole" is merely a medieval form of the word stool, and the groom supervised the king's closet-stool—that is, the privy.

6. George Bernard Shaw, writing under the pseudonym of John Tanner in *Maxims for Revolutionists.*

7. Until 1822 he had been Bishop of Clogher in Ireland, but then was apprehended sodomizing a Coldstream Guardsman in a tavern next to the House of Commons in Westminster. He jumped bail and was forced to find other employment.

8. The Bellamys, whose butler was Mr. Hudson. This part was played by Gordon Jackson in the popular British television series *Upstairs, Downstairs.*

9. At Bly, Mrs. Grose tells the governess the odd story of Miss Jessel and Quint in Henry James' *The Turn of the Screw.* Mrs. Danvers is the sinister and spiteful housekeeper at Manderley in *Rebecca,* by Daphne du Maurier. At Thornfield, Mrs. Fairfax was Mr. Rochester's housekeeper in Charlotte Brontë's *Jane Eyre.*

10. "_____ has been in my employ for two years to the very best of his own satisfaction. If you propose to give him a berth, let it be a wide one."

BIRD WATCHING

1. Why is the missel thrush sometimes known as the storm cock?

2. Which balladeer of Baltimore penned these lines?

> The song of canaries
> Never varies,
> And when they are moulting
> They're pretty revolting.

3. Can birds mate in midair?

4. For which alliterative line in "The Windhover" is the English poet Gerard Manley Hopkins especially remembered?

5. Name six extant birds that are apteroid, or incapable of flight.

6. Can you supply the missing first line of this limerick?

> His bill will take more than his belican.
> He can take in his beak
> Food enough for a week,
> But I'm damned if I see how the helican.

7. The name of which game bird comes from the word fart, and why is it so called?

8. How did the distinguished Bishop Samuel Wilberforce err when he wrote the following:

> If I were a cassowary
> On the plains of Timbucktoo,
> I would eat a missionary
> Cassock, band, and hymn-book too.

9. What is the only bird that can fly backwards?

10. With what words did Prime Minister Winston S. Churchill end this part of his speech before the Canadian Parliament in Ottawa in 1941: "When I warned them [the French Government] that Britain would fight on alone whatever they did, their generals told their Prime Minister and his divided Cabinet, 'In three weeks England will have her neck wrung like a chicken'"?

BIRD WATCHING

1. It sings in all weathers, often perching on some high point and singing into the teeth of a gale.

2. Ogden Nash, in "The Canary" from *The Face Is Familiar*.

3. Yes, some species such as parrots and swifts can. It does not appear to be true that United Airlines took its slogan "Fly United" from this phenomenon.

4.   I caught this morning morning's minion, kingdom
       of daylight's dauphin, dapple-dawn-drawn
       Falcon. . .

   (In the above Hopkins uses the word dauphin in both the literal and figurative French senses of dolphin and heir apparent.)

5. The cassowary, emu, kiwi, ostrich, rhea and penguin.

6. "A wonderful bird is the pelican," in the limerick by Dixon Lanier Merritt.

7. The partridge, which in Latin is *perdix,* from the Greek *perdesthai* (fart), is so named because of the peculiar whirring sound it makes when flushed.

8. The cassowary, which is related to the emu, is native to Australia and New Guinea, but not North Africa. Cassowaries are notoriously vicious and have attacked and killed men with their sharp, spinelike toenails.

9. The hummingbird, which weighs less than a nickel, has a body temperature of 111 degrees and beats its wings 75 times a second.

10. "Some chicken!" [loud applause] "Some neck!" [prolonged applause].

BODY WORK

1. In the Trojan War the foremost Greek hero Achilles was killed when Paris wounded him fatally in the heel. Why was this his only vulnerable spot?

2. What is the operation most frequently performed on American males?

3. Which famous writer lost the use of his left hand in battle, and later remarked that his left hand was destroyed "to the greater glory of the right"?

4. What part of the human body has no function?

5. Why are charley horses so named?

6. Explain the tenuous link between the statue of the Venus de Milo in the Louvre and Ernest Hemingway.

7. A man about to undergo a proctoscopy asked his doctor if it would hurt. "Not at all," the doctor replied, and then added what?

8. Which noted modern painter once said, "I consider it a normal thing to pay close attention to my stools and talk about them"?

9. What is funny about the funny bone?

10. Opticorectalitis is an ailment that is rarely diagnosed correctly. What is it?

BODY WORK

1. When Achilles was an infant his mother Thetis attempted to make him immortal by bathing him in the river Styx, but the heel by which she held him remained vulnerable. From this legend came the phrase "Achilles' heel" for a small but mortal weakness, and the name of the Achilles tendon, which runs from the heel bone to the calf muscle of the leg.

2. Circumcision.

3. Miguel de Cervantes, author of *Don Quixote*, who was a professional soldier before he became a writer. He lost the use of his left hand fighting against the Turks at the Battle of Lepanto in 1571.

4. The appendix, which is considered the vestigial remnant of some previous organ that has become unnecessary to mankind in his evolutionary progress.

5. Old lame horses kept for family use were affectionately called charley horses because of the popularity of the name. The usage gradually was extended to a cramp or stiffness of various muscles in the body, especially in the arm or leg, caused by injury or excessive exertion.

6. The Venus de Milo is armless, and Hemingway's famous World War I novel is *A Farewell to Arms*.

7. "But you'll never forget it as long as you live."

8. Salvador Dali, who has, according to an art critic in *Time* magazine, "The greed of a barracuda, the political views of a Torquemada, and the vanity of an old drag queen."

9. Your funny bone is not a bone at all, but a point near the elbow where the ulnar nerve touches the humerus, the long bone of the upper part of the arm extending from the shoulder to the elbow.

10. Opticorectalitis results when the optical nerve comes into contact with the rectal nerve, causing a generally shitty outlook on life.

BOOK FAIR

1. How did George Bernard Shaw distinguish between journalism and literature?

2. What did T.S. Eliot and Winston Churchill have in common?

3. *The Old Farmer's Almanac,* published annually since 1793, has a unique physical characteristic. Can you say what this is, and explain the reason?

4. Benjamin Disraeli developed which ingenious way of acknowledging receipt of an unsolicited book?

5. *Prominent Black Yachtsmen* and *Italian War Heroes* have often been cited as memorable books that never existed. Name two famous works by Sherlock Holmes that are mentioned by Dr. Watson but are not known to exist?

6. What was Ezra Pound's comment on Henry Miller's *Tropic of Cancer*?

7. Yaddo has been called a cross between Shangri-La and a summer camp, but what precisely happens there?

8. Who observed that "publishing a volume of poetry today is like dropping a rose petal down the Grand Canyon and waiting for the echo"?

9. What got into itself after only nineteen years?

10. The English publisher Leonard Smithers took delight in deflowering virgins. What was Oscar Wilde's observation on this?

1. "The difference between literature and journalism is that journalism is unreadable and literature not read."

2. Winston Churchill and T.S. Eliot were both born in St. Louis, Missouri. Winston Churchill, a minor American novelist, wrote *Richard Carvel, The Crisis* and *The Crossing,* among others. He began his literary career about the same time as did the future Prime Minister of the United Kingdom, who in 1899 wrote him a letter beginning, "Mr. Winston Churchill presents his compliments to Mr. Winston Churchill." In it the English Churchill stated that in the future, to avoid confusion, he proposed to sign his works with the initial of one of his middle names, Spencer.

3. A hole punched in the upper left-hand corner. This is a throwback to the days when the *Almanac,* along with the Sears Roebuck catalogue, was tied to a piece of string hanging in the outhouse.

4. "Thank you very much for sending me the book. I shall lose no time in reading it."

5. *Practical Handbook of Bee Culture With Some Notes Upon the Segregation of the Queen,* and *Upon the Distinction Between the Ashes of Various Tobaccos.*

6. "At last, an unprintable book that's fit to read."

7. Yaddo is a 205-acre retreat in Saratoga Springs, N.Y., providing an environment for artists, writers and composers to work without distractions. The colony was founded and endowed by Spencer Trask, the New York financier, and his wife Katrina.

8. Don Marquis, author of *archy and mehitabel,* in his newspaper column "The Sun Dial."

9. *The Guinness Book of World Records,* first published in 1955. By 1974 it had become the world's fastest-selling book. To date, global sales in 21 languages are estimated at over 50 million copies.

10. "Smithers loves first editions."

BRITISH COOKING

1. England has long been dismissed by foreigners—today rather unfairly—as a gastronomic wasteland. How did W. Somerset Maugham sum it up?

2. What British cooking may lack in finesse it makes up for in fantasy. Just consider these hypocorisms: fadge, oon, rumbledy-thumps, baps, bubble-and-squeak, snoodie, toad in the hole, inky-pinky, haggamoogie, claggum, maids-of-honour, stargazey pie and fairy butter. What, for example, are Bath chaps?

3. Which superb dish is named after an American-born woman who became the highest-ranking lady in the British Empire after Queen Victoria?

4. Name the food customarily served at the Wimbledon tennis championship each June.

5. At one time oysters were plentiful and cheap. Which celebrated character observes: "Poverty and oysters always seem to go together. The poorer the place, the greater call there seems to be for oysters"?

6. Most British pubs serve a Ploughman's, which consists of what?

7. Explain the difference between smoked Scottish salmon and Scottish smoked salmon.

8. Who characteristically once said, "During my life I have often had to eat my own words, and have found them a wholesome diet"?

9. Why do the English traditionally eat goose on September 29, Michaelmas Day?

10. While Burt Reynolds was on location in England, he was offered a piece of the English specialty, jellied eel. After he tasted it, what was his comment?

BRITISH COOKING

1. "If you would eat well in England, you must eat breakfast three times a day."

2. Bath chaps are cured pieces of the cheeks of longjawed, fruit-fed pigs, which are delicious either hot or cold.

3. Lady Curzon soup. This subtle and unusual turtle soup, delicately flavored with curry and sherry and enhanced with cream, was created for Mary Victoria, Lady Curzon, wife of Lord Curzon of Kedleston, Viceroy of India during the British Raj. She was the daughter of Levi Leiter of Chicago, an early associate of Marshall Field.

4. Smoked salmon, and strawberries and cream with champagne.

5. Samuel Weller, in Dickens' *Posthumous Papers of the Pickwick Club*. He was Mr. Pickwick's servant, formerly "boots" of the White Hart in the Borough, and perhaps the greatest character Dickens ever drew.

6. A Ploughman's is a lunch consisting of a large chunk of Cheddar cheese, a thick slice of bread, a pat of butter, and a relish such as Branston Pickle (a dark brown, spicy mixture) or small pickled onions.

7. Smoked Scottish salmon is the aristocrat, processed from salmon caught in Scotland's lochs and coastal waters, whereas Scottish smoked salmon can come from anywhere but is smoked in Scotland.

8. Winston S. Churchill.

9. Queen Elizabeth was eating goose on that day when she heard of the defeat of the Spanish Armada.

10. "That's really—average."

BRITISH ROYALTY AND PEERAGE

1. Name the queen who, in the time of the Emperor Nero, led a gallant but unsuccessful revolt against the Romans in Britain.

2. Who is the Premier Duke and Earl of England, and what is his family name?

3. How did historians err when they called Egbert the first king of England?

4. Which two orders rank just below the peerage, and what is the difference between them?

5. Name the only king since 1066 to be succeeded as monarch by three of his children. Who were they?

6. What can the holder of an Irish peerage do that is denied to all other British peers?

7. Who said, "My father was frightened of his mother, I was frightened of my father, and I am damned well going to see to it that my children are frightened of me"? And to whom was he referring?

8. In which play by whom does this line appear: "You should study the Peerage, Gerald . . . it is the best thing in fiction the English have ever done"?

9. Which peer could, if he wished, call himself Duque de Victoria, Marques de Torres Vedras, Conte de Vilmeira, Duque de Ciudad Rodrigo, and is a Grandee of Spain?

10. Prince Charles' badge as the Prince of Wales consists of three plumes of ostrich feather enfiladed by a coronet. Beneath this is the motto *Ich Dien*, which means what? And what are the two versions of how it came to be adopted?

BRITISH ROYALTY AND PEERAGE

1. Boudicca, or Boadicea, queen of the Iceni (of Norfolk). After sacking Colchester, London and St.Albans, her army was crushed by the Romans, and Boudicca took poison.

2. The Duke of Norfolk, Earl Marshal of England, whose family name is Fitzalan-Howard. His most unusual attribute is that he is a Roman Catholic in a predominantly Anglican country.

3. Although Egbert (802–39), the grandfather of Alfred the Great, successfully ruled a large part of England, there was no conception then of a kingdom of England.

4. Baronet and knight, both of which carry the title of Sir. Unlike a knighthood, a baronetcy is a hereditary honor.

5. Henry VIII, who was succeeded by Edward VI, son of Jane Seymour; Mary I or "Bloody Mary," daughter of Catherine of Aragon; and Elizabeth I, daughter of Anne Boleyn.

6. He or she can sit in the House of Commons without having to renounce the title.

7. George V, referring to his grandmother Queen Victoria, his father Edward VII and his own children, including the rebellious Prince of Wales.

8. Oscar Wilde, in *A Woman of No Importance*.

9. The eighth Duke of Wellington. These are titles bestowed on the first Duke by Portugal and Spain during the Peninsular War.

10. *Ich Dien* means I Serve. One version is that during the Battle of Crécy in 1346, when the blind John of Luxemburg, King of Bohemia, was slain fighting for the French, Edward the Black Prince (so named after his death because of his black armor) plucked the badge from him and wore it as a mark of respect. Some authorities, however, say the motto should read *Eich Dyn,* which means in Welsh Your Man, words uttered by Edward I when he held up his baby son, the first Prince of Wales, in view of the Welsh barons at the first investiture at Caernarvon in 1301.

BUILDINGS

1. Can you describe a ziggurat?

2. Give an explanation for the Egyptian step pyramid.

3. What was Zbigniew Stefanski's principal contribution to the building of America?

4. When he first saw Blenheim Palace, the newly-built seat of the Dukes of Marlborough, what was the English author Horace Walpole's reaction?

5. The concourse of which famous railroad station was a splendid copy of the Tepidarium of the Baths of Caracalla in Rome?

6. Whose official residence is the Palais Schaumburg?

7. Anyone planning to build a house in the country would profit from knowing the pitfalls that lay in wait for a New York advertising man in whose amusing novel?

8. What is the world's largest cathedral?

9. Supply the full name of the famous building that is called the Beaubourg for short and resembles a gaily-painted chemical plant.

10. A certain structure is famous for its concrete roofs, which suggest different things to different people: "A huddle of nuns in the wind"; "an echo of sails of yachts in the harbor"; and "some gigantic, magnificent, but utterly strange hard-shelled sea creature that has come up from the water to rest on Bonnelong Point." What is it, and why was its architect fired?

BUILDINGS

1. A ziggurat is a temple tower of the ancient Assyrians and Babylonians, having the form of a terraced pyramid of successively receding stories.

2. It was believed to afford a staircase by which the entombed king might rise to Heaven.

3. He was one of the six Polish craftsmen who came out in 1608 to the Jamestown colony, which badly needed skilled workers.

4. "It looks like a place built for an auctioneer who had been chosen King of Poland."

5. Pennsylvania Station in New York City, which has since been demolished and made over into what Alistair Cooke calls "airport arcade moderne."

6. The Chancellor of the Federal Republic of Germany. The Palais Schaumburg may be seen in Bonn, the country's capital.

7. Eric Hodgins' *Mr. Blandings Builds His Dream House,* which was made into a 1948 film starring Cary Grant, Myrna Loy and Melvyn Douglas.

8. The cathedral church of the Protestant Episcopal Diocese of New York, St. John the Divine. Started in 1892, the structure is still uncompleted, and is sometimes referred to as St. John the Unfinished. (St. Peter's in Rome is still the world's largest church, but it is a basilica, not a cathedral.)

9. The Centre National d'Art et de Culture Georges Pompidou, in Paris.

10. The Sydney Opera House ("the other Taj Mahal"), whose roofs like soaring sails have made it a national symbol and the only internationally acclaimed building in Australia. Its architect was fired when his board protested that he had not provided parking lots. His parting shot was, "Does the Parthenon have parking lots?"

BUSINESS AND FINANCE

1. Just as marketing know-how was regarded as the key to success in the 1960s and an MBA became the tool for survival in the 1970s, mastery of what is essential for the business executive in the 1980s?

2. Name the three secret words for successful real estate investing.

3. Which famous Chancellor of the Exchequer said, referring to decimal points, "I never could make out what those damned dots meant"?

4. Can you give the gist of Conway's Law?

5. Whose budgetary advice went this way: "Annual income twenty pounds, annual expenditure nineteen nineteen six, result happiness. Annual income twenty pounds, annual expenditure twenty pounds ought and six, result misery"?

6. "The Magic Sixes" refers to a group of stocks, often considered undervalued, that meet certain requirements, all of them having to do with the number six. What are the Magic Sixes?

7. When Standard Oil was forced by a federal court ruling to change the Esso (S.O. phoneticized) trademark, they thought of using the name Enco, which was already one of their brands. Why did they finally decide on the name Exxon?

8. What is said to be the traditional explanation of the Rothschilds for their success?

9. What is the "Rule of 72"?

10. A multinational executive's life can either be halcyon or sheer hell. What is his dream of heaven, and what is his nightmare?

BUSINESS AND FINANCE

1. Mastery of advanced office information technology is taking its place as the strategic priority in the 1980s.

2. Location, location, location.

3. Lord Randolph Churchill, father of Winston S. Churchill.

4. "In any organization there will always be one person who knows what is going on. That man must be fired."

5. Mr. Wilkins Micawber, in Charles Dickens' *David Copperfield*.

6. A Magic Six stock must trade at sixty percent of book value, have a maximum price-earning ratio of six, and the annual dividend, or yield, must be more than six percent.

7. Exxon was chosen after they discovered that Enco means "stalled car" in oil-importing Japan. The double xx occurs in a mere handful of proper names, such as Foxx, and otherwise only in Maltese.

8. "We never buy at the bottom of the lows; we never sell at the top of the highs; and we always take our profits too soon."

9. There is a simple formula called the "Rule of 72" that can be used to approximate the number of years required for money to double itself at any rate of interest. The formula involves dividing the effective annual rate of interest into 72. For example, at 10 percent, the rule obviously gives 7.2 years. The exact time for doubling would be 7.27 years. The rule is surprisingly reliable over a wide range of rates, although the inaccuracy increases at extremely high or extremely low rates. For example, at a 2 percent rate, the rule gives 36 years, while the exact-minded investor would only have to wait for 35 years.

10. His dream of heaven is working in London on an American salary with a Chinese wife and a French chef. His nightmare is working in Paris on a Chinese salary with an American wife and an English cook.

CAPITALS

1. Although the Romans had no formal capital in Britain during their occupation, what is the present-day name of the city that is considered to have fulfilled this function?

2. Is the capital of Kentucky pronounced Lewisville, Louieville or Louahvull?

3. Which European capitals are known as "the Athens of the North" and "the Venice of the North," and why?

4. Who had the strange conceit of laying out the streets of which capital in the form of the Union Jack?

5. Can you name a United States capital and its state that together sound like "Eden without temptation"?

6. How does a famous 19th-century statesman happen to lie between a Shakespearean heroine in *A Midsummer Night's Dream* and a mender of fishing nets?

7. The Arabic name of which East African coastal city means "Haven of Peace"?

8. Which state capital is located on the Colorado River?

9. What is the only capital to be named after an herb?

10. Who described Washington, D.C., as "a city of Southern efficiency and Northern charm"?

CAPITALS

1. Colchester, now a municipal borough of Essex on the Colne River in southeast England. It was one of the great cities of pre-Roman Britain and capital of the ruler Cunobelin (Shakespeare's Cymbeline).

2. Most residents of the Bluegrass State would pronounce it Frankfort. Louisville, however, is pronounced Louahvull.

3. Edinburgh, the capital of Scotland, whose Castle Rock resembles the Acropolis, and Stockholm, the capital of Sweden, which is built on many islands.

4. Horatio Herbert Kitchener, the commander in chief of the Egyptian army in 1898, after he took Khartoum, the capital of the Sudan, on behalf of Britain's puppet state of Egypt. The campaign also carried the moral overtones of avenging the murder in 1885 of General "Chinese" Gordon.

5. What about Annapolis, Maryland (an appleless merry-land)?

6. Bismarck, North Dakota, is equidistant between Helena, Montana, and St. Paul, Minnesota.

7. Dar-es-Salaam, on the Indian Ocean, the capital and chief seaport of Tanzania, formerly Tanganyika. Founded in 1866 by the Sultan of Zanzibar, who built his summer palace there, Dar-es-Salaam remained a small town until German forces occupied it in 1887. The port's commercial importance was enormously enhanced in 1975, when the great Uhuru (Tan-Zam) Railway linked it with the Zambian Copperbelt.

8. Austin, Texas. (There are two Colorado rivers in the United States.)

9. Funchal, capital of the Madeira Islands. In 1420 the Portuguese sailed into a cove so heady with the licorice-sweet scent of wild herbs that they named the spot Funchal, Portuguese for fennel.

10. John F. Kennedy, according to Arthur M. Schlesinger's *A Thousand Days*.

CARTOONS AND COMIC STRIPS

1. What is the origin of the word cartoon, and for what purpose were cartoons first used?

2. What was the earliest magazine drawing to be called a cartoon, a designation that caught on and has been used for political or humorous drawings ever since?

3. Of all the cartoons that have appeared in *Punch,* Britain's humor magazine, which one has been discussed, reprinted and reproduced in numerous variations more than any other drawing in or out of *Punch?*

4. Who assembled a delightfully comic zoo that included the raffish Albert the Alligator; Deacon Muskrat; a prideful hound, Beauregard Bugleboy; a turtle and reformed pirate captain, Churchy La Femme; Howland Owl, a nearsighted sorcerer; a fox, Seminole Sam; Mole MacCarony; Porkypine; Snavely the Snake; a frog, Moonshine Sonata; and a skunk, Miz Ma'm'sell Hepzibah?

5. Which comic strip is unique in being a strip within a strip, and who is the artist parodied in it?

6. In a memorable *New Yorker* cartoon by Peter Arno, three beaming policemen hold erect a drunken man in a rumpled tuxedo as one of the policemen explains to the officer behind the desk. What is the caption?

7. Which popular series of panel cartoons was devoted to the oddities of life?

8. What was the occupation of Superman's father, Jor-El?

9. In the world of comic art there exists a visual vocabulary. You have seen them, but can you define plewds, indotherms and waftavoms?

10. When asked why he drew such weird-looking women, what did James Thurber reply?

CARTOONS AND COMIC STRIPS

1. The word cartoon derives from the Italian *cartone,* meaning pasteboard. The first cartoon was a preliminary sketch, similar in size to the fresco, mosaic, tapestry or the like that was to be copied from it.

2. In 1843 *Punch, or The London Charivari,* printed a series of cartoons commenting on various social evils. The first was a drawing entitled "Shadow and Substance," by John Leech. It portrayed a group of poverty-stricken Londoners at an exhibition regarding with some bewilderment the portraits of gorgeously uniformed and decorated notables.

3. Sir John Tenniel's "Dropping the Pilot," portraying the young German Emperor as a sea captain looking indifferently over the rail as the aged Prince Bismarck, his grandfather's mentor, descends to the pilot boat.

4. Walt Kelly in "Pogo," a mixture of hilarious slapstick, brilliant satire and subtle humor. Pogo, "a possum by trade," is the warmhearted and naïve star performer who is remembered for the line, "We have met the enemy and it is us."

5. Al Capp's "Fearless Fosdick," "the ideal of every red-blooded American boy," which appeared in "Lil' Abner" and is a parody of Chester Gould's Dick Tracy.

6. "Sergeant, this is Mr. J. Stanhope Anderson. He has money, position, many influential friends, and we can't do this to him."

7. "Believe It or Not!" by Robert Ripley. A similar series based on the *Guinness Book of World Records* has replaced it, but "Believe It or Not!" lives on as a television series hosted by Jack Palance.

8. Jor-El was a scientist who put his infant son (later to become Superman) in an experimental rocket and launched it toward Earth before the planet Krypton exploded.

9. Plewds are the droplets that come from the head of an exasperated or exhausted character, and the stars or odd typographical marks that double for curses. Indotherms show that a pot or a pie is hot, while waftavoms show smells.

10. "They look very attractive to my men."

CATNIP

1. "Belling the cat" means taking on a dangerous job for the benefit of others. How did the phrase originate?

2. The English detective story writer Edward Clerihew Bentley has the unique distinction of having a word named after his middle name, a clerihew being a humorous quatrain about a person named in the first line. What did Bentley have to say about Alfred de Musset and his cat?

3. Books about cats, golf and the Third Reich have built-in reader appeal. In what fashion did Alan Coren, the editor of *Punch,* combine these elements in a book he wrote?

4. In his poem "The Naming of Cats" in *Old Possum's Book of Practical Cats,* T.S. Eliot writes:

   > But I tell you, a cat needs a name that's particular,
   >   A name that's peculiar, and more dignified,
   > Else how can he keep his tail perpendicular,
   >   Or spread out his whiskers, or cherish his pride?

   To name a cat Oedipus or Magnificat would seem to follow Eliot's precept, but who or what were they?

5. Where would Hellcats, Tigercats, Wildcats or Bearcats feel at home?

6. What name is given to any of various semiprecious gems displaying a band of reflecting light that shifts position as the gem is turned?

7. "The Catbird Seat" is the title of a James Thurber story, but which famous baseball announcer first popularized the phrase, which means sitting pretty?

8. This post-mortem is a prolix version of which common proverb?

   > The coroner observed: Perpend—
   > The death of this our feline friend,
   > Reflects preoccupation shown
   > With business other than its own.

9. Who was Samuel Johnson's feline companion, and how did "the great Cham of literature" spoil him?

10. Can you give an example of the Rule of Feline Frustration?

1. "Belling the cat" refers to an Aesop's fable in which the mice decided that a bell should be put around the cat's neck to warn them of its approach, until one wise old mouse asked, "But who's to bell the cat?"

2.   Alfred de Musset
              Used to call his cat Pusset.
              His accent was affected;
              That was to be expected.

3. He wrote a book titled *Golfing for Cats,* which featured a large black swastika on the cover. Needless to say, the book had nothing to do with any of these subjects. In a similar vein years ago a book called *Lincoln's Doctor's Dog* was published.

4. Oedipus in Greek mythology unknowingly killed his father Laius, the king of Thebes, and married the king's wife Jocasta, who, unknown to him, was his mother. The Magnificat is the canticle beginning *Magnificat anima mea Dominum,* My soul doth magnify the Lord (Luke 1:46).

5. On the decks or hangars of aircraft carriers. They were the names given to U.S. Navy fighter planes in World War II.

6. Cat's-eye, a name also given to the reflecting studs sometimes placed at the center of a road.

7. Red Barber, who used to announce the old Brooklyn Dodger games. Barber first heard the phrase in a stud poker game when he unsuccessfully tried to bluff another player, who said, "From the start I was sitting in the catbird seat." Red Barber noted, "Inasmuch as I had paid for the expression, I began to use it. I popularized it, and Mr. Thurber took it."

8. "Curiosity killed the cat."

9. Hodge, who was spoiled by meals of fresh oysters. Of Hodge, Johnson had this to say: "I have had cats whom I have liked better than this—but he is a very fine cat, a very fine cat indeed."

10. When your cat is asleep on your lap and looks utterly content, you will suddenly have to go to the bathroom.

CHARIVARI

1.   Wynken, Blynken and Nod one night
              Sailed off in a wooden shoe—
          Sailed on a river of crystal light,
              Into a sea of dew.

According to the author, Eugene Field, who or what are Wynken, Blynken and Nod?

2. Reflecting on which historic moment, who wrote, "I felt as if I were walking with Destiny and that all my past life had been but a preparation for this hour and this trial"?

3. Is Pinyin an advanced Japanese computer, a potent Thai fermented liquor or a new method of rendering Chinese into English?

4. Give the name of the word processor whose writing element is at one end, whose deletion element is at the other, and which produces a magic dust when a deletion is made.

5. What and where are the Nazca Lines?

6. Norwich is an English acronym meaning "knickers off, ready when I come home." A reverse acronym, taken from the Personals column of the London *Times,* is: "Michael, See you when tea is ready. Pamela." Pray interpret this.

7. Explain the connection between "the gamecock of the Revolution" and the outbreak of the Civil War.

8. The K.C.M.G. and the O.B.E. are two esteemed British decorations. What do they stand for?

9. September 1945 marked the end of World War II with the Japanese signing the surrender document on the deck of the battleship U.S.S. *Missouri.* Who signed for the United States?

10. When the grasshopper walked into his pub, the bartender said, "Say, they've named a drink after you." What was the grasshopper's somewhat amazed reaction to this news?

CHARIVARI

1. Wynken and Blynken are two little eyes, and Nod is a little head.

2. Winston S. Churchill, on taking over as Prime Minister from Neville Chamberlain in May 1940.

3. Pinyin (Chinese for phonetic spelling) is a somewhat less cumbersome method of rendering Chinese characters in alphabetic form than the traditional Wade-Giles system. For example, Peking, the capital of the People's Republic of China, is now Beijing. Chou En-lai becomes Zhou En-lai and Mao Tse-Tung, Mao Zedong in their Pinyin form.

4. A pencil.

5. The Nazca Lines are ancient Peruvian desert art created on a 30-square-mile barren plain southeast of Lima. Since their gigantic patterns can be observed only from the air, their discovery in 1939 led many people to believe that they were the work of an ancient culture that had also mastered the ability to fly.

6. "Michael, Cunt is ready. Pamela."

7. During the Revolution, General Thomas Sumter, like "The Swamp Fox" Francis Marion, formed a guerrilla band and harassed the British in the Carolinas. In 1861 the bombardment of Fort Sumter, which was named for him, at the entrance to the harbor of Charleston, South Carolina, marked the start of the Civil War.

8. Knight Commander of the Most Distinguished Order of St. Michael and St. George, and Officer of the Order of the British Empire. These abbreviations can also stand for "Kindly Call Me God" and "Other Buggers' Efforts."

9. Fleet Admiral Chester W. Nimitz. General of the Army Douglas MacArthur signed first as Commander Allied Forces, Southwest Pacific.

10. "Irving?"

CHRISTMAS CHEER

1. In Beatrix Potter's *The Tailor of Gloucester*, what was to happen on Christmas morning that made the tailor so anxious to finish a coat?

2. Merry carolers on many a frosty night over the years have sung the praises of Good King Wenceslas. Where did the good king rule?

3 How did the English Puritans celebrate Christmas?

4. Explain the connection between St. Stephen and boxing.

5. In *A Night At The Opera* Groucho Marx, by way of explaining a legal contract, says, "That's the sanity clause." What is Chico's response?

6. The white-berried mistletoe may inspire Christmas kisses and fond embraces, but to the hardwood trees in which it lives, it is what?

7. Who suggested that "every idiot who goes about with a 'Merry Christmas' on his lips should be boiled with his own pudding and buried with a stake of holly through his heart"?

8. Which Rugby- and Cambridge-educated poet wrote these lines?

> And things are done you'd not believe
> At Madingley on Christmas Eve.

9. Edmund Gwenn won an Academy Award as Best Supporting Actor for his part as Kriss Kringle in *Miracle on 34th Street*. Give the derivation of the name of Kriss Kringle.

10. "Marley was dead, to begin with." And so, of course, did Charles Dickens begin *A Christmas Carol*. But who started as follows?

> One Christmas was so much like another, in those years around the sea-town corner now and out of all sound except the distant voices I sometimes hear a moment before sleep, that I can never remember whether it snowed for six days and six nights when I was twelve or whether it snowed for twelve days and twelve nights when I was six.

CHRISTMAS CHEER

1. The Mayor of Gloucester was to be married, and the coat was for him to wear.

2. Bohemia, which is now part of Czechoslovakia. Vaclav, as Wenceslas was called in Czech, was Duke of Bohemia in the 10th century and later became its patron saint.

3. Not at all. The English Puritans detested it as a papist rite, and there were laws against its observance in the Massachusetts colony.

4. St. Stephen was the first Christian martyr, who was accused of blasphemy and stoned to death in Jerusalem in A.D. 36. His feast day is December 26, Boxing Day in Britain (provided that it is a weekday), when Christmas gifts in boxes were traditionally given to household employees and other service workers.

5. "You can't fool me, mister. There ain't no Santy Claus."

6. An aerial parasitic killer. Mistletoe flourishes on the trunks and branches of hardwood trees, robbing the host of water and nutrients and often killing it.

7. Ebenezer Scrooge, speaking to his nephew at the beginning of Charles Dickens' *A Christmas Carol.*

8. Rupert Brooke, in "The Old Vicarage, Granchester."

9. Kriss Kringle comes from the German *Christkindl,* Christ child.

10. Dylan Thomas, in *A Child's Christmas in Wales.*

CLOTHES MAKE THE MAN

1. In late 18th-century England the Macaronis were a coterie of fashionable fops who had traveled in Italy. They affected long curls, "spying glasses" and narrow-cut jackets resembling tail coats. What lasting but unseen innovation did they introduce to men's clothes?

2. Which famous man of the road was attired in the following fashion:

    He'd a French cocked hat on his forehead,
        a bunch of lace at his chin,
    A coat of claret velvet, and
        breeches of brown doe-skin.

3. When the crusty Lord Brownbottom was being measured for a suit at his Savile Row tailors Sackcloth and Ashes, the fitter for the trousers enquired if he "dressed" on the left or right side. What was his Lordship's response?

4. What is the tartan or check most widely seen in the world today?

5. The journalist Heywood Broun's habitually rumpled appearance reminded his friends of what?

6. Who is remembered for, among other things, wearing soiled "gabardine"?

7. Which former employee of the Hong Kong and Shanghai Bank wrote "The Right Hon was a tubby little chap who looked as if he had been poured into his clothes and had forgotten to say 'When'"?

8. Can you explain what the Duke of Windsor had to do with the Windsor Knot, which is made by tying a tie in such a way that the knot is wider than usual?

9. The theatrical producer Jed Harris was in the habit of working at his desk in the nude. When George S. Kaufman called on Harris, what was his comment on this?

10. An English duke was observed walking down St. James's Street in a remarkably shabby-looking suit. How did he shrug off his tatty appearance?

CLOTHES MAKE THE MAN

1. The inside pockets of jackets, which provide an unbroken narrow-line effect.

2. The Highwayman, in Alfred Noyes' poem of the same name.

3. "None of your bloody business—just make them a little baggy at the knees."

4. No Scottish clan or regimental tartan, but the distinctive beige, black, red and white Burberry check. Originally designed as a trench coat lining, it is now used for everything from scarfs to luggage.

5. "An unmade bed" or "a one-man slum."

6. Shylock, in Shakespeare's play. As he says to Antonio, the Merchant of Venice:

   > For sufferance is the badge of all our tribe.
   > You call me misbeliever, cut-throat dog,
   > And spit upon my Jewish gabardine. . .

7. P.G. (Sir Pelham Grenville) Wodehouse in *Very Good, Jeeves*.

8. Nothing at all. The Duke of Windsor achieved the effect of a thick knot by having all his ties especially made with an extra heavy lining and then tying them in the ordinary way.

9. "Jed, your fly's open."

10. "In the country everyone knows who I am, so it does not matter; in London nobody knows who I am, so it does not matter."

CLUBS AND SOCIETIES

1. The unique facade of which club has three huge bay windows resembling the stern of a 17th-century Dutch *yaghte* and has carved over the entryway the Latin proclamation *Nos Acimus Tumidis Velis* (We Go Forth with Swelling Sails)?

2. Where is the "In and Out" Club, and why is it so nicknamed?

3. When W.C. Fields was asked if he believed in clubs for women, how did he reply?

4. Who were the Molly Maguires, and what was their purpose?

5. During World War II, what did members of the U.S. Army Air Corps have to do to join the Mile High Club?

6. The genesis of country clubs came in the decade after the Civil War when America discovered organized sport and a new generation of men—those with the time and money to be sporting—took to the country to play. Can you name the first country club in the nation?

7. Who recounted this unfortunate account of a clubman?

   They had thrown him out of a club in Bombay
   For, apart from his mess-bills exceeding his pay,
   He took to pig-sticking in *quite* the wrong way.
   I wonder what happened to him!

8. What do a pig, a bull and a fly have to do with clubs?

9. "Speculations on the Source of the Hampstead Ponds, and Some Observations on the Theory of Tittlebats" was the title of a paper delivered by the rotund founder of which famous club?

10. The 1001, a Nature Trust founded by H.R.H. Prince Bernhard of the Netherlands, has a nice ring to it to fauna lovers. What are the two requirements for becoming a member?

CLUBS AND SOCIETIES

1. The New York Yacht Club on West 44th Street in New York City. Its grandest space is the Model Room, filled with more than 1,000 half- and full-model yachts stretching across the 45- by 96-foot area. In addition, glass cases house models of every America's Cup defender and challenger since 1851.

2. In London, at 94 Piccadilly. The Naval and Military Club is called the In and Out because those words appear prominently on the gateposts facing the street as a guide to drivers entering the courtyard.

3. "Yes, if every other form of persuasion fails."

4. The Molly Maguires were a secret organization of Irish-Americans in the anthracite mining districts around Scranton, Pennsylvania, whose purpose was to combat oppressive working and living conditions.

5. Any airman who had sex with a woman in an airplane at an altitude of 5,000 feet or more was automatically a member of the Mile High Club, which never lacked for members.

6. The Myopia Hunt Club in South Hamilton, Massachusetts, which began with a baseball team organized by some Harvard men, including four brothers named Prince. The latter were all nearsighted, hence the club's unusual name.

7. Noël Coward in "I Wonder What Happened to Him" from his revue *Sigh No More*.

8. They are the symbols of three of the most elite clubs at Harvard: Porcellian, A.D. (Alpha Delta) and the Fly respectively.

9. The Pickwick Club, the general chairman of which was Samuel Pickwick, as described by Charles Dickens in *The Posthumous Papers of the Pickwick Club*.

10. $10,000 for a lifetime membership, and approval of your application by H.R.H. Prince Bernhard, the 1001st member. The 1001 is a select group within the framework of the World Wildlife Fund International, the president of which is H.R.H. Prince Philip, Duke of Edinburgh. The tie of this worthy organization is patterned with little white pandas.

COLOR SCHEME

1. Identify the ancient people who were responsible for royal purple.

2. By which name is the aristocratic Gilles de Rais better remembered?

3. Who referred to whom as "the sea-green Incorruptible"?

4. What purplish-red color was named after a famous battle fought in northern Italy in 1859?

5. Why are enthusiasts for an activity called buffs?

6. Can you give the proper name of the World War I award known as the Blue Max because of its blue enameled Maltese cross?

7. In the early part of World War II, who wrote the lovely long poem *The White Cliffs,* which contains these lines?

   I am American bred,
   I have seen much to hate here—much to forgive,
   But in a world where England is finished and dead,
   I do not wish to live.

   And according to a popular song of the day, what will fly over the white cliffs when peace finally comes?

8. How is a variety of the genus *Poa* better known?

9. The freeing of the U.S. embassy hostages by the Iranians in 1981 after 444 days of captivity was symbolized in the United States by the wearing of yellow ribbons, which was inspired by either of two songs. One is the folk song that begins:

   Round her neck she wore a yellow ribbon,
   Wore it for her lover who was far, far away.

   What is the other song?

10. Who penned this verse?

    I never saw a purple cow,
    I never hope to see one;
    But I can tell you, anyhow,
    I'd rather see than be one.

COLOR SCHEME

1. The Phoenicians, who colored their cloth, known as Tyrian purple, with dye made from the anal gland of a small Mediterranean shellfish. Phoenicia is the Greek word for "purple land."

2. Bluebeard, the infamous mass murderer who lived in 15th-century France and was a supporter of Joan of Arc.

3. In his *History of the French Revolution* Thomas Carlyle so described Robespierre, apparently from misreading a line of Mme. de Staël's about the blue-green veins in his forehead.

4. Magenta, discovered in the same year as the Battle of Magenta and named for the battle's bloodiness.

5. Buffalo-hide clothing of a light yellowish brown was for centuries common as a military uniform.

6. The Military Order *Pour le Mérite,* the highest Prussian award for bravery and military merit. It is named the Blue Max because the German aviator Max Immelmann was the first man to receive the award.

7. Alice Duer Miller. A year after she wrote the poem a popular song started:

> There'll be bluebirds over
> The white cliffs of Dover
> Tomorrow—just you wait and see.

8. Kentucky bluegrass, which, despite its name, is native to Eurasia, but is naturalized throughout North America.

9. "Tie a Yellow Ribbon Round the Ole Oak Tree," which became an enormous hit when it came out in 1973, with some 100 million copies sold. The song concerns a man about to be released from jail who tells his wife what to do if she wants him to come home. If he doesn't see it, he will just "stay on the bus and forget about us."

10. Gelett Burgess, who was so plagued by the lines that nineteen years later he felt forced to issue this warning:

> Ah, yes, I wrote the "Purple Cow"—
> I'm sorry, now, I wrote it!
> But I can tell you, anyhow,
> I'll kill you if you quote it.

COMMUNICATIONS

1. Anthony Trollope, one of the great English novelists, spent over thirty years working for the General Post Office. What is he credited with inventing?

2. How did the "sage of Concord," Ralph Waldo Emerson, greet the news that the first long-distance telephone system had been developed?

3. Before 1912 the radio signal CDQ was the traditional what?

4. George Bernard Shaw once received a letter to which was appended the phrase "Dictated but not read." How did he react?

5. In what is probably the shortest amorous exchange of notes, the Prince de Joinville, after seeing the actress Rachel Félix perform, sent his card backstage, having written on it: "Where? When? How much?" What response did he get from Mlle. Félix?

6. Some friends of his, not knowing Mark Twain's current whereabouts, addressed a letter to him as follows:

   > Mark Twain
   > God Knows Where

   The letter reached him in Italy, and he replied with which two words?

7. In 1901 a young man stood on a windy hill near St. John's, Newfoundland, and flew a kite to retrieve an S. Who was he, and what was he up to?

8. Dolly Parton, the well-endowed singer and a favorite of truckers, has her own CB (Citizen's Band) frequency. What is her "handle"?

9. How did it happen that a letter addressed as follows was delivered to the person intended?

   > Wood
   > John
   > Mass

10. An Oxford undergraduate once called on a friend and found him *in flagrante*. What message did he leave?

COMMUNICATIONS

1. The mail box, which is called a pillar box in England.

2. "Now Maine can talk to Florida, but does Maine have anything to say to Florida?"

3. Distress signal. In 1912 it was replaced by SOS, which was easier to transmit and was first used by the sinking R.M.S. *Titanic*.

4. He returned the letter, adding, "Opened but not read."

5. "Your place. Tonight. Free."

6. "He did."

7. Guglielmo Marconi, who used the kite to raise an aerial for picking up the first transatlantic radio signal—the Morse letter S (three dots)—sent from his transmitter in Poldhu, Cornwall.

8. Booby Trap.

9. The post office correctly interpreted the address and delivered the letter to John Underwood, Andover, Mass.

10. "Called to see you but you were in. Sorry to find you out."

COUNTRIES

1. The Romans called it Lusitania. By what name is it known today?

2. Can you identify the oldest important republic in the world, and state why it was founded? Who was the legendary hero of this event?

3. Many countries are ruled by nuts, but what is the only one to display a "nut" on its flag?

4. "Our country! In her intercourse with foreign nations may she always be in the right; but our country, right or wrong!" Who gave this stirring toast at dinner one evening in Norfolk, Virginia, in April 1816?

5. Everyone knows that Count Dracula came from Transylvania, but where is Transylvania—that is, if it exists at all?

6. Which two countries joined in 1958 to form the United Arab Republic?

7. What is the only European country with a Moslem majority?

8. Can you locate the following: Laurania, Freedonia and Gondolin?

9. Which European country's head of state is ex officio head of state of another, jointly with a bishop?

10. Why has the European Common Market recently lost more than half its land area?

COUNTRIES

1. Portugal.

2. Switzerland. In 1291 the three original cantons—Uri, Schwyz and Unterwalden—formed the Helvetic Confederacy as a defensive league to protect themselves from the Hapsburg tyranny. The legendary hero of this union was William Tell.

3. The spice island of Grenada, advertising one of its most famous exports, the nutmeg, which is actually a hard, aromatic seed.

4. Stephen Decatur, the American naval hero, who rose to fame in the wars against the Barbary pirates. In 1815 he forced the Dey of Algiers to sign a treaty that ended American tribute to Algeria.

5. Transylvania is a region of Rumania bounded by the Carpathian Mountains and the Transylvanian Alps.

6. Egypt and Syria. Syria withdrew in 1961, but Egypt continued to be known as the United Arab Republic until 1971.

7. Albania. In 1967, however, the government shut down all mosques and churches and declared itself to be "the world's first atheist state." It is the only country in Europe for which U.S. citizens cannot obtain an entry visa.

8. They are all fictional countries: Laurania is in Winston S. Churchill's only novel *Savrola,* Freedonia in the Marx Brothers' film *Duck Soup* and Gondolin in J.R.R. Tolkien's *The Silmarillion.*

9. France. The French President is joint head of state of Andorra with the Spanish Bishop of Urgel.

10. Greenland seceded when it became independent of Denmark.

CRAZY QUILT

1. Which tree is the source of two commercial spices?

2. Give the meanings of the initials POSSLQ and the acronym BURMA.

3. A certain city in France, whose history goes back over 2,000 years, has been described as "a diadem of towers . . . a profusion of turrets, battlements and draw-bridges." Can you identify it?

4. If an old Etonian went to Eton and an old Harrovian to Harrow, what school did an old Wykehamist attend?

5. How did Sir Isaac Isaacs, the first native-born Australian to become Governor General, reply, while still in Parliament, when an enraged opponent cried, "The learned attorney general [Isaacs] looks as if he wants to eat me!"?

6. Who coined the phrase "Respectable Professors of the Dismal Sciences," and to what was he referring?

7. Can you name six well-known American composers who wrote the words as well as the melodies for their songs?

8. During World War II, what was the function of the motherly "milch cows"?

9. Can you explain the meaning of a vertical wine tasting?

10. When facing the tremendous waves at Sunset Beach, which Hawaiians call "the Pipeline," off the northern coast of Oahu, what did the reluctant surfer say?

CRAZY QUILT

1. The nutmeg tree, which produces both nutmeg and mace. Nutmeg comes from its hard, aromatic seed and mace from the covering of the kernel or seed.

2. People of the opposite sex sharing living quarters—a creation of the U.S. Census Bureau to denote the inhabitants of miscellaneous households. BURMA stands for Be Undressed Ready My Angel.

3. The medieval walled city of Carcassonne in Languedoc in southern France. Sitting high on a hill over the valley of the Aude, its double-battlement walls have been attacked or defended by Visigoths, Franks, Saracens, Huguenots and Albigensians.

4. Winchester College, one of the great English public schools, founded in 1382 by William of Wykeham, Bishop of Winchester.

5. "The honourable gentleman forgets my religion."

6. Thomas Carlyle in *Latter-Day Pamphlets,* referring to political economy and the social sciences.

7. Stephen Foster, George M. Cohan, Irving Berlin, Cole Porter, Frank Loesser and Stephen Sondheim.

8. "Milch cows" was the name given to the submarine tenders designed to supply German submarines at sea, which extended their range dramatically. Six feet broader in the beam than the ordinary U-boat, a single milch cow could carry 700 tons of diesel fuel and 45 tons of supplies in its roomy hull, enough to keep a ten-boat wolf pack at sea for as long as four months.

9. A vertical wine tasting is one in which a single wine is tasted over a span of years. It is essential to a complete understanding of any wine.

10. "They also surf who only stand and wait."

CRIMINAL TENDENCIES

1. Who is acknowledged to be the father of the modern detective story?

2. What is "Asian white," and where is it produced?

3. Experts in which field are called "tops" or "maestros"?

4. In France, what is the generic word used for the police?

5. Name the raffish and inept fictional gang that attempted to smuggle gold out of England in the form of souvenir Eiffel Towers.

6. In which racket is the term "six for five" commonly used?

7. "When constabulary duty's to be done," what is a policeman's lot, according to the sergeant of police in Gilbert and Sullivan's *The Pirates of Penzance?*

8. Who was imprisoned at or in a) Ham, b) Landsberg Castle, c) Holmby House, d) the Château d'If?

9. To custom officials, what is a "mule"?

10. Name the authors who created the following detectives:

    a) Inspector Javert
    b) Mike Hammer
    c) Nick Charles
    d) Perry Mason
    e) Philo Vance
    f) Luis Mendoza
    g) Professor Gervase Fen
    h) Simon Templar (The Saint)
    i) Mr. Moto
    j) Bulldog Drummond

CRIMINAL TENDENCIES

1. Edgar Allen Poe, with such stories of ratiocination as "The Murders in the Rue Morgue," "The Purloined Letter" and "The Mystery of Marie Rogêt."

2. "Asian white" is heroin, 95 percent pure, which is produced in the Golden Triangle, located 500 miles north of Bangkok in northeast Burma where it borders on Laos and Thailand.

3. Pickpockets.

4. Not *gendarmerie,* but simply *police.* A *gendarme* is a member of the armed forces with responsibilities for internal defense, frontier and customs watch, highway patrol and general law enforcement in rural districts.

5. The Lavender Hill Mob, in the film of the same name starring Alec Guinness as a bullion clerk with the Bank of England and Stanley Holloway, who operates a small foundry making metal souvenirs.

6. Loan sharking. "Six for five" is an inflation-resistant favorite of usurers throughout the country. Customers are required to pay back $6 for every $5 borrowed, usually within ten weeks, which works out to about 180 percent a year compounded. This rate is known as "vig" (short for vigorish) or "juice."

7. "When constabulary duty's to be done,
   A policeman's lot is not a happy one."

8. a) Napoleon III, b) Adolf Hitler, c) Charles I,
   d) Edmond Dantès, later Count of Monte Cristo.

9. A "mule" is one who employs "internals" or "internal body carriers" to smuggle drugs, which are enclosed in either fingers of surgical gloves or condoms. They manage this by lubricating their systems with various jellies. As many as 125 to 130 "internals" have been found in the stool of a single "mule."

10. a) Victor Hugo
    b) Mickey Spillane
    c) Dashiell Hammett
    d) Erle Stanley Gardner
    e) S. S. Van Dine
       (Willard Huntington
       Wright)
    f) Dell Shannon
    g) Edmund Crispin
    h) Leslie Charteris
    i) John Philips
       Marquand
    j) Herman Cyril
       McNeile
       ("Sapper")

CURIOUS DERIVATIONS

Give the derivations of the following words:

1. Shambles
2. Ukulele
3. Ostracize
4. Grenade
5. Butterscotch
6. Fiddle
7. Meretricious
8. Bunk
9. Poppycock
10. Clink

CURIOUS DERIVATIONS

1. Shambles, a condition of complete disorder or carnage, comes from a shamble, a table for the display and sale of meat. Hence, a butcher's slaughterhouse.

2. Ukulele in Hawaiian means "jumping little flea"; it was the nickname of Edward Putuis, a 19th-century British officer who popularized the instrument.

3. Ostracize: When voting to banish someone, the Athenians wrote their names on an *ostrakon,* a shard resembling an oyster shell.

4. Grenade derives from the tropical fruit pomegranate because of its shape and its numerous seeds, similar to the "exploding grains" of a grenade.

5. Butterscotch is a cooked mixture of butter and brown sugar which is lightly scored, or "scotched," with a knife.

6. Fiddle is a corruption of Vitula, the Roman goddess of joy and victory, whose celebrations were accompanied by music.

7. Meretricious, which means lacking sincerity or attracting attention in a vulgar manner, derives from the Latin *meretrix,* hired woman or prostitute. Sir Francis Bacon wrote of "the delight in meretricious embracements (where sinne is turned into art) making marriage a dull thing."

8. Bunk is short for buncum, which came from Buncombe County in North Carolina. A congressman from there once made a fatuous speech in which he said, "I'm talking for Buncombe."

9. Poppycock, often used in polite conversation, is actually from a Dutch barnyard epithet, *pappekak,* soft dung.

10. Clink takes its name from the old Clink Prison in Southwark, London, which was destroyed in the 1780 Gordon Riots.

CURTAIN CALL

1. Can you explain the theatrical origin of the phrase "to steal one's thunder"?

2. How did W.S. Gilbert "compliment" the distinguished actor-manager Sir Herbert Beerbohm Tree on his performance in *Hamlet*?

3. At the turn of the century Dublin had two theaters of intellectual stature, the Gate and the Abbey, the former offering international productions, the latter specializing in Irish drama. By what names were they locally known?

4. Why have George Spelvin and Walter Plinge appeared in so many plays?

5. Having agreed to be present at the production of one of his plays at Bury St. Edmunds, Noël Coward was also invited to attend a service commemorating the saint who gave his name to the town. How did he reply?

6. Dylan Thomas's play *Under Milk Wood* was laid in the fictional Welsh town of Llareggub. How did he dream up this name?

7. Alfred Lunt, husband of his equally famous partner Lynn Fontanne, was once asked the secret of his success. What was his advice?

8. Raymond Massey became famous for his various portrayals of Abraham Lincoln both on Broadway and in films, and eventually began to live the part, adopting Lincoln's speech and mannerisms in his private life. What was Dorothy Parker's comment on this?

9. *The Best Little Whorehouse in Texas* was a resounding hit on Broadway. Located in La Grange, Texas, southwest of Austin, its original was known thereabouts as the Chicken Ranch. How did it get this name?

10. What was John Gielgud's reaction after watching a Tennessee Williams play?

CURTAIN CALL

1. For his 1709 play *Appius and Virginia*, John Dennis invented a simulation of thunder, but the show folded. Shortly afterward, Dennis went to see a production of *Macbeth* and heard his thunder sound offstage. Incensed, he cried out, "See how the rascals use me! They will not let my play run, and yet they steal my thunder!"

2. "Superb, my dear fellow—so very funny, and not in the least vulgar."

3. Sodom and Begorrah.

4. When an actor plays two roles in a play, for the second he is identified in the cast list as George Spelvin. In Britain the name Walter Plinge is used.

5. He wired back, "I COME TO BURY ST. EDMUNDS, NOT TO PRAISE HIM."

6. Although it looks Welsh, Llareggub is simply "Bugger all" spelled backwards.

7. "I speak in a loud, clear voice and try not to bump into the furniture."

8. "Massey won't be happy until someone assassinates him."

9. During the Depression clients who could not come up with the money paid for services rendered with chickens.

10. "How different, how very different from the home lives of our own dear queens!"

DAYS AND DATES

1. What happened in London on September 8, 1752?

2. Under whose administration was Washington's Birthday declared a national holiday—Washington's, Lincoln's or Wilson's?

3. Where do we get the term "salad days"?

4. Why is June 16, 1904, memorable in literary annals?

5. TGIF stands for "Thank God, it's Friday." For what is POETS an acronym?

6. On the eve of Saint Crispin's Day, this splendid speech was given:

   We few, we happy few, we band of brothers;
   For he to-day that sheds his blood with me
   Shall be my brother; be he ne'er so vile
   This day shall gentle his condition:
   And gentlemen in England, now a-bed
   Shall think themselves accurs'd they were not here,
   And hold their manhoods cheap whiles any speaks
   That fought with us upon Saint Crispin's day.

   Who is the speaker, and to which battle is he referring?

7. The fourteens are really fifteens, but where?

8. The Bahamian festival called Junkanoo, which features weird masks, is held twice a year—on Boxing Day (the day after Christmas) and on New Year's morning. What is the origin of the term Junkanoo?

9. 1830, 1837, 1901, 1910, 1936 . . . What is the next year in this British sequence?

10. Tennessee Williams once told Gore Vidal that he did not remember anything about the Sixties—he thought he must have slept through them. How did Vidal reply?

DAYS AND DATES

1. Absolutely nothing, from the English point of view. The day was one of the eleven days skipped in order to synchronize English chronology, which was then based on the archaic Julian calendar, with the more accurate Gregorian calendar that had prevailed in the Catholic part of Western Europe since 1582.

2. Under Washington's administration, in 1796. Washington was actually born on February 11, 1731, but the anniversary of his birth was changed to February 22 to conform with the "New Style" calendar.

3. From Shakespeare's *Antony and Cleopatra,* in which Cleopatra says:

   My salad days
   When I was green in judgment, cold in blood.

4. June 16, 1904, called "Bloomsday" in Ireland, is the date of Leopold Bloom's odyssey through Dublin in James Joyce's *Ulysses.* Marathon public readings lasting forty hours have been held in bookstores over the anniversary.

5. "Piss Off Early, Tomorrow's Saturday."

6. Henry V in Shakespeare's play, speaking on the eve of October 25, 1415, when a small English force defeated a vastly superior French army at the Battle of Agincourt, which lies about halfway between Amiens and Calais.

7. In Italy and in the Italian language, in which the century including the years 1400 to 1499 is called *quattrocento*—short for *mille quattrocento* or 14th century. In English-speaking countries, these years are called the 15th century.

8. Junkanoo is a Creole corruption of the French phrase *Jean l'inconnu* (John the unknown).

9. 1952. These are the years of accession to the British throne by William IV, Victoria, Edward VII George V, Edward VIII and George VI and Elizabeth II.

10. "You didn't miss a thing."

DE GUSTIBUS

1. The ubiquitous hamburger is obviously named after the German city of Hamburg, but do you know why?

2. Where were pretzels first made?

3. *Boeuf à la mode* and shrimp *cacciatore* have both appeared on American menus. What is ridiculous about these terms?

4. When Mary Queen of Scots became ill, she felt a particular craving for an orange preserve she had once had in France. This became known to her courtiers as "Marie-malade," and eventually marmalade. True or false?

5. Why is an authentic Brunswick stew hard to find?

6. What one ability should a good restauranteur have?

7. The French gastronome Anthelme Brillat-Savarin called it the "truffle of the poor." Can you identify it?

8. Give the origin of steak tartare.

9.   The man sure had a palate covered o'er
      With brass or steel, that on that rocky shore
      First broke the cozy oyster's pearly coat,
      And risked the living morsel down his throat.

   So wrote the English poet John Gay. In *The Glorious Oyster,* edited by Hector Bolitho, one aficionado believes "they are the loveliest of foods, raw or cooked." To what does he attribute this?

10. Many American establishments advertise their fare as "Continental Cuisine." In view of what is served, one wonders what continent they have in mind. The writer Calvin Trillin thought it might be Australia. Then he decided that the chef had once worked for the Continental Trailways bus company. What continent did he finally settle on?

DE GUSTIBUS

1. In the 18th century France received choice beef from Friesland, now part of the Netherlands, via Hamburg. When the restaurants chopped up the meat, they promoted it as "hamburger steak."

2. Not Germany but Italy, where a monk twisted dough left over from the monastery bread and baked it into little figures representing children with their arms folded in prayer. These were given to those who had learned their catechism and called *pretiola*, Latin for little prayer.

3. *A la mode de quoi? Cacciatore* means hunter's style, but hunters do not catch shrimp.

4. Alas, it is false. Marmalade simply derives from *marmelo*, the Portuguese word for quince, from which it was first made.

5. Very few meat markets carry squirrel.

6. First, the ability to spell the word right: restaurateur.

7. The onion. As Dean Swift put it:

> There is in every cook's opinion
> No savoury dish without the onion;
> But lest your kissing should be spoiled,
> The onion must be throughly boiled.

8. The term steak tartare supposedly arose from the Mongol custom of tenderizing raw meat by sandwiching it between saddles and horses.

9. Their tenderness is a result of their "talent for laziness" and of their being tremendous drinkers, guzzling about 100 quarts of sea water a day.

10. Antarctica, because most of the food was originally frozen.

A DOG'S LIFE

1. What does Noah have to do with a healthy dog's nose, which is cold and wet?

2. According to Aesop's fable, what unattractive habit did the dog in the manger have?

3. Why would you have reason to hold a dog's hind leg?

4. What verse did Alexander Pope, the Wicked Wasp of Twickenham, write for the collar of the dog of Frederick, Prince of Wales?

5. How did Dr. Samuel Johnson compare a woman preacher with a dog that has learned to stand on its hind legs?

6. In the view of Mark Twain in *Pudd'nhead Wilson*, what is the principal difference between a dog and a man?

7. What is the origin of the phrase "Every dog has his day"?

8. When the first Baron Catto was Governor of the Bank of England near the end of World War II, he held forth for an inordinately long time at a meeting at which Prime Minister Churchill presided. What was Churchill's comment afterwards?

9. Dog excrement on city streets and walkways is an ongoing nuisance. What word was coined by Anthony Burgess in *A Clockwork Orange* for this?

10. When asked by two children what two coupling dogs were doing, how did Noël Coward explain the situation?

A DOG'S LIFE

1. According to legend, when the Ark sprang a leak, Noah plugged it with a dog's nose.

2. The fable concerns the dog who would not let the ox come near the hay and could not eat it himself—in other words, a person who keeps another from enjoying what he himself has no use for.

3. To take his pulse.

4.   I am his Highness' dog at Kew,
          Pray tell me, Sir, whose dog are you?

5. "It is not done well; but you are surprised to find it done at all."

6. "If you pick up a starving dog and make him prosperous, he will not bite you."

7. It comes from the poem "Young and Old" in *The Water Babies* by Charles Kingsley:

   > When all the world is young, lad
   > And all the trees are green;
   > And every goose a swan, lad,
   > And every lass a queen;
   > Then hey for boot and horse, lad,
   > And round the world away:
   > Young blood must have its course, lad,
   > And every dog his day.

8. "Catto should have lain doggo."

9. Dogmerd, combining dog with *merde,* the French vulgarism for shit.

10. "Well, you see, my dears, the one in front is blind, and her friend is pushing her all the way to St. Dunstan's." (St. Dunstan's is an agency which helps the blind.)

ENERGY

1. Name the two basic kinds of energy and explain the difference between them.

2. Which is the largest oil-producing nation in the world?

3. How were the Dutch pioneers in one field of energy production?

4. Coal is classified into four varieties. What are these, and which has the greatest heating value?

5. Can you describe hydrogenation? Who first developed it?

6. Aside from coal, what is the most abundant fossil fuel in the United States?

7. Which four Latin American and West Indian countries are the leading oil producers, and which are members of O.P.E.C.?

8. Gasohol, a 90–10 mixture of refined gasoline and ethanol derived from corn, has been suggested as a substitute during an oil shortage. What are its chief drawbacks?

9. What three gases are associated with petroleum, and in which form are they generally shipped?

10. Beneath the surface of the United States, primarily west of the Rockies, lies an untapped source of energy perhaps 5,000 times greater than the nation's total annual energy consumption. What is this?

1. Potential and kinetic energy. The former is associated with position, such as a weight on a pulley or a rock on the edge of a cliff, while the latter involves motion. For example, at the top of its swing a pendulum's energy is entirely potential; as it passes through its point of rest, its energy is entirely kinetic. Kinetic energy is one-half of the product of a body's mass and the square of its speed.

2. The Soviet Union. A controversial study by the C.I.A. predicts, however, that it will become a net importer by the late 1980s.

3. They greatly improved windmills, which today are viewed as a promising source of power.

4. Anthracite, bituminous, subbituminous and lignite. Of these, anthracite has the highest carbon content (85 to 90 percent) and the highest heating value as measured in Btus (British thermal units) per pound.

5. Hydrogenation is the process of getting oil from coal. It involves mixing coal and oil at high temperatures and pressures and then introducing hydrogen.

6. Not oil, nor natural gas, but peat. For example, the amount of peat in Alaska alone outside the permafrost area has the equivalent of 700 quadrillion Btus, which exceeds the value of the total oil reserves of the whole country.

7. Ranked in order of barrels per day: Mexico, Venezuela, Trinidad and Tobago and Ecuador. Only Venezuela and Ecuador belong to O.P.E.C.

8. The existing technology needed to produce the alcohol uses more oil than would be saved, and the cost of producing ethanol is about twice that of gasoline.

9. Methane, butane and propane, which are usually shipped in liquid form.

10. The energy is heat from vast bodies of molten rock (magma) found a few miles down in the earth's crust, usually in regions of geologic instability.

EQUATIONS

Not to fret, this category will not tax your intelligence, verbal ability or talent for math. All that is required is a little creativity. To solve the equation, simply find the missing words that are indicated by their initials. For example, 12 = I. in a F. is 12 = Inches in a Foot.

1. 18 = H. on a G. C.
2. 7 = W. of the A. W.
3. 9 = P. in the S. S.
4. 10 = A. to the B. of R.
5. 3 = P. for a F. G. in F.
6. 54 = C. in a D. (with the J.)
7. 1 = W. on a U.
8. 2 = T. D. and a P. in a P. T.
9. 8 = P. of S. in the E. L.
10. 200 = D. for P. G. in M.

EQUATIONS

1. Holes on a Golf course
2. Wonders of the Ancient World
3. Planets in the Solar System
4. Amendments in the Bill of Rights
5. Points for a Field Goal in Football
6. Cards in a Deck (with the Jokers)
7. Wheels on a Unicycle
8. Turtle Doves and a Partridge in a Pear Tree
9. Parts of Speech in the English Language
10. Dollars for Pass Go in Monopoly

ET CETERA

If "in Hertford, Herefordshire and Hampshire hurricanes hardly happen," what sort of weather might you expect to find in the Iberian Peninsula, according to whom?

Chefs often use zest to enhance the flavor of a dish. What is zest?

Which organization requires of its members a name change and a new birth date?

The celebrated sports writer Red Smith once covered the Masters golf tournament. How did he report the arrival of the players at Augusta, Georgia?

During World War II, what in the Pacific was known as the Japanese Gibraltar?

These are three groups from Greek mythology: Aglaia, Thalia and Euphrosyne; Clotho, Lachesis and Atropos; Megaera, Alecto and Tisiphone. Of these groups, which would you

        a) be forced to accept?
        b) greet with open arms?
        c) flee from, if you could?

Between two clocks, one of which is broken and does not run at all, while the other loses one second every 24 hours, which is the more accurate?

What is the origin of the phrase "to take umbrage"?

One meaning of the word linchpin is a central or cohesive element, as in the statement: "*The Dead* is a linchpin in Joyce's work." It originated in the field of transportation where it means what?

Winston S. Churchill caused consternation among his aides by invariably catching a train or plane at the very last minute. What reason did he give?

ET CETERA

1. "The rain in Spain stays mainly in the plain," according to Dr. Henry Higgins when giving elocution lessons to Eliza Doolittle in Lerner and Loewe's *My Fair Lady*.

2. Zest is the outermost part of the rind of a lemon or an orange. To remove this properly, a special utensil called a zester is required.

3. The French Foreign Legion, a volunteer armed force composed chiefly, in its enlisted ranks, of foreigners. Its international character and tradition of not revealing the men's backgrounds have lent it an aura of mystery and romance. The Legion, which was founded in 1831 by Louis-Philippe, was headquartered at Sidi-bel-Abbès in Algeria until 1962, when it was transferred to Aubagne, near Marseilles, but training is concentrated in the rugged terrain of Corsica.

4. "The happy hookers arrived safely here today, checking into their hotels without incident."

5. The island group of Truk, part of the Caroline Islands.

6. a) The Three Fates or Erinyes: Clotho (who spun the web of life), Lachesis (who measured its length) and Atropos (who cut it).
   b) The Three Graces: Aglaia (brilliance), Thalia (bloom) and Euphrosyne (mirth).
   c) The Three Furies: Megaera (envy), Alecto (pursuit) and Tisiphone (vengeance).

7. The one that does not run at all, since it tells the correct time twice every 24 hours; whereas the other will indicate the time accurately only once every 120 years.

8. To take umbrage is to take offense, to be insulted or angry, or to be overshadowed. It derives from the Latin *umbra,* shadow.

9. A linchpin is a locking pin inserted in the end of a shaft to prevent the wheel from slipping off.

10. "I always like to give it a sporting chance of getting away."

EXIT LINES

Identify the people who uttered or wrote these dying words:

1. "Crito, we owe a cock to Aesculapius. Please pay it and don't let it pass."

2. "I am about to—or I am going to—die; either expression is used."

3. "I have lived as a philosopher. I die as a Christian."

4. "I've had eighteen straight whiskeys. I think that is a record."

5. "Thomas Jefferson survives."

6. "We are all going to heaven and Van Dyck is of the company."

7. "I must go in—the fog is rising."

8. "Ring down the curtain. The farce is played out."

9. "For God's sake, look after our people."

10. "Let us cross over the river and rest in the shade of the trees."

EXIT LINES

1. The Greek philosopher Socrates, after drinking the cup of hemlock by which he was condemned to death for allegedly corrupting the youth of Athens and other impieties.

2. Dominique Bonhours, French grammarian.

3. Giovanni Giacomo Casanova, Italian adventurer, writer, spy, womanizer and, near the end of his life, librarian.

4. Dylan Thomas, Welsh poet and author.

5. John Adams, U.S. President, who died on July 4, 1826, the 50th anniversary of the Declaration of Independence. (Unknown to Adams, Jefferson had died a few hours earlier at his home in Monticello.) Describing John Adams' last moments, Samuel Eliot Morison wrote, "He lingered until the tide turned and crossed the bar at sunset."

6. Thomas Gainsborough, English portrait painter.

7. Emily Dickinson, American poet.

8. François Rabelais, French humanist and satirist.

9. Captain Robert Falcon Scott, English antarctic explorer and naval commander, who reached the South Pole in 1912, only to find that the Norwegian Roald Amundson had been there first. Scott and his party perished on the return trip to their main base. These were the last words he wrote in his diary.

10. General Thomas J. ("Stonewall") Jackson, eight days after having been mistakenly shot by his own men at the Civil War battle of Chancellorsville.

FARRAGO

1. Name the most polluted of the world's major bodies of water.

2. At the annual Academy Awards ceremonies, who was the only person to be nominated for Best Actor and Best Supporting Actor for the same performance?

3. Would top people ever be asked to a dinner party?

4. Who are Cajuns, and from where are they believed to have come?

5. How did the brilliant General "Boy" Bradford, V.C., describe a French waitress?

6. Where would you have to go to see the only Rubens ceiling painting still *in situ*?

7. When a friend taunted Dorothy Parker for being black-listed as a Hollywood screen writer, how did she reply?

8. What have the following ten letters in common, and which one has been omitted?

A H I M T U V W X Y

9. Why were bards, such as Homer, traditionally blind?

10. Henry Ford once said in an interview, "History is more or less bunk." But who wrote, somewhat more gracefully and to the point: "History with its flickering lamp stumbles along the trail of the past, trying to reconstruct its scents, to relive its echoes and kindle with pale gleams the passion of former days"?

FARRAGO

1. The Mediterranean Sea, into which 80 percent of the sewage from 250 million people living on its shores flows untreated. Industrial wastes and 100 million annual tourists add to the problem.

2. Barry Fitzgerald, for *Going My Way* in 1944. He won the Best Supporting Actor Oscar, losing the other to Bing Crosby, his co-star in the film.

3. No, they would be simply asked for dinner.

4. Cajuns are natives of Louisiana whose ancestry includes the French exiled by the English from Acadia, a former French colony of eastern Canada that included Nova Scotia and New Brunswick.

5. "She's got a midriff you could eat poached eggs off."

6. The Banqueting Hall of London's former Whitehall Palace. Painted for Charles I, the work is a celebration of the divine authority of James I and of the peace and wisdom of his reign.

7. Parker, *née* Rothschild, said, "With the crown of thorns I wear, why should I be bothered by a prick like you?"

8. They are the only mirror-image letters (except O, which has been left out) in the English alphabet.

9. At one time bards were actually blinded, so that they would not wander from the tribe.

10. Winston S. Churchill. Although his school days were a bleak and somber period in his life, he later became a distinguished historian, among his other accomplishments.

FICTIONAL CHARACTERS

1. Where would you find the three brothers: Sansfoy, Sansjoy and Sansloy?

2. Which future Shakespearean king lamented his lot as follows?

   Deform'd, unfinish'd, sent before my time
   Into this breathing world, scarce half made up,
   And that so lamely and unfashionable
   That dogs bark at me as I halt by them . . .

3. Which four illustrious gentlemen comprised the Corresponding Society of the Pickwick Club, whose duty was to report on their journeys and adventures and make observations of character and manners?

4. Who "loved the days of old," "sighed for what was not" and "dreamed of Thebes and Camelot"?

5. Who was responsible for Hester Prynne having to wear a scarlet A, signifying Adulteress, in Nathaniel Hawthorne's *The Scarlet Letter*?

6. When he was a seven-year-old boy living in New York City, who did Cedric Errol suddenly find himself to be?

7. In the film *The Thirty-Nine Steps,* based on John Buchan's novel, why was the hero discomfited to find that his host in the Scottish Highlands was missing the tip of the little finger on his right hand?

8. Who was described as looking like "a squashed cabbage leaf" and "a draggletailed guttersnipe," and later, describing her mother, said "Gin was mother's milk to 'er"?

9. As an undergraduate, he was "magically beautiful, with that epicene quality which in extreme youth cries aloud for love and withers at the first cold wind." What was his name, and who was his constant companion when he was at Oxford?

10. Whose world was peopled with such quintessentially English types as Tubby Glossop, Oofy Prosser, Bingo Little, and later with Hollywood moguls like Jacob Z. Schnellenhamer of Colossal-Exquisite and Isadore Fishbein of Perfecto-Fishbein?

FICTIONAL CHARACTERS

1. In Edmund Spenser's *The Faerie Queene*. Sansfoy is the Faithless; Sansjoy, the Joyless; and Sansloy, the Lawless.

2. Richard, Duke of Gloucester, later Richard III in Shakespeare's play of that name.

3. Messrs. Tracy Tupman, Augustus Snodgrass, Nathaniel Winkle and, of course, Samuel Pickwick.

4. Miniver Cheevy, in Edwin Arlington Robinson's poem. The last verse is:

   Miniver Cheevy, born too late,
      Scratched his head and kept on thinking;
   Miniver coughed and called it fate,
      And kept on drinking.

5. The Reverend Arthur Dimmesdale, a seemingly saintly young minister. At the end he makes a public confession on the pillory in which Hester had once been placed and dies there in her arms, a man broken by his concealed guilt.

6. Little Lord Fauntleroy, in the novel by Frances Hodgson Burnett.

7. Richard Hannay, already suspected of murder by Scotland Yard, knew only that the head of the ruthless group out to destroy England had this physical handicap. Robert Donat played the part of Hannay in Alfred Hitchcock's film version of the book, while Godfrey Tearle was the villain, Professor Jordan.

8. Eliza Doolittle, in George Bernard Shaw's *Pygmalion*, which later became the stage musical and film *My Fair Lady,* by Frederick Loewe and Alan Jay Lerner.

9. Sebastian Flyte, the younger son of Lord Marchmain, in Evelyn Waugh's complex social novel *Brideshead Revisited*. While at Oxford, Sebastian created quite a stir by carrying around his teddy bear Aloysius.

10. P.G. (Sir Pelham Grenville) Wodehouse, creator of the immortal Jeeves and Bertie Wooster.

FIRE DRILL

1. What is literally the Land of Fire, and why was it so named?

2.   The boy stood on the burning deck
              Whence all but he had fled.

   In this poem, "Casabianca," by Felicia Dorothea Hemans, why on earth did he keep standing there instead of clearing off?

3. Supreme Court Justice Oliver Wendell Holmes, Jr. had heavy and almost fatal involvements as a young officer in the Union forces during the Civil War at Ball's Bluff and Antietam. Looking back from the vantage point of many decades, he was to say what?

4. Who sagely observed, "Fire is the best of servants, but what a master!"?

5. Those federal officials who frame bureaucratic language are not satisfied with simple words like fire and explosion. What terms have been dreamed up to replace them?

6. Who is remembered for this line: "I'm going to fire some of these people. Give me the fire bell"?

7. Red Adair is preeminent in combatting which type of industrial mishap?

8. Naval vessels such as the U.S.S. *Mauna Loa, Firedrake* and *Diamond Head* belong to what category of ships?

9. According to the *New Columbia Encyclopedia,* Lillian Mountweasel, an American photographer born in Bangs, Ohio, died in a manner consistent with the name of her birthplace. Can you describe the circumstances?

10. On hearing that a theater in Andorra had caught fire and a number of people were crushed to death because there was only one exit, what was George S. Kaufman's advice?

FIRE DRILL

1. Tierra del Fuego, an archipelago, partly Chilean and partly Argentinian, that forms the southern tip of South America. It was discovered by Magellan, who gave it this name because of the fires of the natives burning on shore at night.

2.   The flames rolled on; but he would not go
          Without his father's word.

   During the Battle of the Nile in 1798 Giacomo Casabianca was aboard the flagship *L'Orient,* commanded by his father, when she caught fire. When most of the crew had fled, Giacomo remained behind to help his gallant father.

3. "Through our great good fortune, in our youth our hearts were touched by fire."

4. Thomas Carlyle, in *Past and Present*.

5. Fire becomes "rapid oxidation," while an explosion is an "energetic disassembly."

6. Groucho Marx, in *Cocoanuts* [*sic*], in which he plays the part of Hammer, a shifty Florida hotel operator and auctioneer of resort acreage.

7. Red Adair is considered the world's expert in oil-well fires, whether on land or on drilling rigs.

8. Ammunition ships, whose names are from volcanoes or words suggesting fire or explosives.

9. While on assignment for *Combustibles* magazine, Mountweasel was blown up in an explosion.

10. "Never put all your Basques in one exit."

FRACTURED FRENCH

Fractured French consists of bizarre translations, phonetically influenced, which were collected by Fred S. Pearson II some years ago. For example, *Jeanne d'Arc* (Joan of Arc) might mean "No light in the bathroom," *Hors de combat* (Out of action), "Camp followers," and so on. With these guidelines, give the "fractured French" equivalents of the following:

1. *Au contraire* (On the contrary)

2. *Tout en famille* (In the bosom of the family)

3. *Quelle heure est-il?* (What time is it?)

4. *Mille fois* (Thousand times)

5. *Marseillaise* (French national anthem)

6. *Tête-à-tête* (Private conversation)

7. *Carte blanche* (Free hand)

8. *La petite chose* (The little thing)

9. *Coup de grâce* (Finishing blow)

10. *Tant pis, tant mieux* (Well, it might be worse.)

FRACTURED FRENCH

1. Away for the weekend
2. Let's get drunk at home
3. Whose babe is that?
4. Cold lunch
5. Mother says okay
6. A tight brassiere
7. For God's sake, take Blanche home
8. Your fly's open
9. Lawn mower
10. My aunt feels better after going to the bathroom

FUN AND GAMES

1. Who, on which historic occasion, said, "There's plenty of time to win this game and to thrash the Spaniards too"?

2. A Yarborough is a bridge or whist hand containing no card higher than a nine. How did the term arise?

3. Atari, a division of Warner Communications, has been a leader in the video game craze. What is the origin of the word Atari?

4. In the Gilbert and Sullivan light opera, the Mikado devises appropriate punishment for various social offenders, including "the billiard sharp whom anyone catches":

> His doom is extremely hard—
> He's made to dwell
> In a dungeon cell
> On a spot that's always barred.

But what further torture does the Mikado have in mind?

5. In *My Little Chickadee* W. C. Fields, in the part of Cuthbert J. Twillie, was playing cards when a stranger asked, "Is this a game of chance?" How did Fields respond?

6. Counters, or people with the gift of remembering what cards have been dealt in 21 or blackjack, are usually barred at casinos. What is the technical term for their art, and for whom is it named?

7. What was Dr. Samuel Johnson's idea of a most delightful pastime?

8. When told at a Halloween party that people were ducking for apples, what was Dorothy Parker's observation?

9. In which game is the Crawford rule sometimes invoked?

10. George S. Kaufman, who was a superb bridge player, had spent an exasperating afternoon at the table when his partner arose and said he was going to the bathroom. What was Kaufman's comment?

FUN AND GAMES

1. Sir Francis Drake, who was playing bowls on Plymouth Hoe, when he heard of the approach of the Spanish Armada.

2. The term is named after the 2nd Earl of Yarborough, who made a fortune betting people 1000 to 1 against its showing up. The odds against are 1 in 1728 so he came out nicely ahead.

3. In the Japanese game of Go two players compete on a board, with the advantage shifting from one player to another. Once the outcome becomes inevitable, the winning player cries out, "Atari!"

4.   And there he plays extravagant matches
         In fitless finger-stalls
             On a cloth untrue,
             With a twisted cue
     And elliptical billiard balls.

5. "Not the way I play it."

6. Mnemonics, the science or art of memory training, named for Mnemosyne, goddess of memory and mother of the Muses.

7. "Driving briskly in a post chaise with a pretty woman."

8. "There but for a typographical error, is the story of my life."

9. In tournament backgammon. The Crawford rule, named for the master player John Crawford, states that if a player gets to one point from winning–say, 20 points in a 21-point match—his opponent may not double during the next game only. After that, regular doubling is resumed.

10. "Fine. This is the first time this afternoon I'll know what you have in your hand."

GAFFES AND BONERS

1. How did Lord Raglan, who died of chagrin from his inability to defeat the Russians and win the Crimean War, not help things during the course of the campaign?

2. In the Battle of Spotsylvania Courthouse in 1864, during the Wilderness Campaign of the Civil War, how did General John Sedgwick show himself to be a poor judge of range?

3. J. Pierpont Morgan, who had a very red and prominent nose, was coming to have tea with a lady and her young daughter. The mother warned her child not to mention or stare at Mr. Morgan's nose. What unfortunately happened?

4. Uncle Don conducted a popular program for children in the 1930s. How did his career suddenly become unraveled?

5. When Walter Annenberg presented his credentials as U.S. Ambassador to the Court of St. James's to Queen Elizabeth II, she asked him if he was living in Winfield House, Barbara Hutton's former London house, which was then being redecorated. What was his classic, convoluted reply?

6. When the Nixons first visited the People's Republic of China, a large banquet was given in their honor. When Mrs. Nixon was asked by her hosts how she liked it, what was her response?

7. What comments did Oleg Cassini make about a gown worn by one of his models at a fashion show?

8. After the Reagan assassination attempt outside the Washington Hilton Hotel in March 1981, how did one television reporter recount the incident?

9. The 1983 television movie *S.O.S. Titanic,* produced for E.M.I. by Roger Gimbel, carried subtitles bearing the date to indicate the passage of time as the ship crossed the Atlantic before striking the iceberg. What went wrong with this device?

10. For his verbal pyrotechnics, which former member of the Reagan cabinet might well have been called Gaffemaster General, and what did the President give him after yet another apology?

1. Lord Raglan habitually referred to the enemy, in the presence of his allies—specifically, Marechal Canrobert and his staff—as "the French."

2. Poking his nose over the parapet of an embankment, he said, "Why, man, they couldn't hit an elephant at this dist——."

3. The child behaved like an angel, made an excellent impression and left with her nurse. The mother, said to be Mrs. Dwight Morrow, breathed a sigh of relief, turned to her guest and said, "Do you take sugar in your nose, Mr. Morgan?"

4. At the end of one program, when he thought the microphone was dead, he said, "Well, that should hold the little bastards." Unfortunately for Uncle Don, the mike was not dead.

5. "We're in the embassy residence, subject, of course, to some discomfiture as a result of a need for, uh, elements of refurbishment and rehabilitation."

6. "It was the best Chinese food I ever had."

7. "This is a lovely hostess dinner dress with a very low neckline for easy entertaining."

8. "And to think he's only in the second month of his pregnancy."

9. The ship's maiden voyage occurred in April and not May, as the subtitles read.

10. Interior Secretary James C. Watt. For his repeated gaffes, Reagan awarded him with a plaster foot with a hole shot in it. The last straw, which led to his 1983 resignation, was a remark characterizing the balance of a committee he had appointed: "I have a black, I have a woman, two Jews and a cripple."

GALLIMAUFRY

1. The Brompton cocktail was first concocted at London's Brompton Hospital for terminally ill cancer patients. What are its ingredients?

2. Can you give the origin of the phrase "by the skin of one's teeth"?

3. What was Georges Clemenceau's comment on President Wilson's Fourteen Points at the Versailles Peace Treaty in 1919?

4. Who sings the following, and what is inscribed on the author's monument?

> As some day it may happen that a victim must be found,
>   I've got a little list—I've got a little list
> Of society offenders who might well be underground,
>   And who never would be missed—who never would be missed!

5. It has been reported that Mrs. John F. Kennedy referred to the Vice President and Mrs. Johnson as what?

6. In which cinema classic was a citrus fruit an important prop?

7. After petroleum, what is the second largest item in international commerce?

8. In 1891 Rosemonde, the bride of which famous poet and novelist, wrote to her husband, *"Je t'aime plus qu'hier, moins que demain"* (I love you more than yesterday, less than tomorrow)?

9. Which country defends itself by means of what it calls the Porcupine Principle? And what is the Porcupine Principle?

10. What is 1967 regarded in sporting circles as the year I?

GALLIMAUFRY

1. Sixty percent morphine, 30 percent cocaine and 10 percent gin.

2. It is a Biblical phrase found in Job 19:20, where it says, "And I am escaped with the skin of my teeth."

3. "The good Lord had only ten."

4. Ko-Ko, the Lord High Executioner in Gilbert and Sullivan's *The Mikado*. The inscription on Sir William Schwenck Gilbert's monument on the Embankment in London reads: "His foe was folly and his weapon wit."

5. "Colonel Cornpone and his little Pork Chop."

6. *Public Enemy*, which in 1931 gave James Cagney one of his first juicy roles, especially in the scene in which he squashes half a grapefruit in Mae Clarke's face.

7. Coffee. (The United States, for example, produces no coffee except in the Kona district on the western side of the big island of Hawaii.)

8. Edmond Rostand, author of *Cyrano de Bergerac*.

9. Switzerland, which has not fought a foreign war in nearly 500 years. The Porcupine Principle involves rolling itself into a ball and brandishing its quills.

10. It marked the beginning of the Super Bowl. In this first game Vince Lombardi's Green Bay Packers defeated the Kansas City Chiefs 35–10 in the Los Angeles Coliseum.

GEMSTONES

1. Which stone, once called "gold of the North," is the earliest known gem material?

2. Kohl, or powdered antimony, is widely used in Moslem and Asian countries as a cosmetic round the eyes. Which stone was popular with ancient Egyptian, Greek and Roman women as a powder for eye shadow?

3. The finest quality of which precious gem is called pigeon's blood, and where are stones of this water found?

4. What did Friedrich Mohs contribute to the science of gemology?

5. The special characteristic of which gem is rainbow-like iridescence that changes with the angle of observation? What care should be taken with this stone?

6. Can you describe asterism and name the best-known gemstones that exhibit this effect?

7. Who first observed that "diamonds are a girl's best friend"?

8. Lapidary prose—for example, the best of such widely diverse writers as S.J. Perelman and Winston S. Churchill—is of an elegance suitable for inscription in stone. But what does a lapidary do?

9. How did the turquoise get its name?

10. When a tourist observed to one of the yeomen wardens, or "beefeaters" as they are popularly called, who were guarding the British Crown Jewels at the Tower of London that the Russians had about ten times as many on show, what did the Yeoman reply?

GEMSTONES

1. Amber, which is the fossilized resin of the pine tree. There is a Chinese saying that amber is the soul of the tiger turned to stone.

2. Malachite, a green carbonate of copper.

3. Pigeon's blood rubies come primarily from Burma.

4. The German mineralogist Mohs devised the scale for measuring the hardness of minerals, whereby talc is one and diamond is ten. The latter is the hardest substance known, its name deriving from the Greek *adamas,* unconquerable, the same root as in the word adamant.

5. Precious opal. Since an opal sometimes tends to lose its natural water, it should be stored in moist absorbent cotton to maintain its beauty. Opals once were considered unlucky for anyone not born in October.

6. Asterism is an effect of light rays forming a star; the word derives from the Greek *aster,* star. The rays meet at one point and enclose definite angles. Ruby and sapphire cabochons can show effective six-rayed stars.

7. Lorelei Lee, in Anita Loos' novel *Gentlemen Prefer Blondes,* which later became a musical starring Carol Channing.

8. A lapidary cuts, polishes, carves and engraves gems. The name derives from the Latin *lapis,* stone.

9. Turquoise is named for Turkestan, where it was discovered. The stone can be so porous that it absorbs skin oil and changes color, usually turning from blue to green.

10. "Yes, but ours are still in use."

"THE GLORY OF THE GARDEN"

1. The above is the title of a famous poem by whom?

2. Where would you go to see a most spectacular show of rhododendron hybrids and their azalea subspecies at the peak of their flowering season in May?

3. What was H.L. Mencken's definition of a cynic?

4. Who speaks these lines in which Shakespearean comedy?

   I know a bank whereon the wild thyme blows,
   Where oxlips and the nodding violet grows
   Quite over-canopied with luscious woodbine
   With sweet musk-roses, and with eglantine. . .

5. The Latin phrase *sub rosa* means in secret, privately or confidentially. How did it originate?

6. Acclaimed even by European experts as the world's most beautiful, Magnolia Gardens are more than 300 years old—almost as old as Kyoto's Imperial Gardens, and much larger. Where are they located?

7. The wild arum lily was also known as the priest's pintle or cuckoo pintle, pintle being an old word for penis. What is its more familiar name?

8. Thomas Moore once wrote:

   Our couch shall be roses all spangled with dew.

   What was Walter Savage Landor's rhyming comment on this?

9. Passion fruit, the edible fruit of the passion flower, has become, like the kiwi fruit, a food fad—for example, passion fruit sorbet. How did the passion flower come by its name?

10. Games using long words were popular in Dorothy Parker's day. When asked if she could use the word horticulture in a sentence, what did she come up with?

"THE GLORY OF THE GARDEN"

1. Rudyard Kipling. The last stanza of the poem runs:

   > Oh, Adam was a gardener, and God who made him sees
   > That half a proper gardener's work is done upon his knees,
   > So when your work is finished, you can wash your hands and pray
   > For the Glory of the Garden that it may not pass away!
   > And the Glory of the Garden it shall never pass away!

2. The Gardens of Exbury, covering 250 acres of Edmund de Rothschild's 2,600-acre estate in southern England. An award-winning television film about Exbury titled *The Glory of the Garden,* was made in 1982 by Nicholas de Rothschild and Minnie Cassatt.

3. A man who, when he smells flowers, looks around for a coffin.

4. Oberon, the king of the fairies, in *A Midsummer Night's Dream.*

5. *Sub rosa* comes from the practice of hanging a rose over a meeting as a symbol of secrecy, from the legend that Cupid once gave Harpocrates, the god of silence, a rose to make him keep the secrets of Venus. In medieval council halls a symbolic rose was carved in the center of the ceiling.

6. Magnolia Gardens lie near the Ashley River, about ten miles south of Charleston, South Carolina.

7. Parson-in-the-pulpit.

8. It would give me rheumatism and so it would you.

9. Its beautiful flower, it was thought, resembled the Passion of Christ. The three styles represent the three nails by which Jesus was crucified, and the stamens the wounds in his hands and feet. The crown is the crown of thorns, while the petals and sepals represent the apostles.

10. "You can lead a whore to culture but you can't make her think."

GOLF AND TENNIS

1. Explain the origin of the term links.

2. Who were the youngest players to win one of the Big Four tennis titles?

3. The "positive vetting" of a prospective guest player at the course of the Honourable Company of Edinburgh Golfers at Muirfield involved the following interrogation by the Secretary: "School?" "Eton." "University?" "Oxford." "Service?" "Coldstream Guards." "Rank?" "Brigadier." "Decorations?" "Victoria Cross." After this grilling, what was the Secretary's grudging instruction to the golf pro?

4. How did Teddy Tinling shake the very underpinnings of championship tennis in 1949?

5. In British golfing circles, what do the terms albatross and buzzard mean?

6. Can you name the first woman to achieve the Grand Slam of tennis with her victories in the United States, Great Britain, France and Australia in the same year? What other women players have equalled her feat?

7. Explain the circumstances whereby Alvin Clarence Thomas, also known as Titanic Thomas, won a bet that he could drive a golf ball 500 yards, and how did he come by his nickname?

8. What do the following have in common: dedans, grille, chase, tambour, penthouse?

9. Apart from Gene Sarazen's spectacular double eagle in the 1935 Masters, what is considered the most memorable golf shot in the modern times?

10. Why is Rod Laver, the Red Rocket from Queensland, unique in the annals of tennis?

GOLF AND TENNIS

1. The term links originally denoted broken, sandy ground descending to the sea. As a rule, links courses are more natural than American courses, having been formed by eons of erosion by wind and rain.

2. In 1887 Charlotte (Lottie) Dod was 15 when she won at Wimbledon, and Tracy Austin won the U.S. Open in 1979 at the age of 16. In 1982 Mats Wilander of Sweden was 17 when he won the French Open title.

3. "Give him nine holes."

4. Teddy Tinling designed the highly visible lace panties in which "Gorgeous" Gussie Moran caused a sensation on the courts.

5. An albatross is a double eagle (three under par), while a buzzard is a triple bogey or three over par.

6. Maureen Connolly, who was affectionately known as "Little Mo," in 1953. She was forced to retire when she broke her leg in a riding accident, and died of cancer at the age of 34 in 1969. Margaret Court Smith won the Grand Slam the following year, and Martina Navratilova won it in 1984.

7. Titanic Thomas teed up the ball on the shore of a frozen lake and drove it over the ice. His nickname came from his prowess on the putting green—Titanic could sink the unsinkable.

8. They are all parts of a royal or real tennis court. The game played on it is called court tennis in the United States, and is the forerunner of all racquet games.

9. Tom Watson's dramatic holing of a 20-foot sandwedge shot from the fringe of the green to give him a birdie on the par-three 17th hole of Pebble Beach. He birdied the 18th as well, wresting the lead from Jack Nicklaus in the 1982 U.S. Open.

10. Rod Laver is the only player to win the Grand Slam in tennis twice—in 1963 and 1969. The first person to win all four tournaments in the same year was Don Budge in 1938, the year Laver was born. In 1971, Laver became the first tennis player to pass the $1 million mark in total earnings.

GOVERNMENT

1. Who said, "You have sat too long here for any good you have been doing. Depart, I say, and let us have done with you. In the name of God, go!"? And who had occasion to repeat these words in the House of Commons almost 300 years later?

2. Which U.S. President said, "The budget should be balanced, the treasury should be refilled, the arrogance of officialdom should be tempered and controlled, and assistance to foreign lands should be reduced lest the State become bankrupt. The people should be forced to work and not depend on the government for subsistence"?

3. Which Scotsman in 1888 wrote *The American Commonwealth,* a standard work on the government of the United States?

4. Procedural matters are scrupulously observed in both the U.S. Congress and British Parliament. Among the unwritten rules is a "sense of comity," which is not funny at all. Can you give its meaning?

5. Can you name three former actresses who became dominant forces in the governments of their countries?

6. The view of which political leader was tempered by his country's vast production of cheese?

7. The original signed copy of the U.S. Constitution may be seen at the Library of Congress. Where may the British Constitution be seen?

8. One historic definition of a diplomat is "an honest man sent to lie abroad for the good of his country." How did Adlai Stevenson put it?

9. What are the five M's that Senator Robert Dole listed as essential for political success?

10. The pundit William F. Buckley once ran for Mayor of New York City. What was his reply when asked what his first act would be if elected?

GOVERNMENT

1. Oliver Cromwell, dismissing the Rump Parliament in 1653, when he considered it no longer fit to govern. Leo S. Amery from the back benches of Neville Chamberlain's government in 1940.

2. No President in these exact words, which are those of Marcus Tullius Cicero in 43 B.C., the last year of his life. *Plus ça change, plus c'est la même chose.* (The more it changes, the more it remains the same.)

3. James—later Viscount—Bryce, historian, statesman and diplomat.

4. Comity means civility or courtesy. Under this rule, any unflattering remark must be carefully phrased. For example, a recent Speaker of the House once said, "I hold the gentleman in minimum high regard," and in 1906 Winston S. Churchill distanced himself from his fellow liberals by calling one of their utterances a "terminological inexactitude."

5. Evita Duarte de Peron of Argentina; Jiang Qing, widow of Mao Zedong and a member of the infamous "Gang of Four"; and Melina Mercouri, Cultural Minister of Greece.

6. France's Charles de Gaulle, who once posed the question, "How can you run a country that has 246 kinds of cheese?"

7. There is no single document in Britain. Its "Constitution" starts with the Magna Carta, which limits the power of the sovereign, and embodies a vast body of statutes, declarations, common law principles and precedents that set forth the power of the people acting through Parliament.

8. "A diplomat is a very understandable and easy-to-describe person who is made up of three parts: one part protocol, one part Geritol and one part alcohol."

9. Money, manpower, management, momentum and media attention.

10. "I'd demand a recount."

GRAB BAG

1. If you are being examined by a psychiatrist and he writes on his pad, "O.T.L." or "O.T.W.," what does he mean?

2. For whom did Ernest Hemingway propose to start a subscription to put through Yale?

3. Why would the phrase "No Plan Like Yours To Study History Wisely" prove helpful to a student of English history?

4. It is, perhaps, the Grecian urn that says, "Beauty is truth, truth beauty," in John Keats' famous ode. If so, why was Keats not being strictly accurate here?

5. What is "strine"?

6. The writing of which great poem was interrupted, and could never be resumed, by a person on business from Porlock?

7. Chevy Chase is the name of an actor and a well-known Washington club, and also the title of a Middle English ballad about the Battle of Otterburn in 1388, which arose from a hunt (chase) near the Cheviot Hills on the Scottish border. (From this title comes the verb chivy, meaning to harass.) What haunting lines occur in this ballad?

8. In a math exam an astute but indolent student was asked the following question: "Using a sextant, how would you determine the height of a building?" What was his practical answer?

9. Which ecologically unique group of islands are named for the giant tortoises that live there?

10. The Shan, the oldest son of the Shah, was subject to epileptic fits and a doctor was engaged to be in constant attendance upon him. One day the Shan had a seizure when the doctor was not around. What did the angry Shah have to say to the doctor?

GRAB BAG

1. He thinks you are "Out To Lunch" or "Off The Wall."

2. John O'Hara, whose preoccupation with marks of status among the American upper class got on Hemingway's nerves.

3. The initial letters indicate in chronological order the principal royal houses of England: Norman, Plantagenet, Lancaster, York, Tudor, Stuart, Hanover, Windsor.

4. Keats, it is thought, was writing about a Wedgwood jasper-ware copy of the famous Roman glass vase called the Portland vase in honor of the Duke of Portland, who lent it to the British Museum in 1810.

5. "Strine" (corruption of Australian) is both a dialect and a way of pronouncing English. For example, "Don't come the raw prawn" is strine for "You can't fool me," as is "A bison is used for washing you fice in," and "Emma chissit?" ("How much is it?")

6. "Kubla Khan." Coleridge was reading these lines from *Purchas his Pilgrimage:* "Here the Khan Kubla commanded a palace to be built, and a stately garden there unto. And thus ten miles of fertile ground were enclosed with a wall." About here Coleridge fell asleep, and on awakening feverishly wrote down what he had dreamed. After the "person from Porlock" had left, he found his recollection of the rest of the dream had gone, and the poem was never completed.

7.   But I have dreamed a dreary dream
       Beyond the Isle of Skye;
       I saw a dead man win a fight,
       And I think that the man was I.

8. "Lower the sextant from the top of the building and measure the string."

9. The Galápagos (Spanish for tortoises), which are located in the Pacific 650 miles west of Ecuador, of which they are a province, and consist of 13 main islands and numerous smaller ones.

10. "Where were you when the fit hit the Shan?"

GRAFFITI

During World War II the phrase KILROY WAS HERE became the most ubiquitous of all graffiti, appearing on surfaces from Arnhem to Alamein, from Bizerte to Burma. Kilroy actually existed; he was an inspector in a Quincy, Massachusetts shipyard who chalked the words on ships and equipment to keep men on their toes. The following graffiti have elicited what replies?

1. I like sheep.

2. Jesus is the answer.

3. Pertstroofka Noodleman lives.

4. Keep New York Clean.

5. Sodom is a summer festival.

6. I love Margaret Holmes.

7. All women over forty are lesbains.

8. Lions 7, Christians 0.

9. Faith can move mountains.

10. To be is to do—Plato.

GRAFFITI

1. It's me and ewe, babe!
2. What's the question?
3. And obviously quite alone.
4. Eat a pigeon today.
5. Gomorrah the merrier.
6. Good God, Watson, so do I!
7. But they can spell.
8. Christians in heaven, lions ill.
9. She's a big girl.
10. To do is to be—Socrates.

   [and underneath]

   Do-be-do-be-do—Sinatra.

GREAT BRITAIN

1. The Seven Sisters is another name for what famous British landmark?

2. On which historic site do the ruins of Battle Abbey stand?

3. Where in 1215 did King John sign the Magna Carta, and which later leader is also memorialized there?

4. Besides being cities, what do the following have in common: Aberdeen, Liverpool, Newcastle, Oxford, Salisbury?

5. Who went to King's College, Cambridge, and thought so little of the "townies" that he penned these lines?

   For Cambridge people rarely smile,
   Being urban, squat, and packed with guile.

6. Where in London is one expected to obey the Regency laws, still imposed by top-hatted beadles, forbidding one to whistle, sing or hurry?

7. There are seven regiments of guards in the Household Division, two of horse and five of foot. Can you name them, and state the simplest way to distinguish between the five classes of foot guards when they are in dress uniform?

8. Scottish tartans were originally worn to tell members of one clan from another. What distinction, however, attaches to the Balmoral tartan and the Culloden tartan?

9. For what would you stand in Britain and run in America? And if you moved from green to red seats, what would have happened?

10. Cockney rhyming slang, usually condensed into a single word, came into vogue in the early 19th century to confound the police and baffle authority. Can you give the normal word for the following?

a) weasel	f) titfer
b) Khyber	g) ginger
c) trouble	h) Bristols
d) tiddley	i) Berk
e) briney	j) cobblers or orchestras

GREAT BRITAIN

1. The White Cliffs of Dover, at Beachy Head on the Sussex coast.

2. The Battle of Hastings, in which William the Conqueror defeated Harold in 1066, was fought on that site.

3. Runnymede in Egham on the south bank of the Thames River, west of London. (He did not sign the document, however, as he could not write; he affixed his seal.) There is also a memorial to John F. Kennedy at Runnymede.

4. They were all British prime ministers.

5. Rupert Brooke in the poem "The Old Vicarage, Grantchester."

6. The Burlington Arcade, built in 1819 by Lord George Cavendish. Each of its thirty-eight shops is a precious antique, an enduring legacy of the city's history, preserved as "a Category One national monument."

7. The two mounted regiments are the Life Guards and the Blues and Royals. Listed in order of seniority, the foot guards are: Grenadier, Coldstream, Scots, Irish and Welsh; they are instantly recognizable by the spacing of their tunic buttons.

8. The Balmoral tartan, named for the castle in Aberdeenshire which Queen Victoria bought in 1848, was designed by her Consort H.R.H. Prince Albert. It is reserved for the sole use of the royal family. After the Jacobite defeat at Culloden a scrap of tartan with no clan affiliation was found. Recently woven into cloth, it is called the Culloden tartan and is in the public domain.

9. Elective office. You would have moved from the House of Commons to the House of Lords.

10. a) coat (weasel and stoat)
    b) ass (Khyber Pass)
    c) wife (trouble and strife)
    d) drink (tiddley-wink)
    e) darlin' (briney marlin)
    f) hat (tit for tat)
    g) queer (ginger beer)
    h) titties (Bristol cities)
    i) cunt (Berkshire Hunt)
    j) balls (cobbler's awls or orchestra stalls)

HAUTE CUISINE

1. A *poulet de Bresse* is one of the most tender and flavorful chickens to be found anywhere. What does it have in common with the French flag?

2. Alexander Dumas *père* called it the *sacrum sanctorum* of epicures, George Sand the "fairy apple" and others everything from the "divine tuber" to the "underground princess." What is referred to, and how much do they cost?

3. During the French Revolution, how did the mathematical philosopher the Marquis de Condorcet inadvertently reveal himself to be an aristocrat when ordering an omelet in a café?

4. What do the following have in common: angelot, rascasse, roucaou, loup and vive?

5. Mastering adjectival descriptions in a foreign menu takes a little doing. For starters, interpret the following:

    a) *Bigarade*
    b) *Bolognese*
    c) *Crécy*
    d) *Piedmontese*
    e) *Périgourdine*

6. The title *cordon bleu* denotes a person highly distinguished in his field, and generally refers to a master chef, or *gros bonnet*. How did the term arise?

7. Lamb designated *pré salé* is not to be missed. What is so special about it?

8. What innovation brought fame to the French chefs Paul Bocuse, Michel Guérard and the brothers Paul and Pierre Troisgros?

9. *Poulet demi-deuil* is aptly named. Why?

10. Can you name a delicious dessert first prepared by the chef of a Russian diplomat?

HAUTE CUISINE

1. The colors: a *poulet de Bresse* has a red crown, white meat and blue feet.

2. Truffles, which cost between $450 and $600 a pound—the most expensive food in the world.

3. When the waiter asked him how many eggs he wanted, the Marquis, who had been hiding out with a price on his head, replied, "Twelve," revealing his ignorance of a working man's omelet. Suspicious, the waiter called the police, who arrested the starving philosopher. He escaped the guillotine only by taking poison.

4. They are all Mediterranean fish used in preparing bouillabaisse.

5. a) *Bigarade* is a bitter cooking orange from Spain that is a requisite for a true duck *à l'orange*.
   b) *Bolognese* refers to a red meat sauce served with pasta.
   c) *Crécy,* a small town remembered for a big battle, always connotes carrots as a main ingredient.
   d) *Piedmontese* means risotto with blanched truffles or mushrooms.
   e) *Périgourdine* always contains Périgueux truffles from the region of Périgord.

6. The *cordon bleu* was the blue ribbon worn as a decoration by members of the Order of the Holy Ghost, the highest order of French chivalry under the Bourbon monarchy.

7. *Pré salé* pertains to young sheep that have grazed on pastures near the sea.

8. *Nouvelle cuisine,* which emphasized fresh ingredients and a lighter approach to cooking than was traditional. Some followers of the masters, offering contrived dishes served on immense plates, have produced what is known as *cuisine poseur*.

9. *Demi-deuil* means half-mourning, since slices of black truffle are placed between the skin and flesh of the breast.

10. Nesselrode: a rum-flavored mixture of chestnuts, cherries, preserved oranges and dried fruits used in puddings, pies or ice cream. Count Karl Nesselrode's chef, Moüy, named it in his honor.

HIGH AND LOW

1. In which countries might you find towers of silence?

2. There are two lowest points on earth, but only on one can you stand without support. For whatever help it may be, they are both below sea level. Where are they?

3. Why is the northernmost department of France so aptly named?

4. How did the English mystery writer Edgar Wallace define a highbrow?

5. Where in the contiguous United States is the lowest point only 84 miles from the highest point?

6. "Made it, ma—top of the world!" Which mother's boy and killer cried this out at the end of which film?

7. Which group of employees sought to upgrade their occupational status by calling themselves members of the Vertical Transportation Corps?

8. When Groucho Marx was asked by a hotdog vendor at a baseball game which hotdog he would like, what was his reply?

9. The principal airport for which major city is thirteen feet below sea level?

10. How did Lord Curzon, later 1st Marquess Curzon of Kedleston, show his ignorance of the working class when he saw some soldiers bathing in the vats of a shelled-out brewery?

HIGH AND LOW

1. In India or Iran, where Zoroastrians, known as Parsees to the Indians, expose their dead in towers to be eaten by birds of prey.

2. The first is where the River Jordan enters the Dead Sea, 1,290 feet below sea level. The second is the deepest known depression on the earth's surface—the Marianas Trench, whose depth has been measured at 36,198 feet or nearly seven miles.

3. Curiously enough, it is called Nord, which simply means north.

4. "A man who has found something more interesting than women."

5. California, where Death Valley, at 282 feet below sea level, is not very far from Mount Whitney, which rises 14,494 feet.

6. James Cagney as Jody Garrett, shouting from the top of a gas tank in Raoul Walsh's *White Heat*.

7. Elevator operators at Philadelphia's Hahnemann Hospital. This effort brought them honorable mention from the Committee on Public Doublespeak of the National Council of English.

8. "Give me the one on the bottom. I always root for the underdog."

9. Amsterdam's Schiphol, which in Dutch means ship's graveyard. It lies on land reclaimed from the sea.

10. "I never knew the lower classes had such white skins."

HIGHWAYS AND BYWAYS

1. Everyone knows that the British Prime Minister lives at 10 Downing Street, but who lives at 11 Downing Street?

2. Which short but famous street starts at a church and ends near a river, and what is the reason for its name?

3. What prodigious literary effort was carried out in the garret of a house at 17 Gough Square in London?

4. Name the widely esteemed toiletry product that takes its name from its address on the Glockengasse in Köln-am-Rhein.

5. The well-to-do residents of certain parts of a charming Southern city are called SOBs. Can you explain this?

6. Sidney Kingsley's play (and later movie) *Dead End*, starring Humphrey Bogart and introducing the Dead End Kids, is an engrossing melodrama about New York slum life. The dead end street where the action takes place is readily identifiable by the luxury apartment house that serves as a backdrop. Where is it?

7. Which famous diarist lived at 263 Prinsengracht in Amsterdam?

8. Can you identify the controversial mayor of a large eastern city who made this inane remark: "The streets are safe; it's only the people who make them unsafe"?

9. Why are the Mall and the circular roadway in front of Buckingham Palace the only streets in London paved in red?

10. The forbidding Darien Gap is a fifty-mile missing link in a 16,000 mile chain. Where is this gap located, and what points does the chain link?

HIGHWAYS AND BYWAYS

1. The Chancellor of the Exchequer.

2. Wall Street, which starts at Trinity Church and ends near the East River. Its name comes from the stockade or wall built in 1653 by the Dutch settlers to protect the settled area south of it from assault by the Indians.

3. Dr. Samuel Johnson compiled his famous *Dictionary of the English Language* in this room, which was fitted up like a counting house with a long desk at which several people would write standing. The isolated private house stands surrounded by the printing firms of Fleet Street. Close by is the Cheshire Cheese, one of Johnson's favorite haunts.

4. No. 4711 Eau de Cologne, which is the genuine article, and still the best.

5. People who live in the large, desirable houses south of Broad Street in Charleston, South Carolina.

6. East 53rd Street, near the East River. In the background is the River House, built in 1931, which was the first luxury apartment house to be put up on former tenement land facing the river. A Peter Arno cartoon of the period recaptures its image: A bibulous gentleman in white tie and tails is deposited by two burly cops at the entrance to some smart building, only to be turned away by the doorman saying, "He's not ours. Try the River House."

7. Anne Frank, who wrote her diary in a secret annex there. She was arrested when she was 15 and died of typhus within a year at the Bergen-Belsen concentration camp. The diary has been a play, a movie and a book with a total print run of some 15 million copies in 50 languages.

8. Former Mayor Frank Rizzo of Philadelphia.

9. They are paved in red to indicate their royal status as facing Buckingham Palace.

10. The gap lies between the Panama Canal and northwest Colombia. When it is completed, one will be able to drive from Alaska to Chile on the Pan American Highway.

HODGEPODGE

1. Can you name the only state that has produced seven elected U.S. presidents?

2. A memorable cartoon by Peter Arno shows a man standing next to a bosomy blonde seated at a bar. What are his instructions to the bartender?

3. Who left for France in a Fury on December 12, 1936?

4. An aphorism is an eternal truth packed into a pithy one-liner, but for almost each there is a contra-aphorism. Give the opposites of the following:

   a) Thou shalt not steal. (Exodus 20:15)
   b) Never look a gift horse in the mouth. (Samuel Butler)
   c) No evil can happen to a good man. (Plato)
   d) Haste makes waste. (John Heywood)
   e) Absence makes the heart grow fonder. (Sextus Aurelius)

5. How and why is an elephant given a haircut?

6. What would be a prime blunder for an oarsman in the annual Yale-Harvard crew race held on the Thames at New London, Connecticut?

7. When did the Chief Justice of the Supreme Court serve as Secretary of State at the same time?

8. Horses who win the three races that comprise the Triple Crown are draped with blankets of flowers. Can you match the flowers with the races?

9. When a visitor arrived to see President Lowell of Harvard in the early 1900s, how did the dean apologize for his absence?

10. His accountants once told the last Duke of Buckingham that he would have to economize and that one of his six Italian pastry chefs would have to go. What was the plaintive wail of the impoverished peer?

HODGEPODGE

1. Ohio. Grant, Hayes, Garfield, Benjamin Harrison, McKinley, Taft and Harding were all born there. (Virginia also produced seven presidents—Washington, Jefferson, Madison, Monroe, William Henry Harrison, Tyler and Wilson—but Tyler was not elected. On Harrison's death he became the first vice president to succeed to the presidency.)

2. "Fill 'er up."

3. The Duke of Windsor, after his abdication as Edward VIII, sailed from Portsmouth to Boulogne on the destroyer H.M.S. *Fury*.

4. a) God helps those that help themselves. (Algernon Sydney)
   b) Beware of Greeks even bearing gifts. (Virgil)
   c) Nice guys finish last. (Leo Durocher)
   d) He who hesitates is lost. (Anonymous)
   e) Out of sight is out of mind. (Arthur Hugh Clough)

5. With a blowtorch, so that the elephant's stiff bristles will not scratch circus performers.

6. "Catching a crab"—that is, striking the water with an oar in recovering a stroke or missing it in making one. Not only will this disrupt the rhythm of the other oarsmen, but it could catapult the rower out of the shell.

7. In 1801 John Marshall served in both capacities under President John Adams, and actually tried a crucial case—*Marbury* v. *Madison*—arising from the incompetence of the State Department under his management.

8. Red roses—Kentucky Derby; black-eyed Susans—Preakness; white carnations—Belmont.

9. "President Lowell is down in Washington, seeing Mr. Taft."

10. "What! Can't a fellow even enjoy a biscuit anymore?"

HOLY MATRIMONY

1. Do you recall the tiny connubial claim to fame of Lavinia Warren in 1863?

2. Why does a bride never walk down the aisle of a church?

3. The dancer Isadora Duncan once proposed marriage to George Bernard Shaw for the express purpose of bearing a child by him. "Imagine one with your brains and my body," she rhapsodized. What was Shaw's devastating reply?

4. After marrying a woman twice his age, what did the English politician and journalist John Wilkes say after his wedding night?

5. The speaker revisits the home of his youth and bemoans the fate of his lost love Amy, "shallow-hearted," who abandoned him in deference to her parents' desire for a wordly marriage, in the following lines of whose poem?

> As the husband is, the wife is; thou art mated with a clown,
> And the grossness of his nature will have weight to drag thee down.

6. According to Francis Bacon in "Of Marriage and Single Life," what three roles do wives play in men's lives?

7. How did Sacha Guitry tenuously link woman's infidelity with marriage?

8. Even at the best-ordered weddings, lapses will occur. When H.R.H. Prince Charles married Lady Diana Spencer in St. Paul's Cathedral in July 1981, minor slips were made by each of them. What were they?

9. Louise de Vilmorin and André Malraux were lovers for twenty years. When he finally asked her to marry him, what did she say?

10. How are these women connected: Dorothea of Zelle, Caroline of Anspach, Charlotte Sophie of Mecklenburg-Strelitz, Caroline of Brunswick, Mary of Teck and Elizabeth Bowes-Lyon?

1. Lavinia Warren (2 feet 8) married the famed P.T. Barnum midget "General Tom Thumb" (3 feet 4), who had to contend for her favors with his even tinier amorous rival, "Commodore Nutt." Later President Lincoln threw a lavish reception for them at the White House. After Tom's death at 45, Lavinia married a piccolo player named "Count Primo Magri," who was 3 feet 9.

2. She actually walks down the nave. The aisles are on either side of the nave.

3. "But suppose it had *your* brains and *my* body?"

4. "It was a sacrifice to Ploutos, the god of wealth, not to Venus."

5. "Locksley Hall," by Alfred, Lord Tennyson.

6. "Wives are young men's mistresses, companions for middle age and old men's nurses."

7. "There are women whose infidelities are the only link they still have with their husbands."

8. Prince Charles, in pledging to share all his worldly goods, omitted "worldly." Lady Diana called the Prince "Philip Charles Arthur George," instead of "Charles Philip Arthur George."

9. "Nowadays, chéri, only priests marry."

10. They all married men who were or became King Georges of England, and are the wives of George I to George VI respectively.

"HOME, SWEET HOME"

1. London may well lay claim to having the first luxury apartment house in the world. What is it called?

2. Who live in warrens, setts, earth and yurts?

3. Can you identify the last great estate on the island of Manhattan in New York City?

4. Which famous poem came from the almost forgotten opera *Clari, The Maid of Milan,* with music by Sir Henry Bishop and libretto by John Howard Payne?

5. Who made the following their home?

   a) I Tatti
   b) Haworth Parsonage
   c) Sagamore Hill
   d) Dove Cottage
   e) Pickfair
   f) Finca Vigia
   g) Oak Hill
   h) Tanglewood
   i) Villa Mauresque
   j) Kykuit

6. In the film *Laura,* how did Clifton Webb as Waldo Lydecker, a character loosely based on the literary gadabout Alexander Woollcott, reply when complimented on his apartment?

7. Where do these lines appear: "I pray Heaven to Bestow the Best of Blessings on this House and on All that Shall thereafter Inhabit it. May none but Honest and Wise Men ever rule under this Roof"?

8. In which of England's stately homes would you find the magnificent Double Cube room, and how does it come by its name?

9. The following lines were widely quoted at the time the American hostages were being held by the Iranians. Who is the author?

   So it's home again, and home again, America for me.
   My heart is turning home again, and there I long to be.

10. When Aristotle Onassis visited Beverly Hills with an eye to buying property, he was photographed inspecting Buster Keaton's estate. How was the picture captioned?

"HOME, SWEET HOME"

1. Albany (never preceded with a "the"), set in a discreet courtyard off Piccadilly. Built by the 1st Viscount Melbourne, it was converted into flats in 1804. More distinguished people have lived there than in any other private house in London. It is named for a former owner, Frederick, Duke of York and Albany.

2. Rabbits, badgers, foxes, and Mongolian nomads respectively. (A yurt is a circular, domed portable tent.)

3. Gracie Mansion, the home of New York City's mayors. Located on a beautiful tract of land overlooking the East River and the turbulent waters of Hell Gate, the mansion, built in 1811 by the colonial merchant Archibald Gracie, has been the mayor's home since 1942, when Fiorella La Guardia moved in.

4. "Home, Sweet Home," which contains the lines:

   'Mid pleasures and palaces though we may roam,
   Be it ever so humble, there's no place like home.

   Payne's saltbox house, the original "home, sweet home," may be seen today in East Hampton, Long Island.

5. a) Bernard Berenson
   b) Charlotte Brontë
   c) Theodore Roosevelt
   d) William Wordsworth
   e) Mary Pickford and Douglas Fairbanks
   f) Ernest Hemingway
   g) James Monroe
   h) Nathanial Hawthorne
   i) W. Somerset Maugham
   j) John D. Rockefeller, Jr.

6. "It's lavish, but I call it home."

7. Inscribed on the mantelpiece in the State Dining Room of the White House. The words were written by John Adams, the first President to live in the White House.

8. Wilton House, the seat of the Earls of Pembroke for over 400 years. The Double Cube is 60 feet long, 30 feet wide and 30 feet high, and is so called because it is double the size of the adjoining room, which is a perfect cube.

9. Henry Van Dyke, in the poem "America for Me."

10. "Aristotle Contemplating the Home of Buster."

HORSEFLESH

1. Can you name the two major groups of modern horses?

2. After Dr. Johnson published his *Dictionary of the English Language*, a lady asked him how he came to define pastern as the knee of a horse. What was his forthright reply?

3. The Arabian horse has been prized since earliest times for its superior beauty, speed, spirit, grace of movement, stamina and intelligence. It has served as parental stock for which five strains of modern light horses?

4. Is a Hobson's choice a dilemma or a difficult decision?

5. Devotees of racing will know the names of the three original sires from which every Thoroughbred in the world is descended. Who were they?

6. If you were riding a course that had such formidable obstacles as Becher's Brook, the Canal Turn and the Chair, where would you be?

7. A walkover is a comparative rarity in thoroughbred racing. What kind of race is it, and when did it last spectacularly occur?

8. Why, according to U.S. racing regulations, is the length of a horse's name limited to eighteen characters, including hyphens, apostrophes and spaces?

9. Name the only Triple Crown winner to sire another winner.

10. How did Mrs. Patrick Campbell neatly manage to connect sex and horses in one sentence?

HORSEFLESH

1. The light, swift southern breeds called light horses, and the heavy, powerful northern breeds called draft horses.

2. "Ignorance, madam, pure ignorance." (The pastern is that part of a horse's foot between the fetlock and the hoof.)

3. The Thoroughbred, distinguished as a racehorse; the saddle horse, known for its easy gait; the Morgan and the quarter horse, all-purpose breeds used for riding and cattle herding; and the standardbred, or trotter, used for light harness racing.

4. It is neither. Thomas Hobson ran a livery stable in Cambridge, England, where he insisted that the customer take the horse nearest the door, so that each mount would be exercised in rotation. From this came the expression Hobson's choice, which means no choice at all.

5. Byerly Turk, imported into England in 1683; Darley Arabian, imported in 1702; and Godolphin Barb (short for Barbary), in 1725. For example, Man o' War, or Big Red as he was known, was a 14th-generation offspring of Godolphin Barb.

6. The Grand National Steeplechase, which has been held annually since 1839 at the Aintree course near Liverpool, England. It is the toughest and most dangerous steeplechase in the world.

7. A walkover is a race with only one horse entered, who has only to walk over the finish line to win. The most recent walkover was Spectacular Bid's in the 1980 Woodward Stakes at Belmont.

8. So that it will fit on the official racing sheets.

9. Gallant Fox, the 1930 winner, was the sire of Omaha, who won it in 1935.

10. "My dear, I don't care what they do as long as they don't do it in the street and frighten the horses."

INFORMATION, PLEASE

1. In which sport do you use a racquet but not a ball?

2. Who printed the first Bible?

3. According to Red Skelton, why did so many people attend the funeral service for Harry Cohn, the tyrannical head of Columbia Pictures?

4. Why is a barmecide feast certainly not fattening?

5. During World War II Prime Minister Churchill was in a lavatory for the underground War Rooms when an aide knocked timorously on the door and said that Lord Beaverbrook, then Minister of Aircraft Production, was on the telephone demanding to speak to him immediately. How did Churchill react to this invasion of his privacy?

6. The observance of Christmas as a national holiday came relatively late to the United States. Can you name the first President to give the civil service Christmas Day off?

7. Which great novel begins on this informal note: "Well, Prince, so Genoa and Lucca are now just family estates of the Buonapartes"?

8. Bruce L. Felknor, of the *Encyclopedia Britannica*, who has been intrigued by recent heroic naval rhetoric, has put many famous naval orders into Pentagonese. Give the original versions of the following:

   a) "Disregard anticipated structural damage. Continue as programmed."
   b) "Implementation of aggressive action approved. Time frame to be selected by fire control officer."

9. What is the probable derivation of the casual farewell, "Toodle-oo"?

10. It took an Englishman to devise the best response to the all too pervasive habit in the United States of saying, "Have a nice day." What did he come up with? And what was his reply to "Nice to meet you"?

INFORMATION, PLEASE

1. Badminton.

2. Not Johann Gutenberg, who was the first European to print with movable type cast in molds, but his creditors, who seized his new press and type blocks.

3. "It just goes to show that if you give the people what they want, they'll come."

4. Barmecide means plentiful or abundant in appearance only, or illusionary. It comes from the name of an 8th-century noble Persian family, one of whom served a beggar an imaginary feast in the *Arabian Nights.*

5. "Will you kindly tell Lord Beaverbrook that I can deal with only one shit at a time."

6. Grover Cleveland in 1894, perhaps responding to his experience among the German folk of Buffalo, New York.

7. *War and Peace,* by Leo Tolstoy.

8. a) David G. Farragut, at Mobile Bay in 1864: "Damn the torpedoes—Full speed ahead!"
   b) George Dewey at Manila Bay in 1898: "You may fire when you are ready, Gridley."

9. Toodle-oo is a corruption of the French phrase, *à tout à l'heure,* in a little while.

10. "Thank you, but I have other plans," and "Nice to have been met." To "Do you have children?" the reply is, "Occasionally"; while "What do you do?" (a question considered impertinent in Britain) deserves the response, "About what?"

INNS AND HOTELS

1. Who shared a room with a prince at Peter Coffin's The Spouter Inn, in New Bedford, Massachusetts?

2. In 1886 Theodore Roosevelt, then 28 and a widower, walked from his hotel to be married to his second wife Edith Kermit Carow. In 1905 his distant cousin Franklin D. Roosevelt and the latter's wife, Eleanor, TR's niece, checked into the same hotel on their wedding trip. Can you identify the hotel?

3. Where are the following hotels located?

   a) Peninsula
   b) Hassler
   c) Mount Nelson
   d) Stanford Court
   e) La Réserve
   f) Château Frontenac
   g) Grande Bretagne
   h) St. George
   i) Dolder Grand
   j) Oriental

4. As you enter which *grand luxe* hotel will you find a small bronze statue of Louis XIV astride his favorite charger? And what is particularly noticeable about the horse's raised right knee?

5. In Maxfield Parrish's famous mural in the King Cole room in New York's St. Regis Hotel, why is the King smirking and why have the fiddlers three averted their faces?

6. The main part of which legendary hotel was destroyed by a massive bomb explosion on New Year's Eve in 1980?

7. Horn's Hotel in Pago Pago, the capital of American Samoa, has been the setting for innumerable plays and motion pictures. Can you explain?

8. In a *grand luxe* hotel in Europe, who would arrive if you pressed a button marked *Service Privé* on your night table?

9. Legend has it that he was a wrecker who, by means of false lights to simulate ships in harbor, lured vessels to destruction on the reefs and then plundered their cargo. With his loot he built a stone castle, with massive walls and a crenellated battlement, which has now become a luxury resort hotel. What is its name, and where is it located?

10. Rodney Dangerfield says, "My wife always talks to me while she's having sex." What is his follow-up line?

INNS AND HOTELS

1. The outcast youth Ishmael briefly roomed with Quee-queg, a Polynesian prince who was a harpooner on the whaler *Pequod* in Herman Melville's *Moby-Dick*.

2. Brown's Hotel between London's Albemarle and Dover Streets, which was started by Lord Byron's butler in 1837. Originally it was called Brown's and St. George's Hotel, and this name still appears on a plaque at the entrance on Dover Street.

3. a) Hong Kong   f) Quebec
   b) Rome   g) Athens
   c) Capetown   h) Algiers
   d) San Francisco   i) Zürich
   e) Beaulieu   j) Bangkok

4. The Hôtel de Paris in Monaco. The knee of the horse has been burnished by gamblers over the years rubbing it for luck on their way to the casinos.

5. Apparently Old King Cole had just farted. It seems that Maxfield Parrish drew these expressions because he was dissatisfied with his payment for the mural.

6. The Norfolk Hotel in Nairobi, Kenya. Popular for years as a jumping-off point for safaris, its guests have included Ernest Hemingway and Theodore Roosevelt, who in 1909 set off on a big-game safari with 200 porters, some carrying silver buckets for champagne. The Norfolk has now been completely restored.

7. Horn's Hotel was where most of the action takes place in W. Somerset Maugham's classic short story "Miss Thompson," which has often been dramatically produced on both stage and screen under the titles *Rain* and *Sadie Thompson*. In their film *The Road to Bali* Bob Hope and Bing Crosby share a room that has a sign proclaiming "Sadie Thompson Slept Here."

8. Your personal maid or valet, if you were traveling with either.

9. Sam Lord's Castle in Barbados, West Indies.

10. "The other day she called me from a motel in Cleveland."

ISLAND HOPPING

1. What is the historically special relationship of the Channel Islands to England?

2. Name the flying island in Jonathan Swift's *Gulliver's Travels*.

3. "Undoubtedly the finest island in all the world," wrote Marco Polo seven centuries ago, when he was sent to describe the sacred tooth of Buddha by the Great Khan. Can you identify this "resplendent isle," as he called it?

4. How can we be sure on which island Daniel Defoe's sailor Robinson Crusoe was marooned?

5. Which island, known for its distinctively patterned knitware, is located at the southern tip of the Shetlands?

6. Name three Mediterranean islands that sound like a tree, a tinned fish and streets.

7. Where are the ABC islands located, and what are they?

8. Who warned of a fateful future with these words: "I have watched this famous island [Great Britain] descending incontinently, fecklessly, the stairway which leads to a dark gulf. It is a fine broad stairway at the beginning, but after a bit the carpet ends. A little farther on there are only flagstones, and a little farther on these break beneath your feet"?

9. A certain island group where people can stash away their money or put it to work free of taxes, has been called the "Switzerland of the Caribbean." It is also an off-shore financial center of major importance in international commerce because of unrestricted transactions in Eurodollars. Can you identify it?

10. Why did the self-effacing eyeglass maker move his business to the island of Amchitka?

ISLAND HOPPING

1. Since the Channel Islands are the last surviving scrap of the Duchy of Normandy, which conquered England under William, they may properly be described as having acquired England rather than the latter acquiring them.

2. Laputa, where the wise men are so engrossed in their speculations that they are ignorant about practical affairs.

3. This earthly paradise is Sri Lanka, formerly Ceylon. "Dear me," wrote Mark Twain, "it is beautiful. And most sumptuously tropical . . . Oriental in the last measure of completeness—utterly Oriental, also utterly tropical. . . ."

4. Since Robinson Crusoe mentions being able to see "the great island Trinidad," he could only have been stranded on Tobago. (Alexander Selkirk, on whose adventures Defoe based his story, was marooned on the island of Más Afuera in the Juan Fernandez group off the coast of Chile.)

5. Fair Isle. Local legend has it that the designs evolved from Spanish motifs, after a Spanish ship was wrecked there in 1588. Others believe that the patterns have a Scandinavian ancestry, like many of the people themselves.

6. Cyprus, Sardinia and Rhodes respectively.

7. The ABC islands in the Caribbean comprise Aruba, Bonaire and Curaçao, located off the coast of northwest Venezuela. They make up the Leeward branch of the Netherlands Antilles (St. Maarten, St. Eustatius and Saba form the Windward branch, over 500 miles away), and all the islands are autonomous members of the Kingdom of The Netherlands.

8. Winston S. Churchill, in his prophetic work *While England Slept,* a volume of his most telling speeches from 1932 to 1938, a year before the outbreak of World War II.

9. The Cayman Islands, where more than 460 banks and 10,000 companies are represented.

10. He wanted to become an optical Aleutian.

JUMBLE

1. In which year is the Time Capsule, buried at the site of the 1939 New York World's Fair, scheduled to be opened?

2. Name the multi-faceted man of letters who penned this epigram:

    Dark eyes adventure bring; the blue serene
    Do promise paradise; and yours are green.

3. In Edward Albee's *Who's Afraid of Virginia Woolf?*, Sandy Dennis asks if she can powder her nose. How does Elizabeth Taylor reply?

4. Which artistic genius named his daughter after the dove, the symbol of peace?

5. Iceland must be a bookseller's delight. Why?

6. Who said that a tavern chair was "the throne of human felicity"?

7. The diseases beriberi, scorbutus and rachitis have an alphabetical connection. Do you know it?

8. In which field of airborne activity would you have occasion to use a variometer and a pyrometer?

9. What has a spear and a mirror to do with genders?

10. Timothy Dwight was the last man of the cloth to be President of Yale. When he retired in 1899, he was succeeded by Arthur Twining Hadley. When he was almost 90, he tottered around to see Hadley one evening in a highly agitated state, saying, "Hadley, I have terrible news. I think I have a venereal disease that I must have picked up in the men's room at Grand Central Station." What was Hadley's reaction?

JUMBLE

1. The year 6939.

2. Hilaire Belloc, in *Sonnets and Verse*.

3. "Let me show you to the euphemism."

4. In 1950 Pablo Picasso named his daughter Paloma, Spanish for dove, because she was born in the same year that her father designed his famous dove for the World Peace Conference. Paloma Picasso is now a jewelry designer for Tiffany's in New York.

5. Iceland, where everyone must graduate from school in order to get a job and has to be able to speak three languages, is the only country in the world to have 100 percent adult literacy. In contrast, the United States has 72 million (or almost ⅓ of the population) at a marginal literacy level or below.

6. Who else but that archetypal clubman, Dr. Samuel Johnson?

7. They are diseases caused by deficiencies of vitamins B, C and D respectively. Scorbutus and rachitis are commonly known as scurvy and rickets.

8. In hot-air ballooning: a variometer indicates the rate of ascent or descent, while a pyrometer shows the temperature in the crown of the balloon.

9. The astronomical symbols for Mars and Venus, which are used in science to designate man and woman, are the Spear of Mars behind his shield and the Mirror of Venus.

10. Hadley was visibly upset and said, "Timmy, I'm shocked. You—a man of the cloth and a former Yale President. I must say that's a hell of a place to take a woman."

JUST FOR OPENERS

Identify the authors and titles of the literary works whose opening lines appear below:

1. I wish either my father or my mother, or indeed both of them . . . had minded what they were about when they begot me.

2. On Friday noon, July the twentieth, the finest bridge in all Peru broke and precipitated five travelers into the gulf below.

3.   By the shores of Gitche Gumee,
          By the shining Big-Sea-Water . . .

4. It was the afternoon of my eighty-first birthday, and I was in bed with my catamite when Ali announced that the archbishop had come to see me.

5. Robert Cohn was once middleweight boxing champion at Princeton. Do not think that I am very much impressed by that as a boxing title, but it meant a lot to Cohn.

6. Some of the evil in my tale may have been inherent in our circumstances. For years we lived anyhow with one another in the naked desert under the indifferent heaven.

7. It was a wild and stormy night on the West Coast of Scotland. This, however, is immaterial to the present story, as the scene is not laid in the West of Scotland.

8.   Five black bucks in a wine-barrel room,
          Barrel-house kings; with feet unstable . . .

9. To begin at the beginning:

   It is spring, moonless night in the small town, starless and Bible-black, the cobblestreets silent and the hunched, courters'-and-rabbits' wood limping invisible down to the sloe-black, slow, black, crow black, fishingboat-bobbing sea.

10. I'm no bloody hero, and when the Princess Pats stood at Passchendaele in '17, I was damned careful to be twelve years old and three thousand miles to the rear . . .

JUST FOR OPENERS

1. Laurence Sterne, *Tristram Shandy*
2. Thornton Wilder, *The Bridge of San Luis Rey*
3. Henry Wadsworth Longfellow, "The Song of Hiawatha"
4. Anthony Burgess, *Earthly Powers*
5. Ernest Hemingway, *The Sun Also Rises*
6. T.E. Lawrence, *The Seven Pillars of Wisdom*
7. Stephen Leacock, "Gertrude the Governess or Simple Seventeen"
8. Vachel Lindsay, "The Congo"
9. Dylan Thomas, *Under Milk Wood*
10. S.J. Perelman, "Up the Close and Down the Stair"

KINGS AND QUEENS

1. Which queen was the wife of two English kings, mother of two English kings and stepmother of two English kings?

2. Of the first six, one was bald, one fat, one simple, one fair, one wise and one foolish. Who were they?

3. Who is remembered for singing such hit songs as "Unforgettable," "Mona Lisa" and "Nature Boy"?

4. William the Conqueror invaded England in 1066. Which other foreign ruler invaded the country in that year?

5. Which French king sired an English queen as well as a French king?

6. Which royal personage is referred to in these lines on a plaque in the churchyard of St. Anne's in London's Soho?

> The grave teacher to a level brings
> Heroes and beggars, galley slaves and kings,
> But Theodore, this mortal learn'd ere dead;
> Fate poured its lessons on his living head,
> Bestow'd a kingdom, and denied him bread.

7. In 1740, who was the young queen whose acccession to the Hapsburg throne started a war?

8. A Labour MP, Keir Hardie, said in the House of Commons: "From his childhood onward this boy will be surrounded by sycophants and flatterers by the score and will be taught to believe himself as of a superior creation. A line will be drawn between him and the people whom he is to be called upon some day to reign over. In due course . . . he will be sent on a tour round the world, and probably rumours of a morganatic alliance will follow, and the end of it will be that the country will be called upon to pay the bill." To whom was he referring?

9. When he died in 1983, he was the longest-reigning monarch in the world. Can you identify him?

10. When the Prince of Wales, who became Edward VII, complained to his mistress, Lillie Langtry, "I've spent enough on you to buy a battleship," how did "the Jersey Lily" reply?

KINGS AND QUEENS

1. Emma (Aelfgifa) of Normandy, who died in 1052. She was the wife of Ethelred the Unready and Canute the Great, mother of Edward the Confessor and Hardicanute, and stepmother of Edmund Ironside and Harold Harefoot.

2. Each was a King Charles of France, numbering from I to VI.

3. Nat "King" Cole, the American singer and pianist, who was born Nathaniel Adams Cole in Montgomery, Alabama.

4. King Harold Hardrada of Norway. The English King Harold defeated him at Stamford Bridge, but immediately had to march south to an unsuccessful encounter with William the Conqueror at the Battle of Hastings.

5. Henry IV of France (Henry of Navarre) fathered Louis XIII of France and Henrietta Maria, queen consort of Charles I of England.

6. Theodore I of Corsica, in reality a German adventurer named Baron von Neuhof, who became "King" of Corsica in 1736. After being evicted by the Genoese in 1738, he eventually landed in debtors' prison in London and, through the influence of Horace Walpole, was released only after handing over all claims to his "kingdom" for the use of his creditors.

7. Maria Theresa, Queen of Bohemia and Hungary, whose accession to the throne precipitated the War of the Austrian Succession, as a result of which she lost the Hapsburg lands in Silesia.

8. The eldest son of the Duke and Duchess of York, Prince Edward, who was to become Prince of Wales, Edward VIII, and, after his abdication in 1936, Duke of Windsor. Quoting Keir Hardie's observation more than half a century later, the Duke of Windsor described it as "uncannily clairvoyant."

9. King Sobhuza II of Swaziland, who died at the age of 83, had been king since the age of one. A man of simple tastes, he shunned his two royal palaces, preferring to live at his kraal of mud huts. He is survived by more than 100 widows and an estimated 500 children.

10. "And you've spent enough in me to float one."

KITH AND KIN

1. Of a famous Biblical pair, who was a tiller of the ground and who was a keeper of sheep?

2. How is Nathan Hale's relationship to artificial satellites the same as the Kaiser Wilhelm II's to the theory of games?

3. Dauphin, as the title of the eldest son of the King of France, was in use from 1349 to 1830. What watery derivation does the name have?

4. What relation was Queen Victoria to William IV, whom she succeeded?

5. Which son of a famous statesman was described as being "completely unspoiled by his numerous failures," according to Noël Coward?

6. When the Irish writer Brendan Behan lay dying in 1964, what did he say to the nun who had just wiped his brow?

7. The issue of which marriage, if known by their two family names, would be called Glucksberg-Wettin?

8. Which three sisters from a ladies' finishing school apologize for their naïveté in these lines?

> So please you, Sir, we much regret
> If we have failed in etiquette
> Towards a man of rank so high—
> We shall know better by and by.

9. The *Washington Post* subheaded the article on Princess Diana's pregnancy: "The Heir Will Be Apparent in June." Why is a royal heir not necessarily apparent?

10. According to George S. Kaufman, what is the trouble with incest?

KITH AND KIN

1. The brothers Cain and Abel, respectively.

2. Hale's grandnephew Edward Everett Hale described such satellites in *The Brick Moon,* and the Kaiser's grandnephew Oskar Morgenstern pioneered in the theory of games.

3. Dauphin is the Old French word for dolphin. The title (originally borne by the lords of Viennois, whose coat of arms bore three dolphins) was adopted by the French crown princes when the Viennois province Dauphiné was added to the crown.

4. Victoria was his niece; her father Edward, the Duke of Kent and the fourth son of George III, having died before she was a year old.

5. Randolph S. Churchill, the only son of Winston S. Churchill.

6. "Ah, bless you, Sister, may all your sons be bishops."

7. The children of H.R.H. Prince Philip and H.M. Queen Elizabeth II. By a decree issued by the Queen in 1952, the family name of their children is Windsor.

8. Yum-Yum, Pitti-Sing and Peep-Bo—wards of Ko-Ko, Lord High Executioner of Titipu—in Gilbert and Sullivan's *The Mikado.*

9. If the child was a male, as indeed he was, he would be the heir apparent. If the child had been female, she would become the heiress presumptive, whose claim would be defeated by the birth of a brother, for it is the oldest male child who succeeds to the throne.

10. "The trouble with incest is that it gets you involved with relatives."

KUDOS

1. Distinguish between kudos and kudus.

2. At a ball around 1346 Edward III is said to have returned the Countess of Salisbury's garter to her, with what remark? And of what did this phrase become the motto?

3. Whom is it thought that Robert Browning was attacking in these lines from "The Lost Leader"?

   > Just for a handful of silver he left us,
   > Just for a riband to stick in his coat.

4. To which prize was Walt Whitman referring when he wrote the following and who was the Captain?

   > O Captain! my Captain! our fearful trip is done,
   > The ship has weathered every rack. The prize we
   >   sought is won,
   > The port is near, the bells I hear, the people all
   >   exulting.

5. Rudyard Kipling was a truly gifted writer who was accorded neither a knighthood nor a peerage. What particular poem of his definitely did not amuse Queen Victoria?

6. Who awarded himself 80 engraved silver loving cups, one for each of the enemies that he had killed?

7. According to the great sportswriter Grantland Rice, what was more important than winning?

8. One of the questions in the first fitness report on the young George Marshall was, "Would you wish this officer to serve under you in time of war?" What was the response of his commanding officer, Colonel Haygood?

9. Near the end of World War II, after he had lost in the general election to Attlee, Churchill was asked by King George VI if he would accept the Order of the Garter. Churchill declined, saying what?

10. In 1962 President John F. Kennedy invited 49 recipients of the Nobel Prize to dinner at The White House. How did he begin his remarks?

KUDOS

1. Kudos come from the Greek and means fame and renown resulting from some achievement; kudus are large, grayish brown African antelopes with spirally twisted horns.

2. *"Honi soit qui mal y pense,"* (Shamed be he who thinks evil of it), which became the motto of the Order of the Garter, the oldest and most important of the orders of knighthood in England.

3. William Wordsworth, for putting aside his liberal sympathies, accepting a civil list pension, and becoming poet laureate.

4. The "fearful trip" was the Civil War, and the prize won was Union victory. The Captain, dead upon the deck at the end of the triumphant voyage, was Abraham Lincoln.

5. "The Widow at Windsor," which goes in part:

    > Walk wide o' the Widow at Windsor,
    > For 'alf o' Creation she owns:
    > We 'ave bought 'er the same with the sword and the flame,
    > An' we've salted it down with our bones!

6. Manfred von Richthofen, the Red Baron, who had a cup made to commemorate each allied aircraft he had shot down in World War I.

7. In his poem "Alumnus Football" Grantland Rice wrote:

    > When the One Great Scorer comes to write against your name—
    > He marks—not that you won or lost—but how you played the game.

8. "Yes, but I would rather serve under him."

9. "How can I accept the Order of the Garter from my King when the people have given me the Order of the Boot?"

10. "I think this is the most extraordinary collection of talent, of human knowledge, that has been gathered together at the White House—with the possible exception of when Thomas Jefferson dined here alone."

LAST THINGS FIRST

Here are the answers. But what are the questions?

1. Crick
2. Strontium 90, Carbon 14
3. Chromatic scales
4. About twenty drachmas a week
5. Poetic justice
6. "Out, damned spot!"
7. "A loaf of bread, a jug of wine, and thou"
8. Zip-a-dee-doo-dah
9. February 29th, for example
10. A Greek letter

LAST THINGS FIRST

1. What noise does a Japanese camera make?
2. What was the final score of the Strontium-Carbon game?
3. What has rainbow trout that no other trout has?
4. What's a Grecian urn?
5. What would Oliver Wendell Holmes, Jr. have dispensed if he had his father's poetic talent?
6. What is the motto of the Lady Macbeth Dry Cleaners?
7. What's on a cannibal's menu?
8. What does one say to someone whose doodah is open?
9. What is so rare as a day in June?
10. What's Nu?

LEGAL BRIEF

1. According to Plutarch's *Lives of the Noble Grecians and Romans,* written about 100 A.D., whose laws were written not with ink, but with blood?

2. The U.S. Government's protracted antitrust suit against I.B.M., which was dropped in 1982, reminded many observers of which celebrated fictitious law case?

3. The counsel of a Yorkshire miner who put in a very late claim for compensation was asked by the judge, "Your client is undoubtedly aware that *Vigilantibus, et non dormientibus, jura subserviunt.*" How did counsel respond?

4. In British common law, and in the law of some states in this country, adultery is known by what curious euphemism?

5. During World War II a British major was court-martialed for chasing, while stark naked, a Wren (a member of the WRNS, Women's Royal Naval Service) down a corridor of Cairo's venerable Shepheard's Hotel (sorely missed by travelers to the Middle East). How did the major's army lawyer succeed in getting him acquitted?

6. The partnership of Barratry, Champerty and Replevin might be expected to deal with which legal matters?

7. "I'm wedded to the truth!" a witness told Clarence Darrow during a cross-examination. What did the legendary trial lawyer reply?

8. Can you distinguish between a barrister and a solicitor, and explain what "taking silk" in Britain means?

9. What does a grand jury do in an upward manner and a judge in a downward fashion?

10. What is the difference between a rooster and a lawyer?

LEGAL BRIEF

1. The Athenian lawgiver Draco, who lived in the 7th century B.C. Under the Draconian code, the punishment for almost all criminal offenses was death.

2. The case of *Jarndyce v. Jarndyce,* involving the distribution of an estate of an intestate minor in Dicken's *Bleak House,* went on so long as to become a subject of heartless jest and a source of great profit to those lawyers engaged in it.

3. "In Barnsley, m'lud, they speak of little else." (The Latin translates as "The law will uphold those who are vigilant and not those who sleep.")

4. Criminal conversation.

5. By simply quoting from King's Regulations: "Officers shall be dressed in keeping with the sport in which they are engaged."

6. Barratry would incite or stir up quarrels or groundless lawsuits, while Champerty would illegally share in the proceeds of a suit. Replevin, the straight partner, would try to recover personal property illegally taken.

7. "And just when did you become a widower?"

8. A barrister is a counsel admitted to plead at the bar and undertake the public trial of causes in an English superior court; a solicitor is a lawyer who advises clients, represents them in the lower courts and prepares cases for barristers to try in the higher courts. "Taking silk" means that one can wear the distinctive silk gown worn by a King's or Queen's Counsel, a barrister selected to serve as counsel to the British crown.

9. A grand jury hands up an indictment, while a judge hands down a decision.

10. A rooster clucks defiance.

LITERARY ENDINGS

Give the titles and authors of the works that end as follows:

1. Which of us is happy in this world? Which of us has his desire? or, having it, is satisfied?—Come, children, let us shut up the box and the puppets, for our play is played out.

2.   So, thanks to all at once and to each one,
       Whom we invite to see us crown'd at Scone.

3. He could feel his heart beating against the pine needle floor of the forest.

4.   Stands the Church clock at ten to three?
       And is there honey still for tea?

5. This was a base libel on Badger, who, though he cared little about Society, was rather fond of children; but it never failed to have its full effect.

6. And yes I said yes I will Yes.

7. Catherine, meanwhile, in the parlor, picking up her morsel of fancy-work, had seated herself with it again—for life, as it were.

8. It is also a fact that M. Chauvelin, the accredited agent of the French Republican Government, was not present at that or any other social function in London, after that memorable evening at Lord Grenville's ball.

9. "If he was trying German irregular verbs on the poor beast," said Clovis, "he deserved all he got."

10. My panache!

LITERARY ENDINGS

1. *Vanity Fair,* by William Makepeace Thackeray
2. *Macbeth,* by William Shakespeare
3. *For Whom the Bell Tolls,* by Ernest Hemingway
4. "The Old Vicarage, Grantchester," by Rupert Brooke
5. *The Wind in the Willows,* by Kenneth Grahame
6. *Ulysses,* by James Joyce
7. *Washington Square,* by Henry James
8. *The Scarlet Pimpernel,* by Baroness Orczy (Mrs. Montagu Barstow)
9. "Tobermory," by Saki (H. H. Munro)
10. *Cyrano de Bergerac,* by Edmund Rostand

LONG AND SHORT OF IT

1. How long did the Hundred Years War last?

2. Can you list in the proper order the three longest rivers in North America?

3. Name the author of the following lines and the poem in which they appear:

   > Let not ambition mock their useful toil,
   >   Their homely joys, and destiny obscure;
   > Nor grandeur hear with a disdainful smile,
   >   The short and simple annals of the poor.

4. Although Juneau, the capital of Alaska, is the largest city in the United States in land area, another state capital is almost as long north to south as is the western coast of the United States. How can this be?

5. Who is remembered for saying, "Life is not too short and sweet, but too short and bitter for bitterness"?

6. What train has the longest straight-line run in the world?

7. In the stock market, what is a short sale, and what is the rationale behind it?

8. The eminent bishop, who followed a long list of after-dinner speakers, rose to say that, as he had not known whether a long speech [groans] or a short one [cheers] would be appropriate, he had prepared both and would deliver both. What did he proceed to say?

9. Who, after a chilly night in the English countryside, wrote this?

   > Now fades the glossy, cherished anthracite;
   >   The radiators lose their temperature:
   > How ill avail, on such a frosty night,
   >   The short and simple flannels of the poor.

10. A teacher of short-story writing emphasized to her class the importance of getting the reader's attention at the start by the use of profanity, the nobility or sex. The next day she received a paper which began how?

LONG AND SHORT OF IT

1. 116 years of fighting—from 1337 to 1453, although with long truces and even peace settlements in between.

2. The Mackenzie in Canada, the Missouri and the Mississippi.

3. Thomas Gray, "Elegy Written in a Country Churchyard." This churchyard can still be seen in the village of Stoke Poges, now in danger of being engulfed by Greater London.

4. Honolulu ("sheltered harbor" in Hawaiian), the capital and principal city of Hawaii on the island of Oahu, has a boundary that officially includes Kure Island, some 1,380 miles to the northwest.

5. The British diplomat Lord Vansittart, who throughout World War II continued to advocate a "hard peace" for Germany.

6. Australia's Indian Pacific, which takes its name from the two oceans it joins. Between Sydney in New South Wales and Perth in Western Australia, the train passes over 267 miles of perfectly straight track through the treeless, seemingly endless Nullarbor (Latin for no tree) Plain.

7. A short sale is selling securities one does not own in the hope of buying them back at a lower price and delivering them to the buyer for a profit. If the price rises instead of falling, the short seller incurs a loss. As the speculator Daniel Drew put it,

> He who sells what isn't his'n
> Must buy it back or go to pris'n.

8. "The short speech is 'Thank you' and the long speech is 'Thank you very much.'" The bishop sat down to prolonged applause.

9. Christopher Morley, the Anglophilic American editor, novelist and poet, in a parody of Gray's "Elegy."

10. "Hell," cried the duchess, "take your hot hand off my thigh."

LOSERS

1. This is a nursery rhyme taught to British school children:

   > Divorced, beheaded, died;
   > Divorced, beheaded, survived.

   The first five definitely refer to losers. Who were they?

2. During the Battle of Waterloo, the Earl of Uxbridge's leg was blown off by a French shell while he was riding over to the Duke of Wellington. What reported exchange occurred between the two men?

3. "If you can keep your head when all about you are losing theirs and blaming it on you," you will be what?

4. Captain B.S. Briggs apparently abandoned his with his wife, daughter and seven others, and was never seen again. Captain E.C. Smith went down with his. Captain Hans Langsdorff scuttled his on Hitler's orders and then committed suicide. What were the names of their ill-fated vessels?

5. In 1898 the Spanish Governor of Guam went out in his barge to apologize to the captain of a U.S. cruiser for not having any ammunition to return the warship's salute. When did he discover that he was a loser?

6. David Wilkins will never be remembered as a best-selling author. What one work of his qualifies him as a loser *sans pareil* in this department?

7. How did the Ottoman Empire, of which Turkey is the last surviving country, fare in war between 1812 and 1913?

8. In a best four out of seven series, she beat her opponent in the sixth race by 3 minutes, 25 seconds—the highest margin of victory by a foreign challenger in history—thus tying the series 3–3. Whom or what are we talking about, and who won?

9. What all-too-prevalent phrases today mark the user as a loser in the field of simple communication?

10. Who is a classic loser?

LOSERS

1. The first five wives of Henry VIII. A simple way to remember all six is: Kate, Anne, Jane; Anne, two Kates again.

2. Uxbridge: "By God, Sir, I've lost my leg!" Wellington: "By God, Sir, so you have!" Uxbridge survived, and gave the leg a tomb on the battlefield.

3. In the words of Rudyard Kipling's best-known poem, "If—," voted by generations of college students as their favorite poem:

   Yours is the Earth and everything that's in it,
   And—which is more—you'll be a Man, my son!

4. Captain Brigg's ship, the *Mary Celeste,* was found deserted and drifting in the Atlantic in December, 1877—one of the sea's greatest mysteries. Captain Smith was master of the R.M.S. *Titanic,* which sank after striking an iceberg in April 1912, and Captain Langsdorff commanded the German battleship *Graf Spee* at the battle of the River Plate in December 1939.

5. When the captain informed him that the United States had declared war on Spain and that he was being shelled.

6. Wilkins' translation of the New Testament from Coptic into Latin was published by the Oxford University Press in 1716. When it went out of print in 1907, it had sold only 191 copies.

7. Not too well. In this period the Ottoman Empire lost three wars to Russia, three to Montenegro, one to Greece, one to Italy, and one to Bulgaria, Serbia, Montenegro and Greece combined. In 1914 Turkey joined the losing side in World War I. The Ottoman Empire was not called "the sick man of Europe" for nothing.

8. *Australia II,* the 12-meter wing-keeled yacht which, for the first time in 132 years, wrested the America's Cup from the New York Yacht Club by beating *Liberty* in the 1983 races.

9. The surrogate crutch words "Y'know, I mean, uh, y'know."

10. A pregnant nun driving the wrong way down a one-way street in an Edsel bearing a Nixon bumper sticker.

MACÉDOINE

1. Many Italian restaurants are named Quo Vadis, which means what?

2. "Mego" is a term journalists have long used to label a common reaction to recurring stories about poverty, population control, foreign aid and other worthy concerns. What does Mego stand for?

3. Who was described by Edgar Howe as "The only man in America who could sit on a fence and see himself go by," and by T.S. Eliot as having "a mind so fine that no idea could violate it" and possessing "the wings of a beautiful but ineffectual conscience beating vainly in a vacuum jar"?

4. Newer mountain ranges with jagged peaks are sometimes given the Spanish name for a saw, which is what?

5. Name four famous screen Cleopatras.

6. Which artist, known for his classic images of disquiet, painted a derby hat perched atop a sumptuous head of hair?

7. Does a robin hop or walk?

8. This island in the northwestern Indian Ocean rises so dramatically out of the sea that it has been compared in beauty with Capri and Mooréa. Can you name it?

9. Which movie reached the largest U.S. television audience, and which comes second?

10. When William Howard Taft, who weighed roughly 350 pounds, was Governor General of the Philippines, he cabled Secretary of War Elihu Root from Manila: "TOOK LONG HORSEBACK RIDE. FEELING FINE." What did Root cable back?

MACÉDOINE

1. "Whither goest thou?" (John 16:5), which is translated as *Quo Vadis* in the Vulgate, the Latin translation of the Bible. Legend has it that Peter, fleeing crucifixion in Rome, met Christ and asked *"Domine, Quo Vadis?"* Christ replied that he was going to Rome to be crucified again. This shamed Peter into returning to the capital and his own martyrdom. To commemorate the occasion, the Domine Quo Vadis Church on the Appian Way exhibits the imprints made by Christ's feet facing Rome.

2. My eyes glaze over.

3. Henry James, the American novelist who lived in England from 1878 until he died in 1916, six months after he became a British subject as a gesture of wartime solidarity. Prime Minister H.H. Asquith was one of his references, and later claimed that the only time he had perjured himself was when he testified that James could speak English.

4. Sierra, as in Sierra Nevada. Roy Campbell notes this sawtooth resemblance in his poem "The Albatross":

    The ranges moved like two-handed saws
    Notching the scarlet west with jagged lines.

5. Theda Bara (1917), Claudette Colbert (1934), Vivien Leigh (1945) and Elizabeth Taylor (1962).

6. René Magritte. The painting was titled *Pan de la Nuit (Piece of the Night)*.

7. A robin does both, which is unusual among birds.

8. Mahé, one of the Seychelles, an archipelago of about 90 islands, which were under British rule from 1810 but gained independence in 1970.

9. *The Day After*, ABC's $7 million movie about nuclear devastation, was seen in 1983 by about 100 million viewers—more than half the country's adult population. Until then the record was held by *Gone With the Wind*, which was first aired by NBC in two parts in 1976. (In a written statement at the end of *The Day After*, ABC contributed its bit to the nation's illiteracy by starting off: "In it's presentation. . . .")

10. "HOW IS THE HORSE?"

MANNERS AND MORES

1. An English dowager duchess was having the Aga Khan to dinner and wrote to *Debrett's* to determine the correct seating order. What reply did she receive?

2. What is the proper term for the midday meal: lunch or luncheon?

3. When a pregnant bride and her husband are leaving the church, what is the proper thing to throw at them?

4. Can you give a Scottish definition of a gentleman?

5. John Betjeman's poem, "How to Get on in Society," a parody on pretentious English, begins

   > Phone for the fish-knives, Norman,
   >   As Cook is a little unnerved;
   > Your kiddies have crumpled the serviettes,
   >   And I must have things daintily served.

   But Betjeman aside, why *do* we use fish knives?

6. Branch Rickey, manager of the Brooklyn Dodgers, was a notably messy eater, getting most of the food on his clothes. How did one associate comment on his table manners?

7. When Alexander Dumas *père* was a guest one evening in a crowded salon in Paris, he farted loudly. How did he excuse himself?

8. Hostesses today would be well advised to follow the form used on invitations for diplomatic dinners, which is what?

9. What name has been given to people who get free tickets to paid events?

10. Giving the first dinner of a new season at Newport, how did Mrs. Stuyvesant Fish welcome the assembled crowd?

MANNERS AND MORES

1. *Debrett's* wrote: "The Aga Khan is said to be a direct descendant of God. An English duke takes precedence."

2. Lunch. Luncheon is pure affectation. Lunch comes from the Scottish *lonch,* a hunk of meat. *Nuncheon* is an old Middle English word meaning noon drink. Luncheon is nonsensical, since it means literally "drinking a hunk of meat."

3. Puffed rice, according to *Etiquette for Odd Occasions*.

4. One who can play the bagpipes—but doesn't.

5. Fish oxidizes steel blades, which makes the fish taste unpleasant. In the 18th century, fish knives with silver blades as well as handles were introduced. Stainless steel has long ago made them unnecessary, but fish knives are still seen even if they are not silver.

6. "The boss never worries about his table manners. Everything he eats looks well on him."

7. "Sorry. Stuffy, isn't it. Just had to let in a little fresh air."

8. "Eight for eight-thirty." This makes it clear that drinks will be served at eight o'clock and guests will sit down to eat promptly at eight-thirty. In the old days, the time when guests were supposed to leave was also clearly indicated by "Carriages at eleven."

9. Social cellulite.

10. "Make yourselves perfectly at home, and believe me, there is no one who wishes you were there more heartily than I do."

"MATTERS MATHEMATICAL"

1. Can you explain the difference between an ordinal and a cardinal number?

2. The German mathematician Karl Friedrich Gauss is known as the Prince of Mathematicians. When he was only ten years old, his teacher assigned the class the task of adding up all the whole numbers from 1 to 100. How did Gauss manage to arrive at the correct answer without using pencil or paper, and what is the answer?

3. For what is the Italian mathematician Leonardo Fibonacci, also known as Leonardo da Pisa, best remembered?

4. How did two parallel lines (=) come into being as the mathematical symbol for "equals"?

5. According to whom, what is "the only science that it hath pleased God hitherto to bestow on mankind"?

6. Does the doubling cube in backgammon represent an arithmetic or a geometric progression, and what is the highest number shown on the cube?

7. Name the Oxford mathematician who, before Einstein was born, brought relativistic doctrine into the first philosophical novels for children?

8. If you measure 5 by 12 by 13, what are you?

9. A logarithm is the exponent indicating the power to which a given number, called the base, must be raised to produce a certain number. Who invented logarithms, and what was his other contribution to mathematics?

10. What is the largest number that can be represented by using only three digits and no symbols?

"MATTERS MATHEMATICAL"

1. An ordinal is a number such as 1, 2 or 3 indicating quantity, but not sequence. A cardinal number indicates position in a series or order—for example, 1st, 2nd or 3rd.

2. Gauss noticed that if the numbers were added in pairs, one from each end of the sequence, the sum was always the same: 101. For example, $1 + 100 = 101, 2 + 99 = 101, 3 + 98 = 101 \ldots 50 + 51 = 101$. Since there are fifty pairs of numbers, the answer can be calculated mentally: 5,050.

3. Fibonacci was the 13th-century mathematician who brought the Arabic numeral system to Tuscany in northern Italy, enabling Tuscans to invent double-entry bookkeeping, bills of exchange, credit notes and finally banks.

4. The "equals" sign was invented in the 16th-century by the English mathematician Robert Recorde, who believed that "nothing is more equal than two parallel lines."

5. The English philosopher Thomas Hobbes, writing about geometry in *Leviathan*.

6. A geometric progression. The doubling cube is 6-sided and goes up to 64, or 2^6. "Power blocks" are 14-sided polyhedrons, and go up to 16,384, or 2^{14}.

7. Lewis Carroll, pseudonym of Charles Lutwidge Dodgson. The observation of the White Queen in *Through the Looking-Glass*—"Now, *here*, you see, it takes all the running *you* can do to keep in the same place"—has been hailed by scientists as a classic relativistic statement.

8. A right triangle.

9. The Scottish mathematician John Napier, who also introduced the decimal point in writing numbers.

10. 9^{9^9}, which is $9^{387,420,489}$ and would have 369 million digits.

MEDICINE

1. Who is recognized as the father of medicine?

2. Why is adhesive tape also known as court plaster?

3. If you encountered someone suffering from the disease called kuru, what would you urge him to abstain from?

4. What Biblical proverb might a far-sighted ophthalmologist quite logically put on his business card?

5. The young doctor said to the patient, "Just a harmless little prick." What did the patient reply?

6. One of our most famous Presidents suffered all his life from such severe periodic depressions that he has been referred to by some students of medical history as a "manic-depressive." Can you identify him?

7. Can you name the renowned physician who said, "The desire to take medicine is perhaps the greatest feature which distinguishes men from animals, and it is the physician's task to disabuse him of this"?

8. Which famous athlete died from amyotrophic lateral sclerosis, and what does the disease attack?

9. Can you name the insidious drug whose name was originally a trade name, just as the word aspirin was?

10. "Medicant" is a coined word meaning the use of scientific terminology instead of ordinary words. For example, a doctor might say: "The patient had ecchymosis and exanthematous lesions, had suffered alopecia and was in the process of diaphoresis." What does he mean?

MEDICINE

1. Hippocrates, the Greek physician, whose oath is administered to graduating doctors in many modern universities.

2. The name court plaster comes from its use by ladies at royal courts for ornamental face-plaster. They actually used silk adhesive tape gummed with isinglass.

3. Eating the brains of people. Kuru, a severe neurological disease long endemic to certain areas of New Guinea, is transmitted by the cannibalization of people suffering from it.

4. "Where there is no vision, the people perish" (Proverbs 29:18).

5. "I know you are, but what are you going to do with the needle?"

6. Abraham Lincoln.

7. Sir William Osler, renowned Canadian physician and medical historian, who taught both in his own country, the United States and Canada.

8. Lou Gehrig, the Iron Horse of the New York Yankees, who established the record of playing in 2,130 consecutive league games. ALS, as the disease is known for short, progressively attacks the brain and spinal cord, causing degeneration of nerve cells that control the muscles.

9. Heroin, which was adapted as a trademark by the Bayer pharmaceutical company in Germany around the turn of the century because when tested on company employees it made them feel *heroische,* or, heroic. The drug is diacetylmorphine, a derivative of morphine, which is in turn a derivative of opium.

10. "This guy had a bruise, a rash, was bald and sweating."

1. To what was Lord Thomas Howard referring when he said the following?

   " 'Fore God I am no coward;
   I cannot meet them here, for my ships are out of
      gear . . ."

2. Where in London did the Pickwick Club meet?

3. The confluence of the Potomac and Shenandoah Rivers marks the site of which famous event?

4. What future meeting was planned at a place "where it's always double drill and no canteen"?

5. In George Bernard Shaw's play *Pygmalion,* on which *My Fair Lady* was based, where precisely did the professor of phonetics Henry Higgins first encounter the Cockney flower girl Eliza Doolittle?

6. In his book *A Prime Minister on Prime Ministers* Harold Wilson wrote: "Attlee was already forming his government. He had to leave for the Potsdam Conference of the Allies within hours. Churchill had been negotiating there and had returned to London for what he assumed was the formality of an election. Roosevelt and Stalin were waiting." What is wrong here?

7. Who wrote of which particular part of the United States as "The finest meeting of land and water in the world"?

8. Where does the Green Coat Alumni Association meet each year?

9. During World War II Winston S. Churchill coined the phrase "meeting at the summit." A new diplomatic locution is "sherpa meeting," named after the Tibetan people living on the southern slopes of the Himalayas, who are noted for their mountain-climbing abilities. What is a sherpa meeting?

10. Bilderberg Meetings are top secret and exclusive. Who attends them, and how did the name arise?

MEETINGS

1. As Sir Richard Grenville's scouting boat reports in Tennyson's poem "The Revenge—A Ballad of the Fleet":

   > "Spanish ships of war at sea! we have
   >   sighted fifty-three!"

2. The George and Vulture, a restaurant not far from the Bank of England in the City of London, was used by Charles Dickens as the gathering place for the characters in his novel *The Posthumous Papers of the Pickwick Club*.

3. The raid on the U.S. arsenal at Harper's Ferry, Virginia (now located in West Virginia), by the fiery abolitionist John Brown in 1859. He was hanged and became a Northern martyr.

4. A meeting in hell between Rudyard Kipling's anonymous narrator and the indomitable Gunga Din.

5. Under the portico of Inigo Jones' St. Paul's Church in London's Covent Garden, which is called "the actors' church" because of its proximity to the theater district.

6. Roosevelt could not have been waiting at Potsdam in July 1945, since he had been dead for three months. Wilson meant Truman.

7. Point Lobos, just north of California's Big Sur, was so described by the Carmel poet Robinson Jeffers.

8. At Georgia's annual Masters Tournament at the Augusta National Golf Club, where many previous winners—those entitled to wear the green coat—compete each year.

9. At sherpa meetings aides prepare the documents to be discussed at summit meetings.

10. Bilderberg Meetings occur once a year at various sites and are attended by the world's top bankers and business executives. The name comes from the Bilderberg Hotel near Arnhem, where the first meeting was held in 1954.

MEMENTO MORI

1. Which character in literature says the following?

   Cowards die many times before their deaths;
   The valiant never taste of death but once.

2. Which great Englishman showed commendable composure at his beheading, saying, as he placed his head on the block, "So the heart be right it is no matter which way the head lies"?

3. Give the meaning of the Latin phrase *de mortuis nil nisi bonum*.

4. What did Lord Balmerino say when the House of Lords sentenced him to be drawn, hanged and quartered?

5. Funeral parlor directors, as morticians or undertakers prefer to be known, are loath to use the word ashes for the results of cremation. What word have they dreamed up?

6. How was Ernest Hemingway's death headlined in one newspaper?

7. Why did the English naval hero Horatio Viscount Nelson choose to be buried in St. Paul's rather than in the national shrine at Westminster?

8. As the Hollywood wit Wilson Mizner lay dying, he said, "Well, Doc, I guess this is the main event." But he rejected the services of a priest, giving what reason?

9. In the urn containing the ashes of which movie star is a small silver whistle, commemorating what?

10. What did the English actor A.E. Matthews do each day before he went to work?

MEMENTO MORI

1. Julius Caesar, in Shakespeare's play of the same name.

2. Sir Walter Raleigh—soldier, explorer, courtier and man of letters.

3. Say nothing of the dead unless you have something good to say.

4. "Farewell, my Lords; we shall not meet again in one place."

5. Cremains. Presumably the deceased, if a male, would be known as a "cremainder man."

6. PAPA PASSES—a play on "Pippa Passes," the title of a poem by Robert Browning.

7. He had heard that Westminster Abbey was sinking into the Thames.

8. "Why should I talk to him? I've just been talking to his boss."

9. Humphrey Bogart. The whistle is a reminder of Lauren Bacall's lines to him in their first picture together, *To Have or Have Not*: "You know you don't have to act with me, Steve. You don't have to say anything, and you don't have to do anything. Not a thing. Oh, maybe just whistle. You know how to whistle, Steve? You just put your lips together and blow."

10. "I always wait for *The Times* each morning. I look at the obituary column, and if I'm not in it, I go to work."

MISSING LINKS

What is missing in each of the following groups?

1. Europe, Asia, Africa, North America, South America, Antarctica.

2. Carson City, Delaware, Nevada, Olympia, Oregon, Salem, Washington.

3. Duke of Marlborough, Marquess of Bath, Beaulieu, Longleat, Lord Montagu, Blenheim, Duke of Wellington.

4. Abélard, Beatrice, Dante, Heloïse, Petrarch.

5. Bashful, Doc, Grumpy, Happy, Sleepy, Sneezy.

6. Mohawk, Cayuga, Oneida, Onondaga.

7. Quebec, Dublin, Lisbon, Danube, St. Lawrence, Rome, Budapest, Tagus, Tiber.

8. Parma, Germany, Bayonne, Great Britain, Italy, Westphalian, York.

9. Q W E R Y

10. 45U, 46O, 47NM, 48A, 49A.

MISSING LINKS

1. Australia, the smallest of the seven continents.

2. Dover. They are states and their capitals: Carson City, Nevada; Dover, Delaware; Olympia, Washington; Salem, Oregon.

3. Stratfield Saye. They are stately homes of England and their occupants: Beaulieu—Lord Montagu; Blenheim—Duke of Marlborough; Longleat—Marquess of Bath; Stratfield Saye—Duke of Wellington.

4. Laura. They were all lovers in the Middle Ages: Beatrice and Dante, Heloïse and Abélard, Laura and Petrarch.

5. Dopey is missing from the Seven Dwarfs, according to Walt Disney's famous film.

6. Seneca. These comprised the Five Nations of the Iroquois Confederacy or Iroquois League.

7. Liffey. The list comprises the names of the cities and the rivers on which they stand: Dublin is on the Liffey, Quebec on the St. Lawrence, Lisbon on the Tagus, Budapest on the Danube, and Rome on the Tiber.

8. France. They are types of ham and country of origin: Bayonne—France; Parma—Italy; Westphalian—Germany; York—Great Britain.

9. T. They start the top row of lettered characters on a standard typewriter: QWERTY.

10. 50H. The initials represent the states in chronological order of their joining the union: Utah (the 45th State), Oklahoma, New Mexico, Arizona, Alaska and Hawaii.

MISTRESSES

1. What is the traditional definition of a mistress?

2. Which royal mistress began life simply as "Miss Fish"?

3. Can you explain the dual connection that the slave girl Sally Hemings had with Thomas Jefferson?

4. George Selwyn, a 19th-century wit and member of the infamous Hellfire Club in England, heard that a father, son and grandson all shared the same mistress. What observation did he make on this?

5. After he was found guilty of adultery in a divorce case, he married his mistress. The episode ruined his political influence, yet he had succeeded in bringing one burning issue to the forefront of British politics. Who were the principals involved, and for what was the man fighting?

6. What rustic comparison did William Wycherly make about a mistress in his play *The Country Wife*?

7. Which U.S. President was apparently afflicted with satyriasis, a term used to describe a man with abnormal sexual desire, and had extramarital affairs with numerous women, including Nan Britton (the most notorious) and Carrie Phillips?

8. Mrs. Keppel was the long-time mistress of Edward VII. What did she say on the day Edward VIII abdicated so that he could marry Wallis Simpson?

9. Why did Orson Welles' film *Citizen Kane* really infuriate William Randolph Hearst?

10. According to Lady Windlesham (Prudence Glynn) in her introduction to Douglas Sutherland's *The English Gentleman's Mistress*, why do most Englishmen not have mistresses?

MISTRESSES

1. A mistress is that which lies between a mister and a mattress.

2. La Marquise de Pompadour, *née* Mademoiselle Poisson, one of Louix XV's many mistresses, who assumed the role of prime minister behind the throne.

3. Sally Hemings was a half-sister of Jefferson's wife Martha, having been fathered by Martha's father. She was also reputed to have been for twenty-five years the mistress of Thomas Jefferson, for whom she worked as a house servant in Paris, where he succeeded Franklin as Minister to France, and at his beloved Monticello. Between 1795 and 1802 she gave birth to five children who were very light in color and bore a remarkable resemblance to Jefferson.

4. "There's nothing new under the son," and then he added, "nor under the grandson."

5. Charles Stewart Parnell and Kitty O'Shea. The issues for which Parnell had been fighting were land reform and home rule for the Irish.

6. "A mistress should be like a little country retreat near the town; not to dwell in constantly, but only for a night and away!"

7. Warren G. Harding, who on one occasion hid one of his lady friends in a broom closet in the White House.

8. "Things were done better in my day."

9. It was not the movie as a whole, so much as the fact that Rosebud (the name of Charles Foster Kane's boyhood sled and the last word he uttered) was Hearst's pet name for a particularly private part of Marion Davies' anatomy.

10. "The reason that most Englishmen do not have mistresses is threefold: Firstly, they are too mean. Secondly, they are undersexed. Thirdly, they have no need whatever of the status symbol of wealth or position which is implicit in keeping an obviously very expensive piece of property for display purposes and with a very low return on your investment, at any rate in public."

MIXED GRILL

1. Which political leader was born in Europe, grew up in the United States and became Prime Minister of a country in Asia?

2. The redesigned Food Hall of Harrods, London's superb department store, is not to be missed. In variety and quality of stock, as well as beauty of display, it is unsurpassed. Can you name the items sold there under the sign that reads Offal?

3. Name the ship that holds the record for the greatest number of people ever carried on a single vessel.

4. Where is St. Catherine's, a Greek Orthodox monastery named for a Christian martyred by the Romans, and what famous Biblical event is believed to have occurred on its site?

5. Navvy is a British word for a laborer, especially one employed in excavation or construction work. Can you give its derivation?

6. Which celebrated movie hero was discovered on Skull Island?

7. What did Dr. Gregory Pincus and Dr. Min-Chueh Chang do to help speed up the sexual revolution that has swept the world over the past twenty years?

8. A fairly sure way to win the odd $10 or $20 or even a C-note is to make a bet that someone cannot name the twelve parts of the human body that have only three letters in one minute. (Vulgar slang such as ass or tit are not acceptable answers.) Can you?

9. How do cows standing in a field help a pilot to determine the wind direction?

10. When Dorothy Parker heard that a prominent English actress, known for her affairs with members of the legal profession, had broken her leg, what was her reaction?

MIXED GRILL

1. Golda Meir, who was born in the Ukraine, grew up in Milwaukee, Wisconsin, and became Prime Minister of Israel in 1969.

2. Under Offal you will find such delicacies as brains, hearts, kidneys, liver, oxtail, sweetbreads and tripe.

3. R.M.S. *Queen Mary,* which carried almost 17,000 people on a single trip while serving as a troopship during World War II. Today she is an immobile museum and hotel permanently docked at Long Beach, California.

4. St. Catherine's lies at the base of Mount Sinai (Jabal Musa, the Mountain of Moses). On this site it is said that God spoke to Moses from the burning bush and commanded him to lead the Israelites out of bondage in Egypt.

5. "Navvy" is a slang shortening of navigator, in an obsolete and originally humorous sense of a laborer digging the navigational canals of England in the 18th and 19th centuries.

6. King Kong.

7. In 1959 they invented the oral contraceptive, known as "the pill," at the Worcester Foundation for Experimental Biology. Their aim was population control, rather than giving young people the chance to have a good time without worry.

8. Arm, ear, leg, toe, eye, lip, gum, lid, rib, hip, jaw and gut.

9. Grazing cows always stand with their tails to the wind to keep dust and grass out of their eyes.

10. "She must have done it sliding down a barrister."

MONEY AND WEALTH

1. Who was the King of Lydia whose name became synonymous with riches?

2. To combat counterfeiters, U.S. paper currency has three special features. What are they?

3. Can you give a gustato-monetary description of the "upper crust"?

4. Which Middle Western politician made a fortune out of doing nothing when a great oil company did something?

5. Only two men apart from Presidents appear on U.S. bills now being printed. Who are they?

6. An elderly Palm Beach gentleman of considerable means married a young lady with expensive tastes. After ten years of marriage, what wry comment did he make?

7. How did "two bits" come into the language as slang for a quarter, or 25 cents?

8. Explain the significance of the unfinished pyramid that appears on the Great Seal of the United States, as shown on the obverse side of the one dollar bill.

9. If you are playing for high stakes in Las Vegas or discussing a big deal in Houston, you should be familiar with the local terms "dime" and "unit." What do they mean?

10. After listening to Samuel Goldwyn expatiate on the art of making movies, how did George Bernard Shaw close the conversation?

MONEY AND WEALTH

1. Croesus, who lived in the 6th century B.C. (Huck Finn's simile for wealth: "as rich as creosote.")

2. The paper stock contains minute red and blue "security fibers"; part of the bill has magnetic ink; and the bills are printed by a special intaglio process, using great pressure, which imparts a three-dimensional effect to the portraits.

3. A bunch of crumbs held together by dough.

4. John James Exon, formerly Governor of and now Senator from Nebraska, sold the rights of his family furniture business to Esso (the name of Standard Oil of New York until it was changed to Exxon) to clear the title to the oil company's new name and avoid confusion.

5. Alexander Hamilton on $10 bills and Benjamin Franklin on $100 bills. ($1, $5, $20 and $50 bills carry the likenesses of Washington, Lincoln, Jackson and Grant respectively.) Hamilton was the first Secretary of the Treasury, while Franklin was one of the greatest statesmen of the American Revolution and of the newborn nation.

6. "When I got married, I was a multimillionaire; now I'm a millionaire."

7. The word bit was originally a British usage for any small coin. In the southwest United States two centuries ago Mexican coinage, particularly the *real*—one-eighth of a "piece of eight" and worth about 12½ cents—was used interchangeably with the local currency and was called a bit. When the 25-cent coin first appeared, it was soon called "two bits."

8. The unfinished pyramid means that the United States will always build, grow and improve.

9. In Las Vegas a "dime" is $10,000, while in Houston a "unit" is $10,000,000.

10. "That's the difference between us. You talk of art, Mr. Goldwyn; I think of money."

MOUNTAINS

1. What do these five countries have in common: Argentina, Nepal, the Soviet Union, Tanzania and the United States?

2. Name the longest mountain range in the world, and the two next longest.

3. Where did Goethe's Faust attend a supernatural celebration held in honor of an 8th-century English nun?

4. For the expert skier, proficient on the steepest of pitches, what is considered the most challenging slope in North America?

5. A certain face of which Alp has caused it to be known as "the meanest mountain on earth"?

6. Plumb lines are pulled in the direction of great masses. If you held a plumb line between your fingers in India, would it be pulled north or south?

7. In March 1945 Joe Rosenthal of the Associated Press took a photograph atop a mountain that captured the imagination of the world. What was the occasion?

8. Which symbolic poet and engraver wrote these lines?

> Great things are done when men and mountains
>   meet;
> This is not done by jostling in the street.

9. The Great Smoky Mountains, part of the Appalachian system on the North Carolina–Tennessee border, are named for the smoke-like haze that envelops them. What accounts for this haze?

10. Why is Mount Monadnock in New Hampshire recognized as a special kind of mountain?

MOUNTAINS

1. Each country has the highest mountain in the continent where its capital is located: Aconcagua, Everest, Elbruz, Kilimanjaro and McKinley, respectively.

2. The Andes at 4,500 miles, followed by the Rocky Mountains, at 3,750 miles and the Himalaya-Karakorum-Hindu Kush range, at 2,400 miles.

3. On Brocken peak in the Harz Mountains on Walpurgisnacht (April 30), named after Saint Walpurga, who was born in Wimborne Minster, Dorset, in England.

4. The headwall of Tuckerman's Ravine on Mount Washington in New Hampshire, which drops for a half-mile at a 45- to 50-degree angle—so steep that your knees hit the mountainside as you make the ascent. (There is no lift!)

5. The north wall of the Eiger in Switzerland, one of the severest tests of mountaineering in the world. It was not until 1938 that four German alpinists successfully made the ascent.

6. South. The Himalayas are so high because they consist of light, easily crumpled rock, while the heavy mass that is doing the pushing is the main body of the subcontinent moving north.

7. A group of U.S. Marines raising the Stars and Stripes on Mount Suribachi on Iwo Jima as a signal that the island had finally been wrested from the Japanese. A heroic piece of sculpture by Felix de Weldon, modeled on the photograph, now stands outside Arlington Cemetery.

8. William Blake in *Poems From Blake's Notebooks*.

9. The haze is generated by the volatile oils, called terpenes, generated by the many hardwoods and few evergreens there. The molecules of these terpenes form nuclei around which water condenses and forms the drifting fog banks.

10. Monadnock is a generic term for a mountain or rocky mass that has resisted erosion and stands isolated in a plain or peneplain.

MOVIES

1. Asked to step in and direct a film already being shot, a certain director refused a substantial percentage in favor of a flat fee, declaring the movie to be "the biggest white elephant ever made." Name the director and the film.

2. What was Fred Allen's comment on integrity in Hollywood?

3. Can you name the most edited movie, in terms of total footage ending up on the cutting-room floor?

4. Throughout the 1920s she was Hollywood's top box-office draw, yet her biggest success came in 1950, when she made a film whose script was enlivened by such lines as "I still *am* big—it's the movies that got small" and "We didn't need dialogue—we had faces then." Who was she, and what was the name of the film?

5. Can you name the five stages in the life of a movie actor?

6. To Alfred Hitchcock the MacGuffin was the name he gave for the motive force in his films—the "secret" everyone is intent on keeping or getting. But what is the story of the MacGuffin?

7. What is the sentence most often heard in movies?

8. What do the following films have in common: *Attack of the Killer Tomatoes, Invasion of the Star Creatures, Attack of the Mushroom People* and *Please Don't Eat My Mother*?

9. Name the only one-set film to be shot in eight 10-minute takes, in which the 80 minutes of running time corresponds to the 80 minutes of story action, and even the reel changes are disguised by actors walking in front of the camera. (Francis Coppola take note!)

10. How did Wilson Mizner describe his difficulties in cutting a deal with Warner Brothers?

1. Victor Fleming, director of *Gone With the Wind*, one of the biggest grossing films of its time.

2. "You could take all the integrity in Hollywood, put it in the navel of a flea, and still have room left over for an agent's heart and a caraway seed."

3. Howard Hughes' 1930 film *Hell's Angels*. Hughes shot over 2 million feet of film during the four years it took to make the film. If shown unedited, the movie would have run nonstop for 560 hours.

4. Gloria Swanson, in the Billy Wilder film *Sunset Boulevard*, which also starred William Holden as a screenwriter and Erich von Stroheim . . . Stroheim, playing her former director who is now her butler. In this movie Swanson played the part of Norma Desmond, a reclusive, demented silent-film star living in a decaying mansion in an unreal world while vainly seeking a comeback.

5. Who's X? Get me X. Get me an X type. Get me a young X. Who's X?

6. As Hitchcock told it: A man on the Royal Scotsman from London to Edinburgh kept peeking inside a box beside him, and his traveling companion asked what was inside. "A MacGuffin for hunting lions in Scotland," he replied. When told there were no lions in Scotland, he said, "Then that's not a MacGuffin."

7. According to a survey of 150 movie features, the phrase most often heard is: "Let's get outta here."

8. They were all included by Harry and Michael Medved in their *Golden Turkey Awards*, the definitive study of the worst achievements in Hollywood history. *Attack of the Mushroom People* has the distinction of being the worst vegetable movie of all time.

9. *Rope*, the Alfred Hitchcock movie based on the Leopold-Loeb murder case.

10. "It's like fucking a porcupine—one prick against a hundred."

MURDER, ANYONE?

1. Four U.S. Presidents have been assassinated. How many British Prime Ministers have suffered the same fate?

2. Who was murdered in the swimming pool of his mansion, which was "a factual imitation of some *hôtel de ville* in Normandy"?

3. Boston Corbet first made his name after allegedly killing the actor John Wilkes Booth, who had assassinated President Lincoln. When was he next heard of?

4. Who was the first man to be arrested for murder because of a message by radio (developed only nine years earlier) that was sent by Scotland Yard to a ship on which he was traveling?

5. Which famous gangster and Public Enemy No. 1 was done in as a result of a tip from "a lady in red"?

6. In the United States, how does the number of people murdered compare with those killed in all the country's wars? How does the United States compare with other countries in numbers of murders?

7. Who delivered this eulogy about whom on the snow-covered steps of a church: "He used to be a big shot"?

8. In which memorable short story was a man clubbed to death by his wife with a frozen leg of lamb, which she then cooked and served to the policemen investigating the crime, thus effectively doing away with the murder weapon?

9. Which President had occasion to quote this line written by Winston S. Churchill: "Nothing in life is so exhilarating as to be shot at without result"?

10. Explain the point of the title of James M. Cain's novel *The Postman Always Rings Twice*.

MURDER, ANYONE?

1. One. Spencer Perceval was shot in 1812 in the House of Commons by John Bellingham, a bankrupt madman with a personal grudge against the government.

2. Jay Gatsby, in F. Scott Fitzgerald's *The Great Gatsby*.

3. When he tried to kill the entire Kansas legislature.

4. Dr. Crippen, who was sailing to Canada with his mistress (one Ethel Le Neve, disguised as a boy), was arrested on his arrival in Canada for the murder of his wife.

5. John Dillinger, who was gunned down in 1934 by waiting G-men outside a Chicago movie theater where he had seen *Manhattan Melodrama,* starring Clark Gable, in the company of "a lady in red."

6. Twice as many people have been murdered as have died in battles. The number of murders in the United States is ten times that of the private murders of any other country.

7. Gladys George, over the bullet-ridden body of James Cagney, as the last line of Mark Hellinger's *The Roaring Twenties*.

8. "Lamb to the Slaughter," from Roald Dahl's collection of short stories *Some Like It Hot*.

9. Ronald W. Reagan, after being wounded in an assassination attempt when he was leaving a Washington hotel in March 1981. The line Reagan quoted is from Churchill's first book, *The Story of the Malakand Field Force,* about his experiences in India at the end of the last century.

10. The law will get you in the end. In Cain's story the man was freed after being tried for a murder he did commit only to be executed for a killing of which he was innocent. In Bob Rafelson's steamy remake of the original movie, the second point is missed entirely, and the film might better have been entitled *The Postman Always Rings Once*.

MUSEUMS AND GALLERIES

1. Can you explain the connection of Mnemosyne, the personification of memory, with the word museum?

2. Where was the first museum located?

3. A distinguished aeronautical engineer, after gazing at Nike, the Winged Victory of Samothrace, said that in his opinion, "She'll never get off the ground." Where does she share quarters with another even more famous lady?

4. Where could you see a world-famous collection of pictures in a "meadow"?

5. Name the former Colonial capital where nearly every building is a museum of the way life was lived there over 200 years ago.

6. On which body of water is the Palazzo Venier de Leoni located, and whose fabulous art collection is to be seen there?

7. It is generally accepted that the most representative collection of Impressionist and Post-Impressionist paintings may be found at which museum?

8. Where would you find the following caption on an indefinable sort of artifact: "Wooden vessel which was said to be used for sending portions of Rev. Baker's flesh to nearby chiefs"?

9. Who amassed a superb art collection, built a Venetian palazzo to house it, and left in her will a clause stating that if anything was added or moved, the museum was to be given to Harvard, her husband's alma mater?

10. According to George and Ira Gershwin, what was the weather like when the British Museum had lost its charm?

MUSEUMS AND GALLERIES

1. Mnemosyne and Zeus were the parents of the nine Muses, who collectively gave their name to the word museum, which literally means the seat of the Muses.

2. In Alexandria, where Ptolemy founded what was actually a literary academy. A wit of the time called it "the birdcage of the Muses."

3. In the Louvre in Paris, where the world's most famous and valuable painting, Leonardo's *Mona Lisa* (also known as *La Gioconda*), is also exhibited.

4. At the Prado, in Madrid. The word prado means meadow or, in cities, lawn or walk.

5. Colonial Williamsburg, a living museum of more than 200 acres boasting 88 authentically restored or faithfully reconstructed 18th-century buildings lining three long blocks. John D. Rockefeller, Jr. spent some $80 million restoring the area. Williamsburg was built to be the capital of colonial Virginia, a role it filled from 1699 to 1780, when it was succeeded by Richmond.

6. This dramatic palazzo is on Venice's Grand Canal and houses the Peggy Guggenheim collection embracing every phase of contemporary art, including works by Dali, Man Ray, Giacometti, Pevsner, Brancusi, Rothko and Pollock.

7. At the Musée du Jeu de Paume (a former tennis court, literally game of the palm) on the Place de la Concorde in Paris. Here may be seen works by such Impressionists as Monet, Manet, Pissaro, Renoir and Sisley, and such Post-Impressionists as Cézanne, Gauguin, Seurat, Toulouse-Lautrec and Van Gogh.

8. In the Fiji Museum at Suva. Rev. Baker was a missionary who suffered the most absolute form of martyrdom.

9. Isabella Stewart Gardner, whose museum is at Fenway Court in Boston.

10. It was "a foggy day in London town."

NAVAL AND NAUTICAL LORE

1. Which seat of learning was symbolically established at Sagres on the extreme southwest coast of Portugal in the early 15th century?

2. In 1571 a tremendous naval engagement involving 120,000 men was fought in the Gulf of Patras adjoining the Adriatic. What was the name of the battle, who were the opposing forces and what was the significance of the outcome?

3. A certain famous admiral kept locked in his desk a piece of paper which he always read before going on the bridge of his flagship. On his retirement his steward opened the drawer hoping to discover the secret of the admiral's success. What did he find written there?

4. Life at sea could be a hellish existence in the old days of sail. Which eminent landlubber would have preferred jail to being in a ship?

5. Lord Nelson's famous signal before the Battle of Trafalgar, "ENGLAND EXPECTS THAT EVERY MAN WILL DO HIS DUTY," is familiar to everybody. Historical research has shown, however, that Nelson would not have made a very good signals officer. Why?

6. On a fleet exercise a destroyer captain cut too close to the admiral's carrier and his davits touched the flagship's stern. What signal did the admiral make?

7. How did Captain Henry St. James, who commanded the ferry boat *Golden Fleece* between Gibraltar and Tangier, have the best of it in both ports?

8. Sir Thomas Lipton, the grocery millionaire, made five attempts to win the America's Cup for England in various racing yachts, all named *Shamrock*. Yet when he was proposed for membership in the prestigious Royal Yacht Squadron in Cowes by Edward VII, he was blackballed. Why?

9. During the early days of World War II the Women's Royal Naval Service (the Wrens) was buying up all available blue serge to make trousers. How did the Admiralty put a stop to this?

10. A newly rich millionaire bought a lavish yacht. On boarding it, what was his first order to the captain?

NAVAL AND NAUTICAL LORE

1. The famous school of exploration and navigation, founded by Prince Henry the Navigator, which systematically analyzed earlier random voyages of discovery and organized expeditions that led to European domination of world exploration by the mid-1500s.

2. The Battle of Lepanto, in which the fleet of the Holy League, consisting of Spanish, Venetian and papal ships under the command of John of Austria, the illegitimate half-brother of Philip II of Spain, defeated the Turkish fleet and weakened Ottoman naval power for years to come.

3. "Port left, starboard right."

4. Dr. Samuel Johnson, who wrote: "No man will be a sailor who has contrivance enough to get himself into a jail; for being in a ship is being in a jail, with the chance of being drowned. A man in jail has more room, better food and commonly better company."

5. In his original draft Nelson wrote "confides" instead of "expects." When his signals officer, Lieutenant Pasco, pointed out that "confides" would require eight separate flag hoists, Nelson agreed to substitute "expects," which needed only one.

6. "IF YOU TOUCH ME THERE AGAIN, I SHALL SCREAM."

7. In the film *The Captain's Paradise* Alec Guinness as the captain kept a wife, Celia Johnson, in Gibraltar, where he was a stolid English gentleman, and a mistress, Yvonne de Carlo, in Tangier, where he became a dashing playboy.

8. He was in trade. "My uncle," the Kaiser would say with characteristic loathsomeness, "has gone yachting with his grocer."

9. The Admiralty issued this directive: "Wrens clothing is to be held up until the needs of seagoing personnel have been satisfied."

10. "Commence yachting."

NUMBER, PLEASE?

1. Many people act irrationally at times, but an irrational number is always that way. Why is such a number so named?

2. Can you name two sets of numerically named islands?

3. What is the only integer that can be added to itself and multiplied by itself with the same result?

4. There are twelve in all. The first seven are birds, but what are the next five? What are they doing, and when?

5. How did a seventh happen to be followed by a fifth?

6. A man bought a bottle of wine for $11. The wine cost $10 more than the bottle. How much did the bottle cost?

7. "How do I love thee? Let me count the ways" is a famous line from Elizabeth Barrett Browning's *Sonnets from the Portuguese*. How many ways does she enumerate?

8. Explain the connection between the following numbers: a) the stated length of an old Harrovian's memories; b) they traditionally preserve the purity of the French language; c) they are of enormous help to ships sailing to Europe via Cape Horn.

9. The initials of ten well-known people can be found in the following numbers. Can you recognize them?

   a) 200   f) 1100
   b) 550   g)   90
   c) 400   h) 505
   d) 999   i) 2000
   e) 105   j)   55

10. If Bo Derek is a 10, what is a German virgin?

NUMBER, PLEASE?

1. An irrational number is one that cannot be expressed as a finite fraction.

2. The Dodecanese, a group of 12 islands lying between Crete and Turkey, and the Thousand Islands in the St. Lawrence River between Canada and the United States.

3. Two.

4. They are all gifts sent by "my true love" in the song "The Twelve Days of Christmas." The birds are a partridge in a pear tree, two turtledoves, three French hens, four calling birds (colly birds, which are blackbirds), five gold rings (ring-necked pheasants with their five gold bands), six geese a-laying, seven swans a-swimming. Also received were eight maids a-milking, nine ladies dancing, ten lords a-leaping, eleven pipers piping and twelve drummers drumming. At the end of this time the house was a shambles, and "my true love" is out on his ear.

5. In 1910 Edward VII died and George V became king.

6. Fifty cents—therefore, the wine cost $10.50. (If your answer is $1, the wine would cost only $9 more than the bottle.)

7. Nine ways. However, if "with the breadth,/Smiles, tears of all my life" is considered to be three ways, the total rises to eleven.

8. They are all forty: a) "Forty Years On"—the Harrow song; b) the Forty Immortals—the French Academy; c) the Roaring Forties—westerly winds between latitudes 40 and 50 degrees south.

9. a) Christopher Columbus (200 = CC)
   b) Dorothy Lamour (550 = DL)
   c) Charles Darwin (400 = CD)
   d) Iris Murdoch (999 = IM)
   e) Cornelius Vanderbilt (105 = CV)
   f) Marie Curie (1100 = MC)
   g) Xavier Cugat (90 = XC)
   h) Diego Velasquez (505 = DV)
   i) Marilyn Monroe (2000 = MM)
   j) Louis Vuitton (55 = LV)

10. A *nein*.

ODD MAN OUT

In each group, which is the odd man out?

1. Dublin, New Delhi, Jerusalem, Lima, Reykjavik.

2. Flopsy, Mopsy, Samuel Whiskers, Mr. McGregor.

3. Aldous Huxley, Rudyard Kipling, Robert Louis Stevenson, Thomas Mann, John Steinbeck.

4. John Quincy Adams, Theodore Roosevelt, William Howard Taft, Franklin D. Roosevelt, John F. Kennedy.

5. The Shetlands, Orkneys, Hebrides, Channel Islands.

6. Beluga, Sevruga, Oestra, Malossol.

7. Cowslip, Groundwort, Hawkbit, Eglantine, Dandelion.

8. Keats, Boccaccio, Leonardo da Vinci, D. H. Lawrence, Shelley.

9. Mercury, Venus, Earth, Mars, Jupiter.

10. Missouri, Nevada, New York, Oklahoma, Utah.

ODD MAN OUT

1. Lima, which is the capital of Peru. The countries of which the other cities are the capitals all begin with I.

2. Samuel Whiskers, who appears in Beatrix Potter's *The Tale of Tom Kitten*. The others are characters in her story *The Tale of Peter Rabbit*.

3. Rudyard Kipling is the only one who never lived in California.

4. William Howard Taft graduated from Yale, while Adams, both Roosevelts and Kennedy were Harvard men.

5. The Channel Islands are dependencies of the United Kingdom and lie to the south of England. The remaining islands, lying to the north and west of Scotland, are an integral part of Great Britain.

6. Malossol, which means "lightly salted." The others are all types of sturgeon from which caviar is taken, Beluga yielding the largest and most expensive eggs, followed by Oestra and Sevruga.

7. Eglantine. All the rest are rabbits in Richard Adams' *Watership Down*.

8. Leonardo da Vinci died in France, all the others in Italy. (Leonardo da Vinci, in case you thought he was not a writer, is the author of two *Notebooks*, one a vast work concerning technological principles and the other an intellectual diary spanning fourteen years.)

9. Earth is the only planet not named after a Roman deity. It is also the only planet with artificial satellites and the only one whose surface is predominantly water.

10. New York has the only capital, Albany, that does not have City at the end of its name.

ODDS AND ENDS

1. When the French literary historian and critic Charles Augustin Sainte-Beuve was challenged to a duel by a journalist and offered his choice of weapons, what did he choose?

2. According to mariners, who or what is "The Flying Dutchman"?

3. To what was Longfellow referring in these lines?

   > Shall fold their tents, like the Arabs,
   > And as silently steal away.

4. Name the only South American country never to have had a seacoast.

5. Can you explain how Fred Astaire managed to dance on the walls and ceiling of a room in Stanley Donen's film *Royal Wedding*?

6. On which occasion did a great soldier-statesman grumble, "I never saw so many shocking bad hats in my life"?

7. What is the connection between an ice cream flavor, an orchid and a vagina?

8. At the beginning of which pioneering psychiatric work appeared the quotation: *Flectere si nequeo superos, Acheronta movebo* (If I cannot bend [the gods] above, I will roil the waters of Hell)?

9. In the past 500 years or so, what contributions of significant importance to mankind, in any field of endeavor, have been made by people living in the vast area below the 40th parallel north—a line running roughly through Athens, Madrid, Philadelphia, San Francisco and Tokyo?

10. According to the Dean, how could Oedipus Rex have learned about sex?

ODDS AND ENDS

1. "I choose spelling. You're dead."

2. The Flying Dutchman is the ominous apparition of a full-rigged ship seen off the Cape of Good Hope. The captain is doomed to sail forever because of a blasphemous oath he uttered. Richard Wagner used the tale as the basis of his opera *The Flying Dutchman*.

3. "The cares that infest the day" from "A Day is Done."

4. Paraguay, not Bolivia, which had a seacoast until she lost it to Chile during the War of the Pacific in 1879.

5. The scene was executed simply by putting the room inside a barrel, as in a fun fair, with everything in the room tightly secured. The barrel and the camera turned together, so that the room seemed to be upside down with Astaire dancing on the ceiling.

6. The Duke of Wellington, on surveying the new House of Commons after the Whig landslide of 1832.

7. Vanilla is the pod of *Vanilla planifolia,* an orchid native to Mexico and the West Indies. The name derives from the Spanish *vainilla,* little sheath, which in turn comes from the Latin *vagina,* sheath.

8. *The Interpretation of Dreams,* by Sigmund Freud. This quotation comes from Book VII of Virgil's *Aeneid,* when Juno promises to pursue Aeneas to the bitter end.

9. Practically nothing. The warmer climes do not seem conducive to creative invention.

10.
    > Now word has come down from the Dean
    > That, due to the teaching machine,
    >   Oedipus Rex
    >   Could have learned about sex
    > Without ever touching the Queen.

OLLA PODRIDA

1. Why did Elizabeth Barrett Browning entitle her famous work "Sonnets from the Portuguese"?

2. An irate Italian mother wrote her daughter's suitor, "U, wedding Maria Mr." What was she trying to say?

3. What complimentary word is derived from a parable of Jesus?

4. How did the French author Edmond de Goncourt once describe a dinner at Émile Zola's?

5. Why has the koala rarely been able to flourish outside of Australia, and why do the small marsupials smell like cough drops?

6. For what occasion is Handel thought to have written his celebrated instrumental suite, *Water Music?*

7. How did Dorothy Parker, writing as "Constant Reader" in *The New Yorker,* review A.A. Milne's *The House at Pooh Corner,* and what was Milne's reaction?

8. Annie Palmer, the White Witch of Rose Hall, was reputed to have practiced voodoo and murdered three husbands, among other lurid pastimes. Why are she and her house remembered today?

9. According to Viscount Palmerston, Prime Minister under Queen Victoria, "There have been only three men who have understood the Schleswig-Holstein question." Who were they?

10. Who, in a single day, dreamed that he was a naval commander sending the SN 202, a huge, eight-engined hydroplane, hurtling through the worst storm in twenty years; an eminent surgeon saving the life of the millionaire banker, Wellington McMillan; the greatest shot in the world with any type of firearm; a World War I bomber pilot flying forty kilometers through hell over the German lines; facing the firing squad—"undefeated, inscrutable to the last"?

OLLA PODRIDA

1. Robert Browning's pet name for his wife was "my little Portuguese" because of her dark complexion.

2. "You comma wedding. Maria missed her period."

3. Talent—from the parable of the rich man who entrusted his servants in his absence with various amounts of money, the talents, and held them to account for making a profit. This is taken as an example of God's expecting His children to make use of what He has bestowed on them.

4. "Housewarming at Zola's. Very tasty dinner, including some grouse whose scented meat Daudet compared to an old courtesan's flesh marinated in a bidet."

5. Its sole food source is the leaves and bark of the eucalyptus, also called the gum tree, which flourishes in Australia, and the oil of the eucalyptus leaves is an ingredient of cough drops. Outside of Australia koalas are found only at the San Diego Zoo, where their diet is locally grown eucalyptus.

6. *Water Music* was composed in 1717 for a Royal Progress down the Thames by Handel's patron, George I. It supposedly was first played on a boat following the Royal Barge.

7. "Tonstant weader fwowed up." To this Milne commented, "No writer of children's books says gaily to his publishers, 'Don't bother about the children; Mrs. Parker will love it.'"

8. Her house, Rose Hall, outside of Montego Bay, built at the height of the sugar trade and before the British outlawed slavery, is the greatest of Jamaica's "Great Houses."

9. "One was Prince Albert, who is dead. The second was a German professor, who went mad. I am the third one, and I've forgotten all about it."

10. Who else but that daydreamer *sans pareil*, the title character of the James Thurber short story "The Secret Life of Walter Mitty"?

OMNIUM-GATHERUM

1. Name the four largest countries in the world: a) by area, and b) by population.

2. Near the end of his life, who said, "I am lonesome. They are all dying. I have hardly a warm personal enemy left"?

3. When Lord Whistlebritches returned home early from a shoot, he found his wife in bed with a man. He ordered his valet to load his 12-bore Purdey and bring it to him. He then proceeded to shoot at the bed. How did the valet compliment him?

4. In which comic strip were the words glop, goon and jeep first coined?

5. The first Rolls-Royce model, the Silver Ghost, appeared in 1907. In the mid-1960s, when a new model was to be introduced, why was the name Silver Mist considered but subsequently discarded?

6. Which Latin American country, closely connected with the United States, has a river called Rio Bravo del Norte?

7. One of the nephews of the English actress Dame Edith Evans underwent a sex change and married a black handyman from Charleston, South Carolina. What was the reaction of one kinswoman?

8. After he lost the race for the state legislature, the U.S. Senate and the vice-presidential nomination, what became of him?

9. Why does the color red always appear on striped barbershop poles?

10. His range of film portrayals rivals those of Alec Guinness and Laurence Olivier and includes such memorable roles as Captain Jeffrey T. Spaulding, Professor Quincy Adams Wagstaff, Rufus T. Firefly, Otis B. Driftwood, J. Cheever Loophole, Wolf J. Flywheel and S. Quentin Quail. Who is this performer?

OMNIUM-GATHERUM

1. a) Russia, China, United States, Canada, and
    b) China, India, Russia, United States.

2. James A. McNeill Whistler, American painter, etcher, wit and eccentric.

3. "Good shot, your lordship, you got him on the rise."

4. Elzie Segar's "Popeye."

5. The company learned that *Mist* is the German word for excrement. They then named the new model the Silver Shadow.

6. Mexico. This is the Mexican name for the Rio Grande, which forms our southwest boundary with that country.

7. "I wish she hadn't married a Baptist."

8. Abraham Lincoln became President of the United States.

9. Besides trimming hair and beards, early barbers also "cupped," a term for blood-letting, which was considered a panacea for most ailments in those days.

10. Groucho Marx, in *Animal Crackers, Horse Feathers, Duck Soup, A Night at the Opera, At the Circus, The Big Store* and *Go West* respectively.

OPERA—GRAND AND OTHERWISE

1. In which popular Italian opera is part of "The Star-Spangled Banner" played?

2. The characters Don Alvaro, Florestan and Mauricio share three things in common. What are they?

3. Can you name the only stride pianist to have written an opera?

4. What is missing from this list: Aïda, Britten, Tosca, Carmen, Gloriana, Verdi, Puccini?

5. Which Italian proverb refers to the soporific effect grand opera has on some people?

6. Everyone has heard of Jacques Offenbach's opera *The Tales of Hoffmann,* but who was Hoffmann?

7. Which internationally known singers were known as *La Stupenda* and *La Superba,* and what was La Stupenda's attitude towards money?

8. What happens no matter how late you get to a performance of Wagner's *Tristan and Isolde?*

9. If there were 91 in Turkey, 100 in France, 231 in Germany and 640 in Italy, how many were there in Spain?

10. Enlivened by arias lifted from Bizet, Mozart, Offenbach, Verdi and others, plus a Wagnerian leitmotif or two to lend some tone, the Broque Opera Company's *The Ring of the Fettuccines* encapsulates grand opera with merciful brevity and a refreshing lack of pretentiousness. In the cast are the necessary royal family—king, prince and princess—the obligatory cobbler and witch, the Duchess of Quiche Lorraine, Basil de Gaulle, and the inevitable consumptive soprano, who casts her tubercular pall over the proceedings. What is the setting of this opera, and in which culinary fashion does it conclude?

OPERA—GRAND AND OTHERWISE

1. Puccini's *Madame Butterfly,* which features Lieutenant B.F. Pinkerton of the U.S. Navy ship *Abraham Lincoln.* Although his initials are B.F., he has been called F.B. for obvious reasons.

2. They are all tenors; they are all Spanish; and they are all loved by a Leonora.

3. Scott Joplin, whose music was adapted for the film *The Sting,* wrote an opera called *Treemonisha.*

4. Bizet, who wrote *Carmen. Tosca* is by Puccini, *Gloriana* by Britten, *Aïda* by Verdi.

5. "Bed is the poor man's opera."

6. Amadeus Hoffmann was a famous German romantic novelist, dramatist, composer and lawyer. Among his better known works is the fatalistic novel *The Devil's Elixir.*

7. Maria Callas and Dame Joan Sutherland. "I'm not interested in money," Callas said, "but it has to be more than anyone else gets."

8. There are always two acts left.

9. 1,003, according to Don Giovanni's servant Leporello, when he lists the Don's amorous conquests to Donna Elvira.

10. *The Ring of the Fettuccines* is set in the steamy climes of Scampi and Vermicelli and the damp County of Soave Bolla. In a gastronomic "tour de farce" at the end, Alfredo blends with the House of Fettuccine.

OSCARS

1. Douglas Fairbanks, the first president of the Academy of Motion Picture Arts and Sciences, wanted the Oscar statuette to be durable. To emphasize this, he hurled a prototype over a sound stage. Fairbanks made his point; the statuette was and still is made of what?

2. Name the only two movies to have had their entire casts nominated for Oscars.

3. The list of famous players who never received Oscars is too long to include here, but can you name the performers who have received the most nominations and never won?

4. Besides Walt Disney, who has the distinction of winning four Oscars in two consecutive years?

5. Tedious indeed are the seemingly endless speeches of gratitude. How did Award-winning screenwriter Donald Ogden Stewart's acceptance speech for *The Philadelphia Story* strike a refreshing note?

6. Victor McLaglen was the first Best Actor (*The Informer,* in 1935) to be nominated later as Best Supporting Actor (*The Quiet Man,* in 1952). Can you name the three actresses who have won Awards in these categories?

7. Who is the only performer to win an Award posthumously?

8. The voting of the Academy in 1932 was unique in producing the first tie, between Frederic March for *Dr. Jekyll and Mr. Hyde* and Wallace Beery for *The Champ.* Coincidentally, both actors had adopted children that year, which prompted March in his acceptance speech to say what?

9. Richard Attenborough's *Gandhi* garnered eight Oscars in 1983, which tied it with *Cabaret, From Here to Eternity, Gone With the Wind, My Fair Lady* and *On the Waterfront.* Which film remains the all-time winner?

10. The 1974 proceedings were enlivened by a "streaker" who appeared and ran across the stage just as David Niven was introducing Elizabeth Taylor. How did Niven neatly handle the situation?

OSCARS

1. The statuette of a faceless crusader holding a sword is made of gold-plated Britannia metal. (During World War II, when there was a metal shortage, the statuette was made of plaster.)

2. Michael Caine and Laurence Olivier comprised the entire cast of *Sleuth,* the 1972 film. Both were nominated for Academy Awards. And James Whitmore won an Oscar nomination for the 1975 movie version of his one-man show about President Truman, *Give 'Em Hell, Harry!*

3. Richard Burton and Peter O'Toole, with seven, and Deborah Kerr, Thelma Ritter and Geraldine Fitzgerald with six.

4. Joseph L. Mankiewicz, who took home two statuettes in 1949 for writing and directing *A Letter to Three Wives,* and two more in 1950 for *All About Eve.*

5. Stewart simply said: "There has been so much niceness here tonight that I'm happy to say that I'm entirely responsible for the success of *The Philadelphia Story.* Nobody lifted a finger to help me."

6. Helen Hayes for *The Sin of Madelon Claudet* (1932) and *Airport* (1970), Ingrid Bergman for *Gaslight* (1944) and *Murder on the Orient Express* (1974) and Maggie Smith for *The Prime of Miss Jean Brodie* (1969) and *California Suite* (1978).

7. The Australian actor Peter Finch, who won the Best Actor Award in 1976, two months after his death, for his role as the crazed television personality Howard Beale in *Network.* Beale is remembered for shouting, "I'm mad as hell, and I'm not going to take it anymore," and furthermore urging his audience to shout the sentence out of their windows.

8. "It seems odd that Wally and I were both given Awards for the best male performance of the year."

9. *Ben Hur* in 1959, starring Charlton Heston, with eleven Oscars, followed by *West Side Story*'s ten, and nine for *Gigi.*

10. Niven said, "That's probably the only laugh that man will ever get in his life—stripping off his clothes and showing us his shortcomings."

PAINTING

1. Who painted a remarkable series of eight pictures depicting eight phases in the life of Tom Rakehell, and where may these be seen?

2. In the foreground of which famous picture is a plain wooden box used as a writing stand, bearing these words: *"N'ayant pu me corrompre, ils m'ont assassiné"* (Not having been able to compromise me, they assassinated me)?

3. How did a certain early American painter demonstrate his reverence for the old masters?

4. Who portrayed which painters in these films: a) *The Agony and the Ecstasy,* b) *Moulin Rouge,* c) *Lust for Life*?

5. Which English author observed that "art consists of drawing the line somewhere"?

6. The alleged inventor of the electric telegraph, with a small assist from the author of the *Leatherstocking Tales,* made art history in 1982. How?

7. What distinction attaches to Van Gogh's *The Red Orchard*?

8. Why do Monsieur Carrel, Basil Hallwood, Gulley Jimson and Monsieur Elstir belong together?

9. Which famous picture was commissioned for the Refreshment Room in the British House of Lords, but when the Commons refused to vote the money, was successively bought by a peer, a soap manufacturer, and its present owner, a prominent firm of Scotch distillers?

10. When Titian was mixing some pigments, what did the position of his model suggest to him?

PAINTING

1. *The Rake's Progress* by William Hogarth. This series and another, entitled *The Election,* which satirizes the corruption and animosities incidental to such an occasion in the 18th century, may be seen in the Picture Room of the Sir John Soane's Museum in Lincoln's Inn Fields in London.

2. *The Death of Marat* by Jacques-Louis David, in the Musée des Beaux-Arts in Reims.

3. Charles Willson Peale named four of his seventeen children Titian, Rubens, Raphaelle and Rembrandt, and all these did in fact become painters.

4. a) Charlton Heston—Michelangelo, b) José Ferrer—Henri de la Toulouse-Lautrec, c) Kirk Douglas and Anthony Quinn—Vincent Van Gogh and Paul Gauguin respectively.

5. Gilbert Keith Chesterton, who was known as the Prince of Paradox.

6. *The Gallery of the Louvre,* an 1832 painting by Samuel F.B. Morse, was sold by Syracuse University for $3.25 million, then the highest price ever paid for an American work of art. Depicted in the gallery were the artist and James Fenimore Cooper with his wife and child.

7. *The Red Orchard* is the only picture he ever sold in his lifetime.

8. They are all literary painters—from George du Maurier's *Trilby,* Oscar Wilde's *The Picture of Dorian Gray,* Joyce Cary's *The Horse's Mouth* and Marcel Proust's *A la recherche du temps perdu.*

9. Sir Edwin Landseer's *Monarch of the Glen,* which now hangs appropriately in the Board Room of John Dewar & Sons, Ltd. in Dewar House in London's Haymarket.

10.   While Titian was mixing rose madder,
    His model posed high on a ladder.
          Her position to Titian
          Suggested coition,
    So he leapt up the ladder and had her.

PAIRS

1. In the Great Hall of London's Guildhall are the nine-foot wooden figures of Gog and Magog, survivors of a legendary race of giants that were said to have ruled Britain. In biblical prophecy, what were they?

2. Who said to whom: "For well as I loved thee, mine heart will not serve me to see thee, for through thee and me is the flower of kings and knights destroyed"?

3. In which famous poem will you find this refrain?

   > I was a King in Babylon
   > And you were a Christian Slave.

4. What are the Kattegat and the Skagerrak?

5. They invented the summer season on the Riviera, and F. Scott Fitzgerald used them as models for Nicole and Dick Diver in *Tender Is the Night*.

6. What is an *au pair* girl, and why is she so called?

7. Winston S. Churchill liked to describe himself as the result of an English-speaking union; he was the son of Lord Randolph Churchill and Jennie Jerome from New York. While his mastery of the English language was superb, not so was his command of French. How did he once in a speech in Paris describe his past life as being divided into two parts?

8. Which dour-looking Iowa couple are as familiar as Leonardo's *Mona Lisa* or Gilbert Stuart's *Washington*, and have been the subject of innumerable spoofs ranging from ads and greeting cards to magazine covers?

9. Incongruous as it may seem, two pairs of performers—Ronald Reagan and Ann Sheridan, and George Raft and Hedy Lamarr—were considered for the leads in which famous film?

10. The two boys were in the same class at Harrow, where they detested each other. Both were successful in later life: one became Archbishop of Canterbury, the other First Sea Lord. They did not meet again until one day at a local railroad station when the Archbishop went up to the Admiral and said, "Excuse me, stationmaster, but when does the next train leave for London?" What did the Admiral say?

PAIRS

1. Gog was a ruler in the land of Magog (probably Scythia) whose overthrow by Israel was prophesied by Ezekiel.

2. Queen Guinevere to Sir Launcelot, in Sir Thomas Malory's *La Morte d'Arthur*.

3. "Invictus," the best-known work of William Ernest Henley.

4. The Kattegat and the Skagerrak are straits—the first lying between Denmark and Sweden, the second between Denmark and Norway.

5. Sara and Gerald Murphy, who were the subjects of Calvin Tomkins' 1971 bestseller *Living Well Is the Best Revenge*.

6. An *au pair* girl is generally a governess or baby-sitter who lives in a household on equal terms *(au pair)* with the family, receiving board and lodging but no salary. *Au pair* girls are usually from a good family, and have come to another country to learn the language.

7. *"Quand je regards mon derrière, je trouve que c'est divisé en deux parties."* (When I look at my behind, I find that it is divided into two parts.)

8. The pair in Grant Wood's 1930 painting *American Gothic*, so named for the Gothic window in the house in the background. The actual models were the artist's sister and his dentist from Cedar Rapids, Iowa.

9. *Casablanca*, in which the roles of Rick Blaine and Ilsa Lund were played to perfection by Humphrey Bogart and Ingrid Bergman.

10. The Admiral looked at the portly Archbishop in his clerical robes and replied, "Eleven twenty-two, madam, but are you well advised to travel in your delicate condition?"

PASTICHE

1. Doctors take the Hippocratic oath. What do nurses take?

2. "You have a right to remain silent. Any statement you make may be used in evidence against you. You have a right to counsel during questioning, and an attorney will be appointed for you if you cannot afford one." What name is given to the foregoing?

3. What is Lee Trevino's advice if one is caught on a golf course during a thunder and lightning storm?

4. Eleuthera, which means free in Greek, is a strange name for one of the Bahamian islands. How did it come to be bestowed?

5. Which airplane crash caused the greatest loss of life?

6. Just as ham hocks are a favorite of Southerners, the Alaskan Eskimos are partial to muktuk. What precisely are these delicacies?

7. What sport has been compared to standing under a cold shower tearing up hundred dollar bills?

8. He, who was married to a plain woman older than himself, fell in love with a beautiful young one. He wrote a famous letter telling of his "longing to kiss your titties." After considerable difficulty in arranging for a divorce, he married the young woman, causing much scandal and great controversy. Later, suspecting her of infidelity, he had her killed. They had one child together. Who was the child?

9. In which operas are the following found: a) a gingerbread witch, b) a birdcage, c) a game of cards in hell, d) a silver rose?

10. How did John Barrymore explain the need for drinking five martinis before dinner?

PASTICHE

1. The Florence Nightingale pledge.

2. These are the Miranda warnings, which the Supreme Court deemed in 1966 to be the first step U.S. society takes when it is about to charge one of its members with having done serious injury.

3. "Stand in the middle of the fairway and hold up a one-iron. Not even God can hit a one-iron."

4. Eleuthera was founded by a freedom-loving group of Englishmen who sailed from Bermuda in 1647 and called themselves the Company of Eleutheran Adventurers.

5. 582 lives were lost in March 1973, at the fog-shrouded Santa Cruz de Tenerife airport in the Canary Islands when a KLM Boeing 747 collided on takeoff with a Pan American 747 which was taxiing across the runway. The blame was laid to the KLM pilot, who began his takeoff without permission.

6. Pigs' ankles and raw whale skin.

7. Yachting, when you own your own boat. It has also been described as "the fine art of getting wet and becoming ill while slowly going nowhere at great expense."

8. Elizabeth I of England, daughter of Henry VIII and Anne Boleyn.

9. a) *Hansel and Gretel,* by Engelbert Humperdinck,
   b) *The Magic Flute,* by Wolfgang Amadeus Mozart,
   c) *Schwanda the Bagpiper,* by Jaromir Weinberger,
   d) *Der Rosenkavalier,* by Richard Strauss.

10. "One of the worst things you can do is eat on an empty stomach."

PEJORATIVES

The use of these derogatory terms is in the worst possible taste and is to be avoided. Yet they are not without a certain etymological interest. Can you give the origin of the following epithets?

1. Sod buster, shit kicker
2. Dago, wop, guinea
3. Kike, sheenie
4. Mick
5. Greaser
6. Coon, spade
7. Spic or spick
8. Gringo
9. Dyke, bull dyke
10. Mother

PEJORATIVES

1. These were derisive terms used by cattlemen for settlers who were trying to farm the land.

2. Abusive slang for an Italian or person of Italian descent. Dago is a corruption of the Spanish *Diego*. Wop is another offensive term for Italians, derived from the Sicilian *guappo,* dandy. Guinea originally meant a native of Guinea, but it eventually settled on people of Italian descent.

3. Kike was the name applied by aristocratic U.S. German Jews to poor Polish and Russian Jewish immigrants whose names ended in -ki. The derivation of sheenie is found in the German *schin,* meaning a petty thief or a cheat.

4. A disparaging word for the Irish, possibly from the shortening of the name Michael.

5. A greaser, in which the s is pronounced as z, is an epithet for a Mexican or other swarthy person, because such people's sweat is supposedly oily.

6. A Negro, originally from barracoon, the barracks in which slaves and convicts were temporarily confined. Spade undoubtedly derives from the phrase "as black as the ace of spades."

7. An abusive name of a Spanish-speaking person, possibly shortened from the traditional phrase "No spica da Engleesh."

8. Gringo is a standard Mexican derogatory term for *Yangui,* or *Norte Americano,* because of the way they speak, which was Greek (*Griego* in Spanish) to the Mexican. Originally it meant any foreigner.

9. A lesbian. A bull dyke is a female homosexual who plays the male role, especially a large, masculine-looking woman. The origin of the term is obscure, but may come from the legend of the Dutch boy who plugged the leak in the dike with his finger.

10. This is short for mother-fucker, the most insulting obscenity in modern English. It appears in many pieces of black folklore, such as "The Ballad of Stagolee," and was used in 1960 by Jack Lemmon in the film *The Apartment*. Ordering a second martini, he said, "Give me another of those mothers."

PEREGRINATIONS

1. The prologue of which famous trip includes these lines?

   And smale foweles maken melodye,
   That slepen al the nyght with open ye
   (So priketh hem nature in hir corages);
   Thanne longen folk to goon on pilgrimages.

2. The Pole of Inaccessibility is aptly named. Where is it?

3. In the 1930s, before the advent of air travel, transatlantic liners reached their greatest size. Dorothy Parker managed to convey this sense of immensity when she asked what question aboard R.M.S. *Queen Mary*?

4. Why, according to medieval legend, was the Wandering Jew condemned to wander on earth until Judgment Day?

5. Whom did Bjaaland, Hanssen, Hassel and Wisting accompany?

6. The Danish philosopher and religious thinker Søren Kierkegaard once observed that two groups of people have a saying that one should never revisit a place. Who are they?

7. When Gertrude Stein returned after a brief sojourn in Hollywood, a friend asked her, "What is it like out there?" What was Miss Stein's immortal answer?

8. Train buffs will take to their heart this verse from a poem by which celebrated Vassar graduate?

   My heart is warm with the friends I make,
   And better friends I'll not be knowing;
   Yet there isn't a train I wouldn't take,
   No matter where it's going.

9. Where would you find the spectacular 17-Mile Drive?

10. A man on holiday in England's Lake District wired a friend: "SEND TWO PUNTS AND A CANOE." What reply did he receive?

PEREGRINATIONS

1. Geoffrey Chaucer's *The Canterbury Tales*. The motley crew of 31, including Chaucer himself, left the Tabard Inn in Southwark one April morning, but never got to Canterbury. The Tabard, one of the last of London's galleried inns, survived until 1875.

2. The Pole of Inaccessibility is that point in Antarctica furthest of access from any seacoast.

3. "What time does this place get to Southampton?"

4. He mocked or mistreated Jesus while He was on His way to the Cross. (The Wandering Jew was last reported in Salt Lake City in 1868, having found a place where Jews are Gentile. He has not been heard of again.)

5. Roald Amundsen, in his successful dash to be the first man to reach the South Pole in 1912, beating his English rival Robert Falcon Scott.

6. "Only robbers and gypsies say that one must never return to where one has been."

7. After a moment's thought, she said, "There *is* no 'there' out there."

8. Edna St. Vincent Millay, from her poem "Travel."

9. On the Monterey Peninsula on the Pacific south of San Francisco and just north of Big Sur. There you will drive through Del Monte Forest with its groves of Monterey cypress and along a coastline of singular beauty. You will usually see such wildlife as deer throughout the forest and sea lions, seals and sea otters in the water and on the rocks offshore.

10. "SENDING THE TWO GIRLS BUT WHAT IN HELL IS A PANOE?"

POLITICAL LEADERS

1. What was Oliver Cromwell's real name, and what, on discovering this, did H.G. Wells call him?

2. Which Dutch Colonial Governor was given the occasion to sing the following?

   > But it's a long, long while
   > From May to December—
   > And the days grow short
   > When you reach September.

3. What was Disraeli's comment when he took his seat in the House of Lords as the 1st Earl of Beaconsfield?

4. Can you name the South African soldier and statesman who became a member of the Imperial War Cabinet in London in 1917?

5. What advice did Prime Minister Churchill give about dealing with Mussolini and his son-in-law, the Italian Foreign Minister Count Ciano?

6. Who was Adenoid Hynkel?

7. Which leader of a particularly backward country was said to have eaten the inner organs of his enemies after having skinned them alive, and also terrified his illiterate people by dressing in black and presenting himself as the voodoo god Baron Samedi (Lord Saturday or Sabbath)?

8. When Austen Chamberlain was briefly leader of Britain's Conservative Party, how could he invariably tell how well he was doing?

9. What embarrassment overtook the Michigan Republican party in 1980?

10. "Of course, the trouble with Herbie is, he's his own worst enemy" was said about the Labour MP Herbert Morrison. What was Ernie Bevin's rejoinder?

POLITICAL LEADERS

1. Oliver Williams. (Cromwell was his grandmother's maiden name.) Wells, on hearing this from Lloyd George, called him Williams the Conqueror.

2. Peter Stuyvesant, Director General of New Netherland, on his arrival in New Amsterdam, now New York City. Walter Huston played Stuyvesant and sang "September Song" in *Knickerbocker Holiday* by Maxwell Anderson and Kurt Weill.

3. "Dead! But in the Elysian fields."

4. General Jan Christiaan Smuts, who once fought against the British in the Boer War but later was instrumental in the creation of the Union of South Africa.

5. "Never talk to the monkey when the organ grinder is in the room."

6. Adenoid Hynkel was the name Charlie Chaplin chose for his impersonation of Adolf Hitler in his 1940 film *The Great Dictator.*

7. The Haitian President "Papa Doc" François Duvalier, who died in 1971. His reign of terror was orchestrated by the infamous secret police, the Tontons Macoutes (Haitian Creole for bogeymen). Conditions in Haiti under his son and successor, "Baby Doc" Jean-Claude Duvalier, whose title is President for Life, have deteriorated further.

8. "I can always tell how well I stand politically by the number of fingers Lady Londonderry offers me at her receptions."

9. One of its congressional candidates proved to be in a lunatic asylum, and another a member of the American Nazi party.

10. "Not while I'm alive, he's not!"

POPULAR MUSIC

1. What song is traditionally played before the Preakness, and how does it tie in with Christmas and the Russian Revolution?

2. Can you explain the connection between the blues and Tennessee machine politics?

3. Who was once described as "the songwriter who composed the overture to the Jazz Age," and how did he show his appreciation to his adopted country?

4. On a train trip out to California George Gershwin made the pianist and wit Oscar Levant take the upper berth, citing what difference between them?

5. Which versatile man of the theater, who had a "talent to amuse," penned these lines?

> She refused to begin the Beguine
> Tho' they besought her to,
> And with language profane and obscene
> She curs'd the man who taught her to
> She curs'd Cole Porter too!

6. Louis Armstrong was a jazz trumpet virtuoso whose playing was noted for improvisation, and because of him solo performance attained a position of great importance in jazz. Where did he get his nickname Satchmo?

7. What was Billy Wilder's comment on Cliff Osmond's singing?

8. Green and purple hair, safety pins worn through flesh, razor blades and spitting on audiences are all part of what movement?

9. Which song, written in praise of a baby sitter, was reissued with slightly different lyrics more appropriate to a future queen?

10. What was the comment of one Hollywood cynic on learning of Elvis Presley's death?

POPULAR MUSIC

1. "Maryland, My Maryland," which was written by James R. Randall to the tune "O Tannenbaum," a German song celebrating the Christmas tree. It is also the tune of "The Red Flag," an international leftist song and original anthem of the Soviet Union.

2. W. C. Handy's "Memphis Blues" was originally titled "Mr. Edward H. Crump's Marching Band," Crump having been the long-time Democratic boss of Tennessee.

3. The Russian-born Isadore Baline, who as Irving Berlin assigned the royalties of "God Bless America" to the Boy Scouts, the Girl Scouts and the Campfire Girls.

4. "That's the difference between talent and genius."

5. Noël Coward in "Nina," in his 1945 show, *Sigh No More*.

6. Satchmo refers to Armstrong's mouth—satchel mouth.

7. "He has Van Gogh's ear for music."

8. Punk rock, with its driving insistent beat, which many observers see as an expression of the alienation of Britain's working-class young.

9. "Diana," in honor of H.R.H. The Princess of Wales, *née* Lady Diana Spencer. Paul Anka made his first big hit at age fifteen in 1956 with a recording of "Diana," which originally sold twenty million copies.

10. "Good career move."

POTABLES

1. How did the *Kaffeehaus* come into being in Vienna at the end of the 17th century?

2. Linguistic scholars have for years argued over the origin of the word cocktail, but a consensus seem to have agreed on one probable source. What is it?

3. Which is the odd man out: kirschwasser, mirabelle, quetsch, slivovitz?

4. In *My Early Life* Winston S. Churchill wrote: "When I was a young subaltern in the South African War, the water was not fit to drink. To make it palatable we had to add whisky. By diligent effort I learned to like it." What was he to say later?

5. Can you name the author of the following?

> If all be true that I do think,
> There are five reasons we should drink;
> Good wine—a friend—or being dry:
> Or lest we should be by and by—
> Or any other reason why.

6. What was originally called the Bucket of Blood and later the Red Snapper when it first appeared in Paris in the Twenties, and what is rapidly overtaking it in popularity?

7. According to *Debrett's Etiquette and Modern Manners,* what is the preferred "aiming juice" to be carried in a small flask on a grouse shoot, and what refreshing morning drink was introduced by Captain William Buckmaster at Buck's Club in London after World War I?

8. A sweet Barbadian liquor called Falernum is added to all Mount Gay rum brands and is the sine qua non for making the perfect daiquiri without sugar. What is the curious derivation of its name?

9. How is a Bellini made, and where was it first served?

10. Near the end of a particularly bibulous party, what was Dorothy Parker's reply when she was offered another drink?

POTABLES

1. The *Kaffeehaus* began in 1683 when the Viennese repulsed an invasion by the Turks, who left behind sackfuls of strong-tasting little brown beans.

2. An 18th-century New Orleans apothecary, Antoine Peychaud, dispensed tonics of Sazerac du Forge Cognac and his own Peychaud bitters, which he served in a *coquetier,* or eggcup, from which sprang *coquetel,* and then cocktail.

3. Kirschwasser, which is distilled from cherries and cherry stones; the others are from plums.

4. "I neither want it nor need it, but I should think it pretty hazardous to interfere with the ineradicable habit of a lifetime."

5. Henry Aldrich in *Reasons for Drinking*.

6. The Bloody Mary, which was invented by Fernand Petit, a bartender at Harry's New York Bar. When he went to the St. Regis bar in New York in the Thirties, his concoction became famous as the Bloody Mary. The Bullshot, made with beef bouillon (never consommé, which has a tendency to gel) and vodka, is now becoming increasingly popular.

7. A Rusty Nail, which combines Scotch and Drambuie in equal amounts, and Buck's Fizz, a mixture of champagne and orange juice, which is called a Mimosa in the United States.

8. Once, when a woman was asked for the ingredients, she answered in her dialect, "Haf a learn um"—"Have to learn how it's done." Hence the name.

9. A Bellini is made with fresh peaches and "champagne," the noble sparkling Prosecco from Coneglia, and was first served at Harry's Bar in Venice.

10. "One more drink and I'll be under the host."

POTPOURRI

1. "In retreat: indomitable; in advance: invincible; in victory: insufferable" was whose description of whom?

2. By whom were the following burned: a) the White House (then called The President's House) in 1814, b) the Paris Tuileries in 1871, c) the German Reichstag in 1933, d) London's Crystal Palace in 1936?

3. The offense known as mopery is extremely rare, but can you define it?

4. Who is reputed to be the richest man in the United States?

5. Why did a man who is part Spaniard, was born in Bulgaria, lives in England and writes in German receive $180,000 at the hands of the King of Sweden in 1981?

6. Can you explain the meaning of the acronym COCH? And COTCH?

7. Ling-Ling and Hsing-Hsing are certainly "a pair of star-crossed lovers." Who are they, and where does Chia-Chia come in?

8. What are *paradores* and *pousadas,* and where would you find them?

9. Who spoke of the lowly in these terms and where may these lines be seen today?

> Give me your tired, your poor,
> Your huddled masses yearning to breathe free,
> The wretched refuse of your teeming shore,
> Send these, the homeless, tempest-tossed to me:
> I lift my lamp beside the golden door.

10. In George Cukor's film *Dinner at Eight* Jean Harlow tells Marie Dressler that she has read in a book that machinery is going to take the place of every profession. What was Miss Dressler's comment?

POTPOURRI

1. Prime Minister Winston S. Churchill, commenting on Field Marshal Sir Bernard L. Montgomery during World War II.

2. a) British sailors and marines in the War of 1812, in retaliation for the burning of the government buildings at York, now Toronto, by U.S. troops; b) the Paris mob; c) the Nazis, through the agency of Van der Lubbe and others; d) cause unknown.

3. Mopery is exposing oneself to a blind woman.

4. Not Gordon Getty, but Daniel K. Ludwig, whose wealth is estimated at between $2 and 3 billion. By the age of 40 Ludwig had become the largest fleet owner (National Bulk Carriers) in the world and known as "the father of the supertanker." (Getty has been inaccurately accorded the title because of his control of the family trust, but it cannot be distributed until he and his two brothers die.)

5. Elias Canetti won the Nobel Prize for Literature in 1981.

6. COCH stands for Concorde Out, Concorde Home. Of course, if you lose all your money gaming in London or Monte Carlo, you might have to go COTCH: Concorde Out, Tourist Class Home.

7. Ling-Ling and Hsing-Hsing are the only giant pandas in America. When they seemed unable to produce a baby panda, an English import named Chia-Chia was flown in. Unfortunately, he was a Stanley Kowalski type, who only proceeded to beat Ling-Ling up before being shipped home.

8. *Paradores* and *pousadas* are government-owned and -operated hotels in Spain and Portugal, respectively. They are often situated in fascinating converted palaces, castles, convents and monasteries.

9. Emma Lazarus. The lines from her poem "The New Colossus" are engraved on a plaque inside the base of the Statue of Liberty in New York harbor.

10. "Oh, my dear, that's something you need never worry about."

PSEUDONYMS

By what names are the following better known?

1. Eric Blair

2. David Green

3. Hernia Whittlebot

4. Jean-Baptiste Poquelin

5. Lev Davidovich Bronstein

6. Jacopo Robusti

7. Baroness Karen Blixen

8. François Marie Arouet, lj (*le jeune,* the younger)

9. Hilarius Bookbinder, Constantine Constantius, Johannes de Silentio, Anti-Climacus, Victor Eremita and Johannes Climacus

10. Leading Aircraftsman J.H. Ross 47738294

PSEUDONYMS

1. George Orwell, British novelist, whose most popular books are *Animal Farm* and *Nineteen Eighty-Four*.

2. David Ben-Gurion, Israeli statesman, who became the first prime minister of the newly created state in 1948.

3. Noël Coward, when he wrote *Chelsea Buns*.

4. Molière, French playwright and actor.

5. Leon Trotsky, Russian revolutionary and one of the architects of the Soviet Union. Expelled from the Soviet Union in 1929, he was murdered in Mexico in 1940.

6. The Venetian painter Tintoretto, whose name means "little dyer" and was taken from his father's trade.

7. Isak Dinesen, the Danish author who wrote primarily in English. Her best-known work was *Seven Gothic Tales*.

8. Voltaire, French philosopher and author, who anagrammatized his name, Arouet, lj, substituting v for u and i for j. (These pairs of letters were not yet fully distinguished by printers.)

9. Søren Kierkegaard, Danish existentialist philosopher who wrote on religious subjects.

10. T.E. Lawrence, British adventurer, soldier and scholar who as Lawrence of Arabia became a legend in his own lifetime. The narrative of his Arabian adventures is found in *The Seven Pillars of Wisdom*. Having a passion for anonymity, he legally adopted the name T.E. Shaw. However, when he wrote *The Mint,* an account of his life in the Royal Air Force, he used the pseudonym J.H. Ross. (Noël Coward began a letter to him, "Dear 47738294—or may I call you 477?")

QUARTETS

1. According to early theologians there are seven deadly sins—pride, covetousness, lust, gluttony, anger, envy and sloth—but only four cardinal or natural virtues to which all the virtuous, as children of God, may attain. What are they?

2. Who is supposed to bless the bed that I lie on?

3. Can you name the four state capitals named for American Presidents?

4. Which great writer ennumerated the four descending degrees of drunkenness in these terms?

   Upon the first goblet he read this inscription: monkey wine; upon the second: lion wine; upon the third: sheep wine; upon the fourth: swine wine. These four inscriptions expressed the four descending degrees of drunkenness: the first, that which enlivens; the second, that which irritates; the third, that which stupefies; finally the last, that which brutalizes.

5. The first Swiss communities to win their freedom are known as the Four Forest Cantons (*Die Vier Waldstatten*). What are they?

6. Give the four basic words that describe the sensations of taste.

7. Which powerful dramatic role was played successively by Tallulah Bankhead, Bette Davis, Anne Bancroft and Elizabeth Taylor?

8. How did Edward Lear in *A Book of Nonsense* vividly describe the perils involved in having a bushy beard?

9. In evaluating a wine thoroughly, experts have evolved a tasting ritual that examines which four basic elements?

10. Grantland Rice, the dean of American sports writers, gave a new twist to the phrase Four Horsemen when he wrote this about a 1924 football game in the old New York Polo Grounds when the Irish of Notre Dame upset a favored Army team: "Outlined against a blue-gray sky, the Four Horsemen rode again." How did he continue?

QUARTETS

1. Justice, fortitude, prudence and temperance. These were conceived by the early Greek philosophers and expatiated on by St. Thomas Aquinas in his *Summa Theologica*.

2.   Matthew, Mark, Luke and John,
        The Bed be blest that I lie on.
        Four angels round my head,
        One to watch, and one to pray,
        And two to bear my soul away.

3. Jefferson City, Missouri; Madison, Wisconsin; Jackson, Mississippi; and Lincoln, Nebraska.

4. Victor Hugo, in *Les Misérables*.

5. Schwyz (the origin of the name Switzerland), Unterwalden, Uri and Lucerne.

6. Sweet, sour, bitter and salt.

7. Regina Giddens, in Lillian Hellman's *The Little Foxes*. Tallulah Bankhead opened in the 1939 Broadway play, Bette Davis played the part in the 1941 motion picture, Anne Bancroft in the 1967 revival and Elizabeth Taylor in the 1981 dramatic production.

8.   There was an Old Man with a beard
        Who said, "It is just as I feared!—
           Two Owls and a Hen,
           Four Larks and a Wren,
        Have all built their nests in my beard!"

9. Appearance, bouquet, taste and aftertaste.

10. "In dramatic lore they are known as Famine, Pestilence, Destruction and Death. These are only aliases: Their real names are Stuhldreher, Miller, Crowley and Layden, a Notre Dame backfield second to none."

QUIZ MASTER

1. On a grouse shoot on the moors of northern England or Scotland, what is the largest number of birds an exceptionally good shot might bag in a single flight of grouse?

2. The idea for which famous play came in a flash to the author one night at the Imperial Hotel in Tokyo, the complete draft being written in a Shanghai hotel room in four days while he was felled by a bout of influenza?

3. In the motion picture *The Entertainer,* Laurence Olivier plays an aging music hall comedian named Archie Rice. One rainy day, how did he twist one of Churchill's famous lines?

4. Miguel de Cervantes once observed that "all women are good—good for something or good for nothing." In which poem did Rudyard Kipling equally disparage women?

5. Why were the terms "Reef in and max out" heard at the XXIII Olympiad, held in Los Angeles in the summer of 1984?

6. A petitioner before the Internal Revenue Court declared, "As God is my judge, I do not owe the tax assessed." How, with commendable brevity, did the judge reply?

7. "That was a great game of golf, fellows" were the last words of which noted entertainer?

8. Who was Oliver Herford parodying in these lines?

> Gather Kittens while you may,
>   Time brings only Sorrow:
> And the Kittens of today
>   Will be Old Cats Tomorrow.

9. To some ancient Greeks, an ephebe would have been an appealing dish. Why?

10. The American dramatist Maxwell Anderson wrote many of his plays in blank verse. What was Noël Coward's comment to Alexander Woollcott after attending an Anderson opening?

QUIZ MASTER

1. Three brace, or six grouse: four coming in and two flying away from the butt. Of course, to accomplish this feat a matched pair of shotguns and the services of a loader are required.

2. *Private Lives,* by Noël Coward, as recorded in his auto-biography *Present Indicative*.

3. "This is our finest shower."

4. In "The Vampire" Kipling wrote:

   > A fool there was and he made his prayer
   > (Even as you and I!)
   > To a rag and a bone and a hank of hair
   > (We called her the woman who did not care)
   > But the fool called her his lady fair—
   > (Even as you and I!)

5. These are terms used in wind surfing or board sailing, a new open event in the summer Olympics.

6. "He is not, I am, you do."

7. Bing Crosby, who died as he undoubtedly would have wished. In October 1977 he had finished the 18th hole at La Moraleja, just outside Madrid, and was walking towards the clubhouse when he suffered a massive heart attack.

8. Robert Herrick's "To the Virgins, to Make Much of Time":

   > Gather ye rosebuds while ye may,
   > Old time is still a-flying:
   > And this same flower that smiles today,
   > Tomorrow will be dying.

9. An ephebe was a youth between eighteen and twenty years of age.

10. "Isn't it a shame Maxwell Anderson's poetic license has expired?"

QUOTE OR MISQUOTE?

Can you complete these popular quotes correctly?

1. _____ on, Macduff.

2. I must _____ to the seas again.

3. Man doth not live by bread _____.

4. _____ thing, sir, but mine own.

5. 'Twas the night before Christmas, _____ all through the house.

6. And there is _____ under the sun.

7. _____ as remembered kisses after death.

8. _____ lady doth protest _____.

9. Laugh where we must, be candid where we can;
   But _____ the ways of God to man.

10. She may very well pass for forty-three
    In the _____ with the light behind her.

QUOTE OR MISQUOTE?

1. lay (William Shakespeare, *Macbeth*)
2. down (John Masefield, "Sea Fever")
3. only (Deuteronomy 8:9)
4. An ill-favored (William Shakespeare, *As You Like It*)
5. when (Clement Moore, "A Visit from St. Nicholas")
6. no new thing (Ecclesiastes 1:8)
7. Dear (Alfred, Lord Tennyson, "The Princess")
8. The _____ too much, methinks (William Shakespeare, *Hamlet*)
9. vindicate (Alexander Pope, "An Essay on Man")
10. dusk (W.S. Gilbert, *Trial by Jury*)

RANDOM NOTES

1. Why is Tom a good name for a computer?

2. In the last 900 years England has had eight of two of them, and two of one of them. Who or what are they?

3. Can you name one country's best-seller that was originally titled *Four-and-a-Half Years' Struggle Against Lies, Stupidity and Cowardice*?

4. It is unique in being the only article of clothing to be named after the hero of a poem. What is it?

5. How did a poisonous metallic liquid and a messenger of the gods become, in the 1980s, "the right stuff"?

6. In Greek mythology Jason sailed in the *Argo* in search of the Golden Fleece. Why was the fleece golden?

7. "One of those squat, plump little cakes which look as though they had been moulded in the fluted valve of a scallop shell" has been called the cake with the greatest literary clout. What is it, and what went wrong in the translation of the title of the work the cake inspired?

8. Can you name the first planet to be identified in modern times with the aid of a telescope, a discovery that overnight doubled the size of the solar system?

9. Which well-manicured winter resort is known as God's Waiting Room because of the advanced age of its "snowbirds," and has many daily pauses that definitely do not refresh?

10. According to W.H. Auden in *American Graffiti*, on which occasion was Oscar Wilde "greatly beguiled"?

RANDOM NOTES

1. A computer is a totally obedient moron.

2. Kings. There have been eight Edwards and eight Henrys, but only two Charleses.

3. Adolf Hitler's *Mein Kampf* (My Struggle), which shows that every verbose author needs an editor.

4. The tam-o'-shanter, named for the hero of Robert Burns' poem of the same name.

5. The story of America's space pioneers—Wally Schirra, Gordon Cooper, Scott Carpenter, Gus Grissom, Alan Shepard, Deke Slayton and John Glenn, who were the seven Mercury astronauts—is told in Tom Wolfe's *The Right Stuff*.

6. The Golden Fleece came from gold refining. The underside of the fleece, being sticky, as golden because it was used to line the sluices to catch gold particles in mining operations around Colchis, an ancient country on the Black Sea.

7. The madeleine, which Marcel Proust ate with an infusion of tilleul, a tea prepared from the dried blossoms of the linden tree. As he wrote, "An exquisite pleasure had invaded my senses." The title of the work, *A la recherche du temps perdu,* has nothing to do with Shakespeare's phrase, "Remembrance of Things Past"; it should have been translated *In Search of Lost Time*.

8. Uranus, which was discovered in 1780 by Sir William Herschel, who originally thought it to be a comet. In the 1840s Henry Silver, a drama critic of the British magazine *Punch,* posed this question: What do you see when you put your head between your legs? Answer: Uranus.

9. Palm Beach, Florida. PBP means "Palm Beach Pause" when all conversation becomes impossible because of the roar of the jet liners taking off from the nearby airport.

10.   Oscar Wilde
    Was greatly beguiled
    When into the Café Royale walked Bosie
    Wearing a tea cosy.

    (Bosie was Wilde's pet name for his dear friend Lord Alfred Douglas.)

RELIGION

1. Fourteen men of God officiated at Washington's first inauguration. Thirteen were Protestant clergymen. Who was the fourteenth?

2.   In good King Charles's golden days,
          When loyalty no harm meant,
          A furious High Churchman I was,
          And so I gain'd preferment . . .

   So spoke the Vicar of Bray, a village on the Thames, who preached that "Kings are by God appointed" and so accommodated his religious beliefs to the successive reigns of James, William, Anne and George. How does the verse end?

3. Where would you go to see a pulpit shaped like the prow of a ship?

4. To the well-traveled person, what is the difference between heaven and hell?

5. Who defined religion as "a daughter of Hope and Fear, explaining to Ignorance the nature of the Unknowable"?

6. The menorah, a nine-branched candelabrum, symbolizes the unity and permanence of the Jewish faith. What miracle does the candle lighting—one for each of the eight days of Hanukkah—symbolically reenact?

7. Who coined the line: "An atheist is a man who has no invisible means of support"?

8. Name the only church in the world where Easter mass is celebrated daily.

9. During World War II tight security measures were imposed in June 1944, before the D-Day landings on the Normandy beaches. How were orders to the military and naval chaplains designated?

10. Bing Crosby always invited a Roman Catholic priest to his annual golf tournament in California. One tournament was held in unusually fine weather, and Crosby thanked the priest for his intervention with God. What was the priest's reply?

RELIGION

1. A Sephardic rabbi.

2.   And this is the law, I will maintain,
          Unto my dying day, Sir,
          That whatsoever King shall reign,
          I will be the Vicar of Bray, Sir!

3. The Seamen's Bethel in New Bedford, Connecticut, across the street from the Whaling Museum. This was the setting for Father Maple's sermon at the beginning of *Moby-Dick*. In the John Huston film, the fiery preacher was played by Orson Welles. (This prow-shaped puplit is actually a reconstruction built in 1961 to approximate what Melville saw in his imagination and symbolized to him that "The world's a ship on its passage out . . . and the pulpit is its prow.")

4. In heaven, the police are British, the chefs are French, the mechanics are German, the lovers are Italian, and it is all organized by the Swiss. In hell, the chefs are British, the mechanics are French, the lovers are Swiss, the police are German, and it is all organized by the Italians.

5. Ambrose Bierce in *The Devil's Dictionary*.

6. Upon reoccupying the Second Temple of Jerusalem by Judas Maccabeus, the Jews found a cruet of oil, scarcely enough for one evening of light from one lamp. The supply lasted for eight days.

7. Monsignor (later Bishop) Fulton J. Sheen, who conducted an inspirational television program in the 1950s, "Life is Worth Living." Sheen pointed out that he was blessed with good material, and added, "I feel it is time that I also pay tribute to my writers—Matthew, Mark, Luke and John."

8. The Church of the Holy Sepulcher, officially the Church of the Resurrection, in Jerusalem.

9. SACRED and TOP SACRED.

10. "Don't thank me, Mr. Crosby. That's management. I'm in sales."

REMARKABLE PHRASE ORIGINS

Give the probable sources of these phrases or expressions:

1. Stripped to the buff
2. Forlorn hope
3. Taken aback
4. Shot glass
5. To pull the wool over one's eyes
6. Skid row
7. Lay it on her
8. Flash in the pan
9. Around Robin Hood's barn
10. Dressed to the nines

REMARKABLE PHRASE ORIGINS

1. Stripped to the buff, meaning naked. Buff is a light yellow color whose name came from the soft, undyed leather made from the skins of buffalo.

2. Forlorn hope is an Anglicized version of the Dutch *veloren hoop,* meaning lost troops, a body of men picked to lead the attack. Today they would be called shock troops.

3. Taken aback is a sailing term: when a change of wind direction presses the sails back against the mast, forward motion is halted.

4. A shot glass was a small glass into which people who had game for dinner dropped the shotgun pellets.

5. To pull the wool over one's eyes, meaning to delude or hoodwink, goes back to the days when gentlemen wore wigs. Their purses could be snatched more easily if their wigs, or wool, were pulled over their eyes.

6. Skid row was originally Skid Road in Seattle where loggers, pimps and easy ladies hung out. On the skid roads of the logging camps, bull teams dragged heavy logs across greased cross ties called skids.

7. Lay it on her, as when a man gives a girl a present, is far from modern jive talk. The phrase can be found in the Bible. The Book of Ruth 3:15 says: "He measured six measures of barley and laid it on her."

8. Flash in the pan, referring to someone who starts in a showy and ostentatious manner and then fails to come through, goes back to the days of the flintlock musket. The powder in the pan was the primer by which the charge was exploded. If this did not happen, there was only a flash in the pan. The phrase was reinforced when the western miners began panning for gold in the days of the California gold rush.

9. Around Robin Hood's barn is a rambling roundabout course, as his "barn" was Sherwood Forest and the surrounding fields of grain.

10. Dressed to the nines: In Chaucer's day a courtier decked out in parti-colored tunic and a gilt-embossed surcoat was said to be dressed "to the eyne," meaning "to the eyes." This evolved into "to the nines."

RESORTS

1. Which resort has a sign reading "_____ has been welcoming visitors since 1066"?

2. On the beaches of St. Tropez, topless bathing is the norm rather than the exception. How did someone who was really topless, in a loftier sense, give the resort its name?

3. Where would you go to see the Baths, a natural wonder of pools, grottoes and caves, formed by massive boulders scattered upon one another like a giant's building blocks?

4. Name a resort, now drastically changed in character, that is commemorated in a popular game.

5. The following resort hotels are world famous. Where are they located?

   a) The Cloister   f) Las Brisas
   b) Pitrizza   g) Hôtel de Paris
   c) Brenner's Park   h) Schloss Fuschl
   d) Fisherman's Cove   i) Cipriani
   e) The Broadmoor   j) Camelback Inn

6. Which literary doctor played a large part in popularizing the French Riviera as a winter resort?

7. Marion, Massachusetts; Key West, Florida; Augusta, Georgia. What do these have in common?

8. What hotel did Winston S. Churchill find particularly amenable to the pursuit of one of his favorite pastimes—painting?

9. Where in England might you have to queue for your fish 'n' chips during the last two weeks in August?

10. Can you give the meaning of the acronym EPCOT, and state where it is to be found?

RESORTS

1. Hastings, on the southeast coast of England, where William the Conqueror landed in 1066. The decisive Battle of Hastings was fought nearby in what is now the village of Battle.

2. When a Roman legionary named Torpes rashly embraced Christianity, his head was chopped off by the Emperor Nero. Some converts placed the body on a boat in the River Arno and set it adrift. The boat with its decapitated passenger eventually fetched up in a small cove which was thereafter called St. Tropez.

3. Virgin Gorda in the British Virgin Islands, the site of the Rockresort of Little Dix Bay. It was called Virgin Gorda (Fat Virgin) by Christopher Columbus, who thought it resembled a plump, reclining girl.

4. Atlantic City, New Jersey, now a mecca for gambling; it figures prominently in the game of Monopoly.

5. a) Sea Island, Georgia; b) Porto Cervo, Sardinia; c) Baden-Baden, West Germany; d) Mahé, Seychelles; e) Colorado Springs, Colorado; f) Acapulco, Mexico; g) Monte Carlo, Monaco; h) Salzburg, Austria; i) Venice, Italy; j) Scottsdale, Arizona

6. The novelist Tobias Smollett, who traveled and practiced as a surgeon. Returning home from Egypt one winter because it was too hot, he stopped off in Nice because England was too cold. From there he wrote so many enthusiastic letters that his friends joined him.

7. They were resorts favored by three U.S. Presidents: Grover Cleveland, Harry S Truman and Dwight D. Eisenhower, respectively.

8. The Hotel Al-Mamounia in Marrakech, Morocco, where from the balcony of his suite Churchill painted many scenes of the rose-walled town and the snow-covered Atlas Mountains in the background.

9. Blackpool, on the Irish Sea—the largest seaside resort in England. At the end of August when the Midlands factories close down, Blackpool is completely booked.

10. EPCOT stands for Experimental Prototype Community of Tomorrow, located in Orlando, Fla.

RESTAURANT NOTES

1. The three-star (Michelin) restaurant La Tour d'Argent—with its penthouse setting overlooking the Seine and Notre Dame, which is lit up every evening at 9:30, and its ground floor gastronomic museum—is one of the world's great visual delights. Its legendary *canetons à la presse* have been individually numbered for decades. How did the restaurant get its name?

2. What is the oldest eating establishment in the United States run by a single family?

3. At a top house such as Lutèce, name the one thing a guest would never find on the menu?

4. Some California restaurants have been known to serve "phony abalone." How is it prepared?

5. A pseudo-smart Indian-owned French restaurant in New Delhi boasted a menu that was printed in French on one side and English on the other. How was *ragoût de notre chef* translated? And how was *paté maison* interpreted?

6. Can you describe a *croque monsieur,* and say who is credited with originating it?

7. The interior decor of Ernie's, one of San Francisco's top restaurants, is plush and rococo and reminiscent of what?

8. Why is the name Le Bec Fin so appropriate for a good French restaurant?

9. Rocky Mountain oysters are delicious and nutritious, but not necessarily to everyone's taste. Why not?

10. The name of which famous restaurant is taken from a character in Victor Hugo's *Les Misérables* and means a feisty child of the streets?

RESTAURANT NOTES

1. The name originally came from the nearby Château de la Tourelle, which had a tower built of granite—blocks of stone shot through with bits of mica that glistened like silver in the sunlight. In 1582 the adjoining country auberge on the bank of the Seine adopted the name and used a picture of the tower as its official symbol.

2. Antoine's in New Orleans has been run by the Alciatore family since 1840.

3. The prices. Only the host gets a carte showing these.

4. A boned breast of chicken is pounded to a thickness of a quarter inch, marinated in clam juice with chopped clams for 24 hours, then sautéed for five minutes on each side.

5. *Ragoût de notre chef* was translated as stew from our cock, while *paté maison* came out as house paste potted by our chief.

6. A *croque monsieur* is a grilled ham and cheese sandwich, invented by Commendatore Cipriani, who founded Harry's Bar in Venice, where it is known simply as a *tost*. (Harry's Bar is named for a Boston playboy, Harry Pickering, who provided the funds for Cipriani, then a bartender at the Danieli Hotel, to start his own establishment.)

7. A turn of the century brothel, and one indeed did occupy the premises.

8. The term, literally The Fine Beak, is synonmous with a gourmet.

9. Rocky Mountain oysters are lamb's testicles. As delicate as sweetbreads, they are usually breaded and fried and served garnished with ketchup and lemon wedges and resemble fried oysters.

10. La Gavroche, on London's Upper Brook Street, which in 1982 became the first restaurant in Britain to receive three stars from Michelin. It is run by Albert and Michel Roux, who also own Gavvers, two restaurants in the City—Le Gamin and Le Poulbot—and outside London, the Waterside Inn at Bray and Paris House at Woburn Abbey Park, the ancestral estate of the Duke of Bedford.

RIPOSTES

1. How did Henry VIII respond when the Pope made Bishop Fisher, whom Henry was holding prisoner, a cardinal?

2. Congressman John Randolph of Roanoke, Virginia, once compared Edward Livingstone, "so brilliant, and yet so corrupt," to "a dead mackerel by moonlight—he both shines and stinks." When a stranger said, "I had the pleasure of passing your house recently," what was Randolph's response?

3. What was the Duke of Wellington's reaction when, after the war, the French marshals concertedly turned their backs on him at a reception at the French court?

4. How did Benjamin Disraeli use his rival William Gladstone to illustrate the difference between a misfortune and a calamity?

5. When the 8th Marquess of Queensberry, the father of Oscar Wilde's friend Lord Alfred Douglas, sent him a case of rotten cauliflowers, how did Wilde thank him?

6. In 1910 President Taft appointed Theodore Roosevelt special ambassador to the funeral of Edward VII. Afterwards Kaiser Wilhelm of Germany said to Roosevelt, "Call on me at two o'clock. I have just 45 minutes to give you." What was Roosevelt's reply?

7. One day on the Côte d'Azur the rotund critic Alexander Woollcott got annoyed when the playwright Charles MacArthur kept interrupting him and demanded, "Are you trying to cross me?" What did MacArthur come back with?

8. What was Margot, Lady Asquith's delicate correction of Jean Harlow when the latter called her Margott?

9. The Yale Corporation once debated whether to require a compulsory science course. Up spoke Senator Robert A. Taft, "Mr. President, when I was at Yale, I never took any science." What comment did Dean Acheson make to President Seymour of Yale?

10. A rapacious agent said to the screen writer Herman J. Mankiewicz, "I was swimming for home in shark-infested waters, but I got away." What was Mankiewicz's observation?

1. "Since the Holy Father is good enough to give the Bishop a hat, I'll even send the head to go into it."

2. "I am glad of it. I hope you will always do so, sir."

3. "I have seen their backs before."

4. "If Mr. Gladstone were to fall into the Thames it would be a misfortune, but if someone dragged him out again it would be a calamity."

5. "My dear Queensberry, how very kind of you. They remind me of you."

6. "I will be there at two, Your Majesty, but unfortunately I have but 20 minutes to give you."

7. Gazing at the vast expanse of the Woollcott paunch, MacArthur said, "Not without an alpenstock."

8. "The 't,' my dear, is silent, as in Harlow."

9. "Your Honor, the prosecution rests."

10. "I think that's what they call professional courtesy."

ROUND AND ABOUT

1. Somewhere, with all these clouds, and all this air,
   There must be a rare name, somewhere . . .

   What name did the playwright settle on?

2. What of historical interest happened at L'Anse aux Meadows on the northern tip of Newfoundland in the early part of the 11th century?

3. Edgartown, Massachusetts, and Johannesburg, South Africa, are named for whom?

4. This island belonged seven times to the English and seven times to the French. Can you name it?

5. What is missing from this list: Austria, Belgium, Denmark, East Germany, Czechoslovakia, France, the Netherlands, Switzerland?

6. There are eight seas to be found in the Mediterranean. How many can you name?

7. Why would it prove difficult to climb the highest known volcano?

8. After World War I the Serbs, Croats and Slovenes got together to form what?

9. What do these state capitals have in common: Annapolis, Augusta, Boston, Helena, Jackson, Jefferson City, Lansing, and St. Paul?

10. The George Washington Bridge across the Hudson River links upper Manhattan with New Jersey. When a lower roadway was added, how did the public refer to it?

ROUND AND ABOUT

1. "Cloud-cuckoo-land," which Aristophanes used in his play *The Birds*.

2. The Vikings established the first European settlement in continental North America at L'Anse aux Meadows, perhaps encouraged by the discovery of bog iron there, about 500 years before the Spanish or English reached America.

3. Edgartown was named for the young son of the Duke of York, who became James II, but the child died before learning of the honor bestowed upon him. Johannesburg was named for Johannes Paul Kruger, known as Oom Paul, the first president of Transvaal.

4. St. Lucia, one of the Windward Islands of the British West Indies.

5. Luxembourg. They are the countries bordering West Germany.

6. Reading from west to east, the eight seas are the Alboran, Balearic, Ligurian, Tyrrhenian, Adriatic, Ionian, Aegean and Sea of Crete.

7. The highest known volcano is Mons Olympus on Mars. It is over fifteen miles high, about three times the height of Mount Everest.

8. In December 1918, the Kingdom of Serbs, Croats and Slovenes was officially proclaimed. Its name was changed to Yugoslavia only in 1929.

9. They are all capitals of states whose names begin with M: Maryland, Maine, Massachusetts, Montana, Mississippi, Missouri, Michigan and Minnesota.

10. They called it Martha.

SALMAGUNDI

1. The rake of one segment of which famous train consists of cars bearing the names Cygnus, Ibis, Iona, Minerva, Perseus, Zena, as well as Audrey, a car from the Brighton Belle, and Phoenix, originally Charles de Gaulle's private car?

2. Who said, quite rightly and succinctly, "I screwed it up. I paid the price."?

3. Randolph Scott in the Thirties, Henry Fonda in the Forties, Burt Lancaster in the Fifties and James Garner in the Sixties all donned gun belts to portray whom?

4. Which Inca deity sailed across the Pacific in 1947?

5. Arthur Stanley Jefferson was a thin chap, born in Ulverston, in the north of England. When he went west, he lost both ends of his names but added a victor's wreath. Teaming up with a fat fellow, he became part of an enormously successful team. Who was he?

6. What is the world's largest and most luxurious yacht?

7. Name the first Conservative British Prime Minister chosen in this century to serve in successive Parliaments.

8. In John Houston's film *Moulin Rouge*, how does José Ferrer, playing Henri de la Toulouse-Lautrec, cynically define marriage?

9. Toward the end of 1983 a few million select people received a solicitation which began "The Honorable Ronald Wilson Reagan . . ." and which was sent out by the Republican National Committee. The envelope stated "R.S.V.P. Requested," while the invitation said "Please R.S.V.P." What boner is compounded here?

10. According to the Hollywood restaurateur Dave Chasen, "Humphrey Bogart was all right until 11:30." Then what happened?

SALMAGUNDI

1. These historic and splendid cream and brown carriages form the London/Folkestone/London section of the Venice Simplon-Orient-Express. A new rake of equally luxurious cars takes passengers on the continental run from Boulogne to Venice via Paris and Milan.

2. Richard M. Nixon, after resigning following the Watergate cover-up.

3. Wyatt Earp, law officer and notable gunfighter.

4. Kon Tiki, the Inca sun god, who lent his name to the primitive balsa raft that Thor Heyerdahl, the Norwegian explorer and anthropologist, sailed from Peru to the Tuamotu Islands in French Polynesia to support his theory that the first settlers of Polynesia were of South American origin.

5. Stan Laurel, who was Oliver Hardy's partner in film comedies starting in 1926.

6. The *Abdul Aziz,* built in Denmark and decorated in England for King Fahd, whose full name is Fahd ibn Abdul Aziz, of Saudi Arabia at a cost of $56 million. It is also a floating fortress with armor-plated windows, a missile-detection system and antiaircraft missiles.

7. Margaret Thatcher, who established a record unmatched by such illustrious predecessors as Winston S. Churchill and Harold Macmillan.

8. "Marriage is like a dull meal, with the dessert at the beginning."

9. R.S.V.P. stands for *Répondez s'il vous plaît,* or Please Reply. Therefore, if "R.S.V.P. Requested" is gauche, "Please R.S.V.P." is ridiculously redundant.

10. "After that, the trouble is he thinks he is Humphrey Bogart."

"SCHOOL DAYS, SCHOOL DAYS"

1. Which university was founded on acres of diamonds?

2. Name the famous headmaster to whom Thomas Hughes paid tribute in *Tom Brown's School Days*.

3. Who said: "Training is everything. The peach was once a bitter almond; a cauliflower is nothing but a cabbage with a college education"?

4. What have the following in common: Corpus Christi, Jesus, Pembroke, St. John's and Trinity?

5. Can you name the outstanding prep school that was founded by the widow of a prosperous munitions manufacturer?

6. Whose novel starts as follows: "Mr. Snigg, the Junior Dean, and Mr. Postlethwaite, the Domestic Bursar, sat alone in Mr. Snigg's room overlooking the garden quad at Scone College"?

7. What did the physician and author Oliver Wendell Holmes have to say about a child's education?

8. After receiving an honorary Doctor of Laws degree in 1962 from Yale, President John F. Kennedy made what rather apt remark?

9. In an early comic strip Beetle Bailey, a lackadaisical college student, is berating himself for flunking the history exam as he pulls crib notes from his sleeve. What is the final line?

10. When the general manager of the Teletrack off-track betting center in New Haven, Connecticut, realized that his horse-playing clientele were getting on in years, what ingenious plan occurred to him?

"SCHOOL DAYS, SCHOOL DAYS"

1. Not Kimberly U. in South Africa, but Temple University in Philadelphia, which was founded in 1884 on the proceeds of 6,000 repetitions of the lecture "Acres of Diamonds," all given by the Reverend Russell H. Conwell.

2. Dr. Thomas Arnold, who was headmaster of Rugby from 1828 to 1842 and was the father of the poet Matthew Arnold.

3. Mark Twain, in *Pudd'nhead Wilson*.

4. Colleges bearing these names are to be found at both Oxford and Cambridge.

5. The Hotchkiss School, in Lakeville, Connecticut, which was founded in 1892 by Maria Hotchkiss, the widow of the inventor of the Hotchkiss machine gun. Hotchkiss is notable for being the one of the few prep schools to start with a full enrollment.

6. Evelyn Waugh's *Decline and Fall*.

7. "A child's education should begin at least one hundred years before he is born."

8. "It might be said that now I have the best of both worlds—a Harvard education and a Yale degree."

9. "I wore my chemistry shirt."

10. He approached the officials of Yale University suggesting that he conduct a ten-week noncredit seminar, to be called "The Sport of Kings," on the history of thoroughbred horse racing. The university eagerly accepted his offer. Only when it became evident, however, that the major thrust of the course was to be the finer points of horse betting did Yale hurriedly drop the idea and try to forget the whole thing.

SCIENCE

1. We seem to owe the greatest outburst of scientific creativity in history to the closing of a university. How did this happen?

2. Which is the odd man out: argon, boron, krypton, neon, radon, xenon?

3. From the following list, match each scientist with his discovery or invention: Faraday, x-rays, Galileo, Cavendish, dynamo, Roentgen, thermometer, hydrogen.

4. Samuel F. B. Morse, most assuredly, did not do what? But on the other hand, what did he lend his hand to?

5. Which renowned man of science said, "In the fields of observation, chance favors only the mind that is prepared"?

6. After viewing the first atomic bomb explosion in the desert wastes of New Mexico, who thought prophetically of this verse from the sacred Hindu epic Bhagavad-Gita?

> If the radiances of a thousand suns
> Were to burst at once into the sky,
> That would be like the splendor of the
>   Mighty One.
> I am become Death,
> The shatterer of worlds.

7. A radioactive carbon isotope with a mass number of 14 is often used for what?

8. Name the only person to win two undivided Nobel Prizes.

9. Most swimming pool maintenance men speak earnestly about the proper pH level, a term used to measure the acidity or alkalinity of a solution, but it is a good ten to one bet that none of them know what pH stands for. Do you?

10. Archimedes' Principle states that a body immersed in a fluid is buoyed up by a force equal to the weight of the displaced fluid. What is Archimedes' second principle?

SCIENCE

1. In the two-year period from 1664 to 1666, when Cambridge was closed because of the plague, Isaac Newton retired to his home town of Woolsthorpe, where he established the law of gravitation, began to develop calculus, and discovered that white light is composed of all the colors of the spectrum.

2. Boron, which is a nonmetallic element. All the others are gases—the so-called "noble gases," which combine only with great difficulty with other gases.

3. Cavendish—hydrogen, Faraday—dynamo, Galileo—thermometer, Roentgen—X-rays.

4. Morse did not invent the electric telegraph; the American inventor Joseph Henry should get the credit. Morse, however, was a good promoter; he wheedled $30,000 out of Congress to build the first telegraph line between Baltimore and Washington and transmitted the first message: "What hath God wrought?" He gave his name to the Morse code, which did not differ greatly from earlier codes.

5. The French chemist, Louis Pasteur.

6. J. Robert Oppenheimer, director of the atomic energy research center at Los Alamos, New Mexico, from 1942 to 1945.

7. Carbon-14, which has a half-life of 5,730 years, is used to date archeological or anthropological finds. If the material was originally living, you can tell the age of the object by determining how much carbon-14 there is left. Carbon-14 comes from the atmosphere and will have been absorbed only in the plant's or animal's lifetime.

8. Dr. Linus Pauling, who won the Nobel Prize for Chemistry in 1954 and for Peace in 1962. (Marie Curie won twice but shared her 1903 prize with her husband, Pierre, and A. Henri Becquerel.)

9. The French *pouvoir Hydrogen,* which translates as hydrogen power.

10. When the human body is immersed in a bath, the telephone always rings.

SCULPTURE

1. The Colossus of Rhodes, one of the Seven Wonders of the World, was a large bronze statue of the sun god Helios, standing astride the entrance to the harbor of Rhodes. True or false?

2. How does it happen that Michelangelo's *Pietà* in St. Peter's in Rome is his only signed piece?

3. Many people associate the derivation of the word sincere with early Greek sculpture. Why?

4. What name was given to a statue consisting of the head or bust of the Greek god Hermes mounted on a square stone post?

5. Which extremely well-known object, seventeen feet high, was the work of E.H. Bailey, R.A.?

6. What woman has more monuments built to her than any other woman in the United States?

7. There exist two smaller replicas of the Statue of Liberty. One is in Paris on an island in the Seine. Where is the other?

8. The statues of three U.S. Presidents are in London. Who are they, and where may the statues be seen?

9. Where in South America would you find two enormous statues of Christ?

10. If you received a medal with three naked men with their hands on each others' shoulders, what would you have won?

SCULPTURE

1. False. The statue did not stand astride the harbor entrance, but was sited on a promontory overlooking the harbor.

2. On hearing a visitor attributing his work to another, Michelangelo stole in one night and chiseled his name on the sash.

3. It was said that Roman art dealers filled in chipped Greek statuary with wax to conceal the defects. This practice became so prevalent that a law was passed requiring all statues be sold without wax, or *sine cera,* which became the word sincere, meaning without deception. Unfortunately, this is what is called "folk etymology," having no basis in fact.

4. A herm or a herma. Such statues were frequently seen along public roads, since Hermes was, among other things, the god of commerce and the patron of travelers.

5. The statue of Nelson on top of Nelson's 145-foot column in Trafalgar Square. At the base of the column are depictions of the battle in the form of four bronze reliefs that were cast from the captured French guns.

6. Sacajawea, the Indian who served as interpreter and guide to the Lewis and Clark expedition through the West.

7. The second replica is atop the Liberty Warehouse building on West 64th Street in New York City.

8. George Washington is in Trafalgar Square, Abraham Lincoln in Parliament Square, and Franklin D. Roosevelt in Grosvenor Square.

9. One is on top of the Corcovado overlooking the harbor of Rio de Janeiro and the other, called the Christ of the Andes, is on the Chilean-Argentinian border.

10. The Nobel Peace Prize.

SEA CREATURES

1. Did Moby-Dick, Herman Melville's great white whale, ever exist?

2. Nessie, as the mysterious monster said to inhabit Loch Ness in Scotland is affectionately known, is no newcomer. Who was the first recorded person to see it?

3. Why is the halibut considered a holy fish?

4. What do the following have in common: crayfish, cuttlefish, jellyfish, shellfish, silverfish, starfish?

5. Who made the acute observation that "fish and visitors smell in three days"?

6. From which poem are these lines excerpted?

> I should have been a pair of ragged claws
> Scuttling across the floors of silent seas.

7. Who "fished alone in a skiff in the Gulf Stream and had gone eighty-four days without taking a fish"?

8. Which naval disaster during World War II produced what is considered to be the largest number of deaths in a single shark attack?

9. The Pribilof Islands are of particular interest to which eared, aquatic mammal?

10. The whale and the herring were drinking companions. One day the herring came into the bar and the bartender inquired about his missing friend the whale. What was the herring's reply?

SEA CREATURES

1. Yes, indeed. Melville named it for Mocha Dick, a leviathan that was first sighted near Mocha Island off the coast of Chile.

2. Saint Columba, who brought Christianity to Scotland in the 7th century, while on a trip from the Hebridean island of Iona to visit King Brude's castle overlooking Loch Ness near the present town of Inverness (mouth of the Ness).

3. In Middle English *butt* was the common name for flatfish such as flounder, skate, turbot and plaice. The largest one was reserved for eating on holy days and was called the holy butt, which in time became halibut.

4. None of them are fish.

5. That ultimate pragmatist Benjamin Franklin, who thought up this axiom and printed it in his vastly popular *Poor Richard's Almanac* in 1736.

6. "The Love Song of J. Alfred Prufrock," by T. S. Eliot.

7. The old man in Ernest Hemingway's novella *The Old Man and the Sea*.

8. The sinking by Japanese torpedoes of the U.S.S. *Indianapolis* after the cruiser had delivered to the island of Tinian the atomic bombs that were dropped on Hiroshima and Nagasaki, which effectively ended the war. Of the crew of over 1,000 men, only 317 survived the explosions and subsequent shark attacks.

9. The Alaskan fur seal, which uses these islands north of the Aleutians for breeding. Before 1911, competition and ruthless hunting methods threatened extinction of the seals. The islands are now administered by the U.S. Bureau of Fisheries.

10. "Am I my blubber's kipper?"

SECONDS

1. Who was second-in-command of the British fleet at the Battle of the Baltic in 1801?

2. Can you name the second largest living bird?

3. Who were the only two Vice-Presidents to serve under two U.S. Presidents?

4. In 1841 the Royal Yacht Squadron, headquartered at Cowes, England, held a competition for the Hundred-Guinea Cup, to be won by the fastest yacht in a 60-mile race around the Isle of Wight. The schooner *America*, owned by members of the New York Yacht Club, won handily. Queen Victoria, who was watching at the finish line from the royal yacht, was told that *America* was leading, whereupon she asked the sailing master who was second. How did he reply?

5. In 1893 Arthur Wing Pinero's best-known play was produced in London. What was its name, and why did it arouse bitter protests?

6. What was the second prize in the competition that had as its first prize a week in Albania?

7. For years the world's longest single-span suspension bridge was the Verrazano-Narrows Bridge connecting Brooklyn and Staten Island. What has now surpassed it?

8. Who was the second filly ever to win the Kentucky Derby?

9. Name the second largest Polish-speaking city in the world after Warsaw.

10. How did Ronald W. Reagan in 1979 neatly combine politics and prostitution in one sentence?

SECONDS

1. Horatio, Viscount Nelson. Then a vice-admiral, he was under the command of Admiral Sir Hyde Parker.

2. The emu, a large, flightless Australian bird related to the ostrich, which is the largest.

3. George Clinton, who served under Thomas Jefferson and James Madison, and John C. Calhoun, who served under John Quincy Adams and Andrew Jackson.

4. "If it please Your Majesty, there is no second."

5. *The Second Mrs. Tanqueray,* which dealt sympathetically with a divorced woman seeking to regain acceptance by "respectable" society.

6. Two weeks in Albania.

7. The Humber Bridge, over the last major unbridged river in England. Its center span of 4,626 feet eclipses the 4,200-foot center span of the New York bridge. Unfortunately, the bridge, a civic dream for a century, does not really go anywhere and hardly anyone shows signs of wanting to use it.

8. Genuine Risk in 1980, ridden by Jacinto Vasquez and owned by Mrs. Bert Firestone. The first filly to win was Harry Payne Whitney's Regret in 1915.

9. Chicago, Illinois.

10. "I used to say that politics was the second oldest profession, and I have come to know that it has a great similarity to the first."

SEX

1. Which son of Dionysus and Aphrodite was the god of procreation as well as the guardian of gardens and vineyards?

2. How did some prostitutes in ancient Greece advertise their wares?

3. Did the word "fuck" originate as a police blotter acronym for "felonious unlawful carnal knowledge," and why does the word "swive" come to mind?

4. Which son of Priam, King of Troy, lamented to his beloved the limitations of a man's sexual performance in these terms: "This is the monstruosity [*sic*] in love, lady, that the will is infinite and the execution confined, that the desire is boundless and the act a slave to limit?"

5. S/M is short for sado-masochism, or getting sexual pleasure from inflicting pain either on oneself or others. Which two outré writers and practitioners are remembered in the word, and what did they have in common at the end?

6. Why was John Ruskin unable to consummate his marriage?

7. A friend who thought he had talked Oscar Wilde out of homosexuality called on him at the Savoy Hotel. Finding him in bed with a bellboy, he said, "Oscar, you told me you were going to turn over a new leaf." What was Wilde's reply?

8. What does the French phrase *feuille de rose* (rose petal) mean?

9. After making love, what is the typical reaction of a Russian girl, a French girl, an English girl and an American girl?

10. Who said, "Don't knock masturbation. It's sex with someone you love"?

1. Priapus, who was also the personification of the erect phallus.

2. They had a mirror-image script of the words "follow me" tooled on the soles of their sandals.

3. No. Fuck comes from an old German verb *ficken,* to strike or penetrate, whose slang meaning was to copulate. Before people fucked, they swived.

4. Troilus to Cressida, in Shakespeare's tragicomedy.

5. The Marquis (he was actually only a count) de Sade and Leopold von Sacher-Masoch, both of whom died in insane asylums.

6. As his knowledge of female nudity derived exclusively from painting and sculpture, he had never before seen pubic hair on a woman—the sight of which made him impotent.

7. "I am as soon as I get to the bottom of this page."

8. *Feuille de rose* refers to lingual stimulation of the perineum, making it a brief layover on the sexual act known as "around the world."

9. The Russian girl says, "Igor, now I know you love me for my body and not for my soul"; the French girl, "You buy me a new dress, no, Pierre?"; the English girl, "Awfully nice having you, Algernon, really it was"; and the American girl, "Feel better, George?"

10. Woody Allen, in his 1977 film *Annie Hall.*

SHIPS AND BOATS

1. What has the distinction of being the only warship to be saved by a poet?

2. For what is the great and gloriously named Isambard Kingdom Brunel remembered?

3. Can you locate the poop, and explain the derivation of the word?

4. The last lines of which poem are these?

   > Christ save us all from a death like this,
   > On the reef of Norman's Woe!

5. During the Spanish-American War the U.S. Navy named two ships *Harvard* and *Yale*. It liked the sound so well that it instructed Admiral Dewey to rename all captured Spanish ships after colleges. The Admiral did not agree with the Navy and cabled back what two proposals?

6. Back in the days of bootleg liquor, the rum-running boats raced off the coastal waters of the North Atlantic. Fastest of them all was a 65-foot pirate boat named the *Cigarette*, which overtook other rum-runners and made off with their booty. How does the legend of the *Cigarette* survive today?

7. What is the largest sailing yacht ever built?

8. The covers of the bar stools on Aristotle Onassis' yacht *Christina* were made from something intimately connected with one of Onassis' enterprises. What was it?

9. The Cunard liner the *Queen Elizabeth 2*—the *QE2*, as she is commonly known—does not suffer from false modesty. "The greatest ship in the world," she calls herself. For whom or what is she named?

10. What signal did the flotilla captain make to the destroyer *Virago*, which had just collided with a carrier?

SHIPS AND BOATS

1. The U.S.S. *Constitution*. In 1830, when the Navy Department decided to scrap the aging warrior, the young Oliver Wendell Holmes wrote "Old Ironsides," which ignited such a public protest that the ship was saved.

2. Brunel was the engineering genius who built the *Great Western* (1838), the first transatlantic steam vessel, the *Great Britain* (1845), the first ocean screw steamship, and the *Great Eastern* (1858), the longest steam vessel of its time.

3. The poop is the stern superstructure of a ship. The word comes from the Old French *poupe,* meaning doll, from the practice of early sailors of hanging a doll image of the Virgin Mary in that part of the ship.

4. "The Wreck of the Hesperus" by Henry Wadsworth Longfellow, which begins:

   > It was the schooner Hesperus,
   >   That sailed the wintry sea;
   > And the skipper had taken his little daughter,
   >   To bear him company.

5. "MASSACHUSETTS INSTITUTE OF TECHNOLOGY AND VERMONT NORMAL COLLEGE FOR WOMEN." The Navy then dropped the whole idea.

6. Today's Cigarettes are a much faster and tougher breed of boat. Twin turbo-charged 450-horsepower engines hurl the sleek racers across the ocean at speeds exceeding 70 miles per hour.

7. The *Sea Cloud,* a square-rigged, four-masted barque 316 feet in length. Originally named the *Hussar,* she was built in 1931 in Kiel, Germany.

8. Whale's testicles; Onassis maintained a sizable whaling fleet.

9. The *QE2* is named for the magnificent Cunard liner *Queen Elizabeth*. If she were named for the present Queen, she would be known as the *Queen Elizabeth II*.

10. "IN SPITE OF YOUR NAME YOU MUST GET OUT OF THE HABIT OF SNAPPING AT THESE GREAT BIG MEN."

SNOBS

1. The French epigrammist Sébastien Chamfort told of a fanatical social climber who noticed that round the Palace of Versailles it stank of urine. What measures did he take to emulate the court of Louis XIV?

2. What remark of Prince Metternich, the Austrian statesman and arbiter of post-Napoleonic Europe, ensures his inclusion here?

3. Snobbery of residence is often encountered. Many years ago, a Boston banker moved his family on Beacon Hill two blocks in the wrong direction from Louisburg Square. How did Mrs. Mark Anthony deWolfe Howe, trying to be polite, react?

4. One must take great care in dealing with wine snobs. For example, it is considered gauche to say, "This wine has excellent body." What comment is acceptable?

5. The acme of religious snobbery was probably reached by the prominent French family of the Duc de Lévis-Mirepoix, which is reputed to be descended from the sister of the Virgin Mary. When they pray, how are they said to begin?

6. Between the two most recent World Wars, Sybil, Lady Colefax and Emerald, Lady Cunard, were notorious London arrivistes. The aristocratic Lord Berners stayed in a room next to Lady Colefax in Rome. What did he have to say after a sleepless night?

7. Regional snobbery may appear unconsciously. During World War II a schoolboy on Nantucket Island was assigned to write a theme on the then Duce of Italy. How did he begin his paper?

8. What indispensable advice for ladies does the 13th Duke of Bedford provide in his *Book of Snobs*?

9. Give a true snob's capsule comment on society today.

10. What temptation must inevitably occur to a guest at a pretentious Palm Beach party?

SNOBS

1. He told his own servants and tenants to make water around his own château.

2. "For me mankind begins with barons."

3. She said, "Oh, yes, people are beginning to live there now, aren't they?"

4. "This wine has narrow shoulders but very broad hips."

5. *"Ave Marie, ma cousine . . ."*

6. "She never stopped climbing all night."

7. "Mussolini is an off-Islander."

8. "A tiara is never worn in a hotel, only at parties arranged in private houses or when royalty is present."

9. "Society today is sitting next to either your hairdresser or your dress designer at dinner."

10. The urge to ask the hostess, "Did you invite these people or advertise for them?"

SPORTS SECTION

1. In which sport is the technique known as *wedeln* performed, and what does it mean?

2. What is the oldest American intercollegiate sports rivalry?

3. Earl Warren, former Chief Justice of the United States, always turned to the sports page of the newspaper first. What reason did he give?

4. In the late 1930s the United States mounted their first and only 40-goal polo team. Who comprised this "Dream Team," and how, in one memorable sentence, did the sports writer Bob Considine record their victory over the British?

5. Rocky Marciano is the only heavyweight boxing champion to have been undefeated in his entire professional career, but who held the title longer than any man in history?

6. Who played for three New York professional teams, in different sports, in the same season?

7. Some have called it the ultimate laxative, others the Englishman's answer to Russian roulette, although it does not take place in England. Still another compared it to his regiment, which had been completely wiped out three times in the last two centuries—"damn fine show." What is it?

8. The "hat trick" in hockey refers to three goals by a player in the same game. How did the term originate?

9. Which annual sporting event is seen by the largest number of actual (not TV) spectators?

10. During spring training, how did New York Yankees manager Casey Stengel introduce a group of rookies to his unique brand of verbal virtuosity?

1. Skiing. *Wedeln,* which means to "wag" in German, is a series of smooth, short turns punctuating a generally straight run down the mountain.

2. The Yale-Harvard boat race, which started as a two-mile event in 1852 on Lake Winnipesaukee in New Hampshire. In 1876 the contest moved to the Thames River at New London, Connecticut, where it became a four-mile race in 1878.

3. "The sports page records people's accomplishments. The front page usually records nothing but man's failures."

4. Thomas Hitchcock, Jr., Stewart B. Iglehart, Michael G. Phipps and Cecil Smith. Considine opened his story: "Yankee Doodle went to town today, a-riding on a pony."

5. Joe Louis, the Brown Bomber, who held it from June 1937 to March 1949—a reign of eleven years and eight months. In his long career in the ring Louis knocked out five heavyweight champions: Max Schmeling, Jack Sharkey, Primo Carnera, Max Baer and Jim Braddock.

6. Gladys Gooding, who played the organ for the New York Knicks, the Brooklyn Dodgers and the New York Rangers in the Forties and Fifties.

7. The Cresta Run at St. Moritz. The run, which was started by the British in 1884, is a pure ice chute, from St. Moritz Dorf to the village of Celerina, on which you ride a sixty-pound, one-man sled, called a skeleton.

8. The term "hat trick" originated in cricket to describe the feat of a bowler taking three wickets in successive balls. The bowler's reward was a new hat from his cricket club. The term cropped up in hockey around 1900, and the fans still continue to throw their hats onto the ice when the "hat trick" is accomplished.

9. The Tour de France, the most strenuous, grueling bicycle race in the world, which covers almost 3,000 miles through city streets and alpine mountains and extends through several countries. It is estimated that over its 24 days, the race is watched by about 15 million people by the sides of the road.

10. "Now all you fellas line up alphabetically, by height."

STATES OF THE UNION

1. The man who coined the name United States of America was indicted for treason in England and later jailed in France. Can you identify him?

2. Which famous spot in the United States is a corruption of Cayo Hueso (Bone Islet)?

3. The name of Samuel Francis Smith should be familiar to everyone who loves America. Why?

4. Bestowing honorific military titles, such as colonelcies, is an old established practice in the South, particularly in Kentucky. What was the observation of one Chief Justice of the Supreme Court on this? (The term Chief Justice of the United States only came into use in 1888.)

5. Name the only territory the United States acquired through neither exploration, purchase nor war.

6. John Wilkes Booth was shot either by himself or his pursuers while hiding out in Garrett's Farm in Bowling Green, Virginia. What did he have in common with that state?

7. What did Woody Allen have to say about New Jersey?

8. Which Pulitzer Prize winner wrote these lines?

   > I have fallen in love with American names.
   > The sharp names that never get fat,
   > The snakeskin-titles of mining-claims,
   > The plumed war-bonnet of Medicine Hat,
   > Tucson and Deadwood and Lost Mule Flat.

9. New York and California rank first and second in total number of millionaires, but what state has more millionaires per capita than any other state?

10. Florida has been termed a multibillion dollar "mailbox economy" that feeds on Social Security, retirement and dividend checks. If the present trend continues, Florida will soon be recording more deaths than births. But how would you compare yogurt to the state of Florida?

STATES OF THE UNION

1. Thomas Paine, who was persuaded by Franklin to move from England to America where his popular tract *Common Sense* propagandized the American Revolution. He died impoverished and largely forgotten in 1809. Even his bodily remains were lost.

2. Key West, Florida. The Spanish sailors called it Cayo Hueso because of the human bones they found there.

3. A Baptist clergyman and poet, Smith wrote the words of the national hymn "America," which begins "My country, 'tis of thee . . ."

4. In 1825 John Marshall wrote:

> In the blue grass country
> A paradox was born;
> The corn was full of kernels,
> And the colonels full of corn.

5. The Chamizal district on the Rio Grande, which was transferred to the United States by the river changing its course in the 1860s and was finally returned to Mexico 99 years later.

6. When Booth assassinated Lincoln, he cried out, *"Sic semper tyrannis"* (Thus always to tyrants), which happens to be the motto of the state of Virginia.

7. "A certain intelligence governs our universe except in certain parts of New Jersey." It has also been described as a second-rate state with third-rate bars.

8. Stephen Vincent Benét, who won the Pulitzer Prize for *John Brown's Body,* a long narrative poem of the Civil War.

9. Idaho, which has over 25,000 people, or almost 3 percent of the state's population, whose assets exceed $1 million.

10. Yogurt has an active culture.

STOP THE PRESSES!

1. Napoleon once said, "Four hostile newspapers are more formidable than a thousand bayonets." Which English writer put this thought into more enduring words, and how did Mark Twain compress these somewhat priapically?

2. The "bulldog edition" was the term used by every Hearst newspaper for the early edition printed in the late afternoon with the next day's date on it. How did the term arise?

3. What sign did an English editor come up with for the lavatory door?

4. William Randolph Hearst's castle at San Simeon was called La Cuesta Encantada—The Enchanted Hill—where he lived openly with his mistress Marion Davies. After Dorothy Parker had misbehaved one evening, she received a note requesting her to leave the premises. What revenge did she take?

5. Legend has it that when H. L. Mencken was editor of *The American Mercury* he had what standard reply to readers who wrote in, either in praise or complaint?

6. "The lobster shift" refers to those working late into the night on newspapers. What is the origin of the expression?

7. Evelyn Waugh took a dim view of newspapers: "News is what a chap who doesn't care much about anything wants to read." Along the same line, how did Gilbert Keith Chesterton define journalism?

8. Headline writers are prone to using puns whenever the occasion presents itself. For example, a story about women falling for priests and religious gurus was headed "Hooked by the Celibait." What head was given to a report about an economic revival underway in Tirana, the capital of Albania?

9. In a memorable column Art Buchwald employed Pèlerins, Peaux-Rouges and Kilomètres Deboutish to explain to the French what American national holiday?

10. Each year R. Emmet Tyrell, Jr., Editor in Chief of *The American Spectator,* and a distinguished panel of judges, confers the J. Gordon Coogler Award upon whom? And who was J. Gordon Coogler?

STOP THE PRESSES!

1. In his play *Richelieu,* Edward George Earle Bulwer-Lytton wrote:

   > Beneath the rule of men entirely great
   > This pen is mightier than the sword.

   Mark Twain put the following twist on this in his poem, "A Weaver's Beam:"

   > Behold—the Penis mightier than the Sword
   > That leapt from Sheath at any heating Word
   > So long ago—now peaceful lies and calm
   > And dreams unmoved of ancient conquests scored.

2. The newsboys used to fight to get the bundles of early papers because they were the easiest to sell.

3. The Editorial Wee.

4. Before her departure, she opened the visitor's book and wrote:

   > Upon my honor I saw a Madonna
   > Standing alone in a niche,
   > Above the door
   > Of a well-known whore
   > And a first-class son of a bitch.

5. "Dear Sir, You may be right"—a response that saved time and avoided arguments.

6. The "lobster shift" started in New York in the 1890s when there were about 15 papers in the metropolitan area. The night workers often ordered lobster, which was then cheap, at a restaurant called The Lobster.

7. "Journalism consists largely of saying 'Lord Jones Dies' to people who never knew Lord Jones was alive."

8. "Tirana Boom Today."

9. Thanksgiving Day, or *Le Jour de Merci Donnant.* Pèlerins means Pilgrims; Peaux-Rouges, Indians; and Kilomètres Deboutish, Miles Standish.

10. The award is given to that author adjudged the year's worst. J. Gordon Coogler, a poetaster of the rarest water, is chiefly remembered for this couplet:

    > Alas for the South, her books have grown fewer—
    > She was never much given to literature.

SUPERLATIVES

1. Who was the first poet to be buried in what was to become Poets' Corner in Westminster Abbey?

2. Where is the Cabo da Roca, and if you were standing there, what distinction would you have?

3. The game originated in 18th-century England, probably in debtors' prison, but was soon adopted by the upper classes. The hardness and speed of the ball makes it the world's fastest game. What is it called?

4. Can you name the most powerful vertically mobilizing force at work on earth?

5. According to Clarence Darrow, who was "the greatest man who ever came out of Plymouth, Vermont"?

6. A pair of lions—alternatively named Patience and Fortitude, Leo and Leonora, and Lord Lenox and Lady Astor—stand watch over what great institution?

7. Who is the world's biggest party-giver?

8. How close can you come to the correct yardage of the longest punt in football?

9. When it was sold in 1983, it fetched a price of $11,925,000—the largest sum ever spent at an auction for a work of art. Can you identify it?

10. The largest of its kind occasionally hangs around the Verrazano Narrows Bridge at the entrance to New York Harbor. What is it?

SUPERLATIVES

1. Geoffrey Chaucer—as a parishioner, not as a poet.

2. Cabo da Roca is a cape in Portugal facing the Atlantic. Standing on it you would be on the westernmost point in Europe.

3. Racquets, which survives in a handful of exclusive men's clubs in the United States, Canada and Great Britain. Played on a four-wall 60- by 30-foot court, the ball careens off the polished cement surfaces at speeds of up to 150 miles per hour. Squash, a related but slower game, evolved from it.

4. The sun, which each day evaporates a trillion tons of water from the oceans and continents into the atmosphere, and each day the same amount of vapor condenses and falls as rain, snow, sleet or hail.

5. Calvin Coolidge.

6. The New York Public Library, the largest nonstatutory library in the world, which began with a gift of the libraries of James Lenox and John Jacob Astor.

7. Queen Elizabeth II, who entertains no less than 24,000 people at her three garden parties at Buckingham Palace each year. On special occasions such as a Jubilee year Her Majesty gives four.

8. A 98-yard punt was kicked by Steve O'Neal of the New York Jets in a 1969 game with the Denver Broncos.

9. The Romanesque *Gospels of Henry The Lion,* a manuscript rich in illuminated folio miniatures. Henry The Lion was a 12th-century Duke of Saxony and Bavaria.

10. The Old Glory, an American flag larger than a football field, measuring 410 by 210 feet.

TELEVISION

1. "No wonder they call television a medium," observed comedian Ernie Kovacs, adding what?

2. At the start of the Seventies, when ABC had not reached its present ratings status, by what rocky nicknames were the three networks known?

3. Name the only TV series that uses a former royal palace as an important establishing shot at the beginning of each program.

4. Alan Alda, Victoria Principal and Bob Hope are the most popular TV stars in their categories, according to the secret Performer Q list. What does the Q list mean, and to what use is it put?

5. Who is the rumpled man of the law who drinks Châteauneuf de Fleet Street at the local wine bar and heeds "She Who Must Be Obeyed"—his wife?

6. A transponder is an integral part of cable television and communication satellites. What does it do?

7. Which popular series has as its theme song "Moving On Up," and why is it often called the Zebra Show?

8. A movie that was a box-office failure when it was first released more than forty years ago has been broadcast on prime-time television more than any other movie in history. What movie is it?

9. As skipper of the yachts that won the 1973 America's Cup and the stormy 1979 Fastnet race, he was known as "Captain Courageous." He is now called the "Mouth of the South." Who is he?

10. When asked on Hollywood Squares, "What can make a monkey cry?", how did Paul Lynde respond?

TELEVISION

1. "It's neither rare nor well done. And no matter how it is cooked, television often seems to consist of left-overs."

2. NBC was known as 30 Rock from its location at 30 Rockefeller Plaza, CBS as Black Rock from its black granite building on the Avenue of the Americas, while third-place ABC was derisively tagged Little Rock.

3. *Hawaii Five-O,* the long-running series starring Jack Lord, in which Iolani Palace, home of the Hawaiian royal family, is shown as the supposed headquarters of this police group.

4. The Q list, taken from the Q (recognition and likability quotient) study, is used by networks, studios and advertisers to cast actors whom viewers recognize and like. Alda won for situation comedies *(M*A*S*H)*, Principal for dramatic series *(Dallas)* and Hope for comedy.

5. *Rumpole of the Bailey,* the brilliant British series shown on Masterpiece Theater, starring Leo McKern and based on the stories by John Mortimer, who is himself a Queen's Counsel.

6. A transponder is the element on a communications satellite that receives and transmits signals. There are 24 transponders on the newer satellites, allowing each satellite to distribute 24 channels of cable programming instantaneously.

7. *The Jeffersons,* starring George Hemsley and Isabel Sanford as George and Louise Jefferson. It is called the Zebra Show because of its constant interplay of black and white characters.

8. *The Wizard of Oz,* starring Judy Garland as Dorothy, Ray Bolger as the Scarecrow, Jack Haley as the Tin Woodsman, and Bert Lahr as the Cowardly Lion.

9. R. E. (Ted) Turner, founder of CNN and WTBS, which for the past five years have taken in about half of the entire cable industry's advertising revenues and gone into about 30 million homes.

10. "Learning that Tarzan swings both ways."

THIS AND THAT

1. The name of a once popular game of divination is one of the rarest of words in that it is a combination of two languages. What is it?

2. In what country did ketchup originate?

3. Explain the meaning of the phrase "ringing grooves" in these lines by which poet laureate?

> Not in vain the distance beacons. Forward
> forward, let us range.
> Let the great world spin forever down the
> ringing grooves of change.

4. Pressrooms and press lords are familiar newspaper terms, but what did a press gang do?

5. In the last scene of *Some Like It Hot*, Billy Wilder's hilarious spoof of the Roaring Twenties, Jack Lemmon, posing as a bass player in an all-girl orchestra, nips off his wig to convince the aging millionaire playboy, played by Joe E. Brown, that he is not a girl. What was Brown's response to the news that his bride-to-be is a man?

6. During the Nixon-Humphrey presidential campaign of 1968, an unflattering photograph of Nixon was circulated, bearing this query: "Would you buy a used car from this man?" How did the Republicans retaliate?

7. A mule is a sterile hybrid of a male ass and a female horse, but what is a hinny?

8. Crispus Attucks and Matthew Henson were black men who participated in two events in American history widely separated in years. Can you explain why these men are remembered?

9. In which famous restaurant would you find a section called the Omnibus?

10. The actor-manager Sir Herbert Beerbohm Tree returned an unsuitable play to a would-be dramatist with what brief note?

THIS AND THAT

1. Ouija, which means yes in both French and German.

2. China. In the 18th century the Dutch imported this condiment, originally a spiced mushroom sauce called *ketsiap,* as *ketjap.*

3. The phrase "ringing grooves" refers to the emerging railroad tracks of the future in Alfred, Lord Tennyson's "Locksley Hall." (Apparently Tennyson was unaware that trains have flanged wheels that run on rails, not grooves.)

4. A press gang was a company under an officer detailed to press men into military or naval service. According to all accounts, being pressed into service did not come under the heading of fun.

5. "Well, nobody's perfect."

6. They circulated a picture of Humphrey bearing the caption: "Would you buy a used war [Viet Nam] from this man?"

7. A hinny is the hybrid offspring of a male horse and a female ass.

8. Crispus Attucks was one of the men killed in the Boston Massacre of 1770 (a bit of a misnomer, as only five men were killed) when British troops fired into a rioting street gang. Matthew Henson accompanied the Arctic explorer Robert E. Peary, as his servant and chief dog-driver, when he became the first man to reach the North Pole in 1909.

9. Maxim's, on the rue Royale in Paris. The Omnibus is the narrow section between the front room and the Grand Salon, and is an ideal spot for people-watching.

10. My Dear Sir,
    I have read your play. Oh, my dear Sir!
    Yours faithfully,
    Herbert Beerbohm Tree

THREE OF A KIND

1. What were Michelangelo's three main themes in painting the ceiling of the Vatican's Sistine Chapel?

2. Can you describe the three ages of men and women?

3. In his essay *On Studies,* Francis Bacon gives the three benefits to be gained from reading, speaking and writing. What are they?

4. Which English poet wrote these lines and to whom was he referring?

    Three poets, in three distant ages born,
    Greece, Italy and England did adorn.

5. What happened to the three wise men of Gotham?

6. In one of his relentless letters of instruction to his illegitimate son, Philip Stanhope, what three reasons did the 4th Earl of Chesterfield give in warning him against sexual promiscuity?

7. Name the British statesman who said, "There are three kinds of lies: lies, damned lies and statistics."

8. Can you name Caesar's three wives?

9. The *gluteus maximus* is the largest one of three what?

10. Three old ladies were walking down the street when they were confronted by a flasher. What did they do?

THREE OF A KIND

1. Creation, sin and redemption.

2. Young, middle-aged and "How well you look."

3. "Reading maketh a full man; conference a ready man; and writing an exact man."

4. John Dryden in "Lines on Milton," referring to Homer, Virgil and Milton.

5. According to the old nursery rhyme, they apparently drowned.

> Three wise men of Gotham
> Went to sea in a bowl:
> And if the bowl had been stronger,
> My song had been longer.

6. "The pleasure is fleeting, the posture ridiculous and the expense damnable."

7. Benjamin Disraeli, later 1st Earl of Beaconsfield.

8. Cornelia, Pompeia and Calpurnia.

9. The *gluteus maximus* is the largest of the three muscles that form the buttock, the other two being the *gluteus medius* and the *gluteus minimus*.

10. The first old lady had a stroke and so did the second, but the third would not touch it at all.

TIME MARCHES ON

1. Going by radioactive dating of the earliest rocks, the earth is estimated to have been formed between 4.5 and 5 million years ago. If this period were put into the framework of a single year, when would the first evidence of the Stone Age appear?

2. Which character in literature says the following?

   > The time is out of joint; O cursed spite,
   > That ever I was born to set it right.

3. What was old at fifteen and young at forty-five?

4. When the clock struck thirteen, what was Dr. Samuel Johnson's reaction?

5. According to Henry Wadsworth Longfellow's poem, what happens "between the dark and the daylight"?

6. The eminent Supreme Court Justice Oliver Wendell Holmes, Jr., was taking a stroll in Washington on his 90th birthday, when an extremely pretty girl passed by. What did Holmes say to his companion?

7. In this couplet "On a Sundial" from *Sonnets and Verse,* Hilaire Belloc reflected on the passage of time:

   > How slow the shadow creeps: but when 'tis past
   > How fast the shadows fall. How fast! How fast!

   When Sam Goldwyn saw a sundial for the first time, he had to be told what it was used for. How did he express his wonderment?

8. A dog watch at sea is either of two short periods of duty, from 1600 to 1800 hours or from 1800 to 2000 hours. Can you explain the origin of the term?

9. In whose celebrated realistic-satiric fantasy is the superintendent of a Hartford arms factory knocked unconscious in a fight and transported in a time warp back to 6th-century England?

10. A publicist wired Cary Grant's agent: "HOW OLD CARY GRANT?" Grant himself opened the telegram and sent back what reply?

TIME MARCHES ON

1. A little after eight o'clock on the evening of December 31st.

2. Hamlet to Horatio and Marcellus, after seeing the ghost on the battlements of Elsinore Castle.

3. The Stuart claim. James Edward Stuart, the Old Pretender and son of James II, tried in 1715 to establish his claim to the throne of Britain by an abortive rising in Scotland known as the "'15." His son, Charles Edward, the Young Pretender, known as Bonnie Prince Charlie, led another Jacobite rebellion in Scotland and England in 1745, known as the "'45."

4. "It is not only disconcerting, but it makes one doubt the past."

5.   Between the dark and the daylight,
         When the night is beginning to lower,
         Comes a pause in the day's occupations,
         That is known as the Children's Hour.

6. "Oh, to be eighty again!"

7. "What will they think of next!"

8. A dog watch is a corruption of dock watch—that is, a watch that has been docked or shortened.

9. Mark Twain's *A Connecticut Yankee in King Arthur's Court*.

10. "OLD CARY GRANT FINE HOW YOU?"

TITLE SEARCH

Give the quotations from which the following titles are taken, naming also the work and the author:

1. *Blithe Spirit,* by Noël Coward

2. *Of Mice and Men,* by John Steinbeck

3. *A Handful of Dust,* by Evelyn Waugh

4. *The Razor's Edge,* by W. Somerset Maugham

5. *Inherit the Wind,* by Jerome Lawrence and Robert E. Lee

6. *Alien Corn,* by Sidney Howard

7. *All the Conspirators,* by Christopher Isherwood

8. *The Golden Bowl,* by Henry James

9. *Slouching Towards Bethlehem,* by Joan Didion

10. *Kind Hearts and Coronets,* by Robert Hamen and John Dighton

1. Hail to thee, blithe spirit
   Bird thou never wert . . .
   —"To a Skylark," by Percy Bysshe Shelley

2. The best laid schemes o' mice an' men
   Gang aft a-gley.
   —"To a Mouse," by Robert Burns

3. I will show you fear in a handful of dust.
   —"The Waste Land," by T. S. Eliot

4. We did not flinch but gave our lives to save
   Greece when her fate hung on a razor's edge.
   —"Cenotaph at the Isthmos," by Simonides

5. He that troubleth his own house shall inherit the
   wind.
   —Proverbs 11:29

6. She stood in tears amid the alien corn . . .
   —"Ode to a Nightingale," by John Keats

7. All the conspirators save only he
   Did that they did in envy of great Caesar . . .
   —*Julius Caesar,* by William Shakespeare

8. Or ever the silver cord be loosed, or the golden
   bowl
   be broken . . .
   —Ecclesiastes 12:6

9. But now I know
   That twenty centuries of stony sleep
   Were vexed to nightmare by a rocking cradle,
   And what rough beast, its hour come round at last,
   Slouches towards Bethlehem to be born?
   —"The Second Coming," by William Butler Yeats

10. Kind hearts are more than coronets
    And simple faith than Norman blood.
    —"Lady Clara Vere de Vere,"
    by Alfred, Lord Tennyson

TOWNS AND CITIES

1. Which city was already six thousand years old when it entered history?

2. Where would you go to find Pittsburg?

3. Once called *Aquae Sulis,* after the local deity Sul whom the Romans identified with Minerva, it was formerly one of the most elegant spots in Europe. What is its name today?

4. Which famous lover of London penned these lines?

   > Forgive my transports on a theme like this;
   > I cannot stand a French metropolis.

5. How did Gotham become a name signifying New York City?

6. In a note to his friend and later biographer Cole Lesley, how did Noël Coward announce his return to England after a trip to Istanbul?

7. In the early 1800s, this town was one of the main seafaring ports in the United States, and in fact more people in certain parts of the world recognized its name than they did America's. The name of the town comes from *Shalom,* the Hebrew word for peace, hello and goodbye. Can you identify it?

8. No matter which direction you travel—north, south, east or west—from this U.S. town, you will enter another state, but it will be the same state. Which town are you in, and what state will you enter?

9. What do the following cities have in common: Belgrade, Bratislava, Budapest, Ulm and Vienna?

10. What city was described as a "big hard-boiled city with no more personality than a paper cup," and who called it that?

TOWNS AND CITIES

1. Jericho, whose storming by Joshua, recorded in the Bible, cannot have been earlier than 1450 B.C., but which goes back at least to 8000 B.C., making it the oldest known settlement in the world.

2. Either California, Kansas, Kentucky, New Hampshire, Oklahoma or Texas. To find Pittsburgh you would, of course, go to Pennsylvania.

3. Bath, a city in southwestern England on the Avon. In the 18th century it became the country's most fashionable spa under the auspices of the social arbiter Beau Nash. Its mineral baths are still filled from a reservoir built by the Romans in the first century A.D.

4. Dr. Samuel Johnson, in "London, A Poem."

5. Washington Irving called New York City Gotham in *Salmagundi,* an 1807 series of satirical essays and poems. The name came from a legendary "town of wise fools" in England.

6. "Have just returned from Istanbul where I was an English delight."

7. Salem, Massachusetts, now only an inlet on Massachusetts Bay, its once famous harbor having silted up. Its early history was darkened by the witchcraft trials of 1692.

8. Greenwich, Connecticut. To the north and west is Westchester County, New York, while to the south and east is Long Island, New York.

9. They are all on the Danube.

10. Los Angeles, California, as described by Raymond Chandler's private investigator, Philip Marlowe. In Woody Allen's opinion, the most culturally exciting thing about Los Angeles is that you can turn there on a red light.

TRANSPORTATION

1. Who invented the first American steamboat?

2. The word chauffeur literally means stoker and derives from the French word *chauffer*, to warm. Why is this?

3. What is a portage, and where is a portage not a portage?

4. Kenneth Brown wrote these lines about *Le Train Bleu*, the famous royal blue, all-steel cars of the *Compagnie des Wagons-Lits*, which made their debut at Calais in 1922:

   However dark the times may be
   I oft times in a mirage see
   The sleek blue coaches of the Wagons-Lits
   That greet the traveler on Calais quai.

   Le Train Bleu is, alas, no more, but what two famous trains de luxe of today have the same color?

5. When Joseph H. Choate, the United States Ambassador to the Court of St. James's, left a reception at Claridge's, someone came up to him and said, "Call me a cab." How did the Ambassador reply?

6. Can you name the only moving national historic landmark in the United States?

7. What spot has more vehicular traffic flowing through it than any other place in the world?

8. Many taxi drivers deserve to be called Jehus. Who was Jehu?

9. Between which two northern cities does a train known as the "Moose Gooser" operate?

10. Loelia, Duchess of Westminster, was not much given to riding in buses. What did she have to say about them?

TRANSPORTATION

1. Not Robert Fulton, but John Fitch, who built and operated the first steam vessel on the Delaware River in 1786, 21 years before Fulton's *Clermont* was launched on the Hudson. As the latter was the first steamboat to be commercially successful, Fulton got the credit for inventing it.

2. Many of the early French cars ran on steam, and it was the chauffeur's job to get the steam up before setting off on a trip.

3. A portage is the carrying of boats and supplies overland between two waterways. In the Adirondacks, however, where the use of a French derivation is shunned because of the animosity created during the French and Indian Wars, the word carry is used.

4. The magnificent South African Blue Train *(Die Blautrein)* that runs between Cape Town and Johannesburg. It is usually fully booked a year in advance. The cars of the European segment of the Venice Simplon-Orient-Express are painted a deep royal blue.

5. "You are a cab, sir, but not a hansom cab." A variation on this occurred when Robert Benchley emerged from a Hollywood nightclub and asked a uniformed man to call a cab. The man brusquely informed him that he was an admiral, so Benchley simply said, "Then would you mind getting me a battleship?"

6. San Francisco's hill-climbing cable cars, one of the city's most popular attractions for over a hundred years.

7. The spectacular four-level freeway interchange in downtown Los Angeles, where the Harbor, Hollywood, Pasadena and Santa Ana freeways cross above and below each other.

8. Jehu was a King of Israel whose rapid and reckless chariot driving has become proverbial.

9. The "Moose Gooser" runs between the seaport of Seward and the inland city of Fairbanks, Alaska. The moose use the right of way as a winter highway and sometimes charge the trains during the fall rutting season.

10. "Anyone seen in a bus after the age of thirty has been a failure in life."

U.S. PRESIDENTS

1. Can you name four Presidents who are not buried in the United States?

2. In the event of a President dying in office, what is the order of succession after the Vice-President?

3. What curious aspect attached to John Tyler's cabinet?

4. When he was a young lawyer practicing in Springfield, Illinois, Abraham Lincoln tore the seat of his trousers just before appearing in court. The other lawyers passed a subscription paper to buy him a new pair of pants. What did Lincoln write after his name?

5. Whose Presidency was such a disaster that Senator Charles Sumner, chairman of the committee on foreign relations, told the Senate that the country was suffering from "a dropsical nepotism swollen to elephantiasis"?

6. Unknown to the public, one Chief Executive became critically ill with cancer of the jaw and underwent successful surgery aboard the private yacht *Oneida*, cruising near New York City, before it headed up Long Island Sound to his summer home in Marion, Massachusetts. Who was he?

7. After President Theodore Roosevelt explained to his cabinet the recognition of the Republic of Panama and twelve days later signed a treaty authorizing the construction of a canal there, he asked whether he had explained his actions satisfactorily. What was Secretary of War Elihu Root's reply?

8. Who quoted his father as saying, "If you were a girl, you'd be in a family way all the time. You can't say no"?

9. "I haven't checked these figures, but 87 years ago, I think it was, a number of individuals organized a governmental setup here in this country." Whose speaking style is parodied here?

10. During the Democratic Convention of 1960, Lyndon B. Johnson, referring to the possibility of sharing the ticket with John F. Kennedy, confided to Clare Boothe Luce, "Clare, honey, no way will I ever join that son of a bitch." Later, at an inaugural ball, how did he cynically explain to her his change of mind?

U.S. PRESIDENTS

1. Richard M. Nixon, Gerald R. Ford, James E. Carter and Ronald W. Reagan.

2. Two elected officials—the Speaker of the House and the President *pro tempore* of the Senate—and two appointed officials—the Secretary of State and the Secretary of the Treasury.

3. Tyler's first Cabinet, inherited from William Henry Harrison, all resigned to protest his policies, and his subsequent Secretaries of State and of the Navy were blown up when a ten-ton gun exploded aboard the U.S.S. *Princeton*.

4. "I can contribute nothing to the end in sight."

5. U.S. Grant's, because he appointed so many old friends to office.

6. Grover Cleveland. The news of both the illness and the operation in 1893 was kept from the press and the public until many years after he left the Presidency.

7. "You certainly have, Mr. President," Elihu Root assured him. "You have shown that you were accused of seduction and have conclusively proved that you were guilty of rape."

8. Warren G. Harding, revealing how his genial, complacent nature had once been characterized by his father.

9. Dwight D. Eisenhower's, whose syntax, particularly at ad-lib conferences, was notoriously convoluted. This parody of the beginning of Lincoln's Gettysburg Address was written by the historian Oliver Jensen.

10. "Clare, I looked it up: One out of every four Presidents has died in office. I'm a gambling man, darlin', and this is the only chance I got."

1. After President Bonaparte made himself Emperor Napoleon III, Nicholas I of Russia would only address him as *"Mon ami,"* not, as Emperor to Emperor, "Mon frère." When the Russian Ambassador had rather awkwardly given him the first dispatch so indited, what was Napoleon III's amiable comment?

2. *Modern Warfare,* by General Tom Thumb, and *Hansard's Guide to Refreshing Sleep* (Hansard prints the full text of parliamentary speeches) were part of Charles Dickens' library at Gad's Hill. How do you account for these curious titles?

3. If you went into a store in Paris and asked to see a *brassière,* what would you be shown?

4. When H.R.H. Prince Philip was asked how he liked living in Buckingham Palace, what did he answer?

5. During World War II, who was second in command to General Eisenhower of the Allied invasion forces?

6. The person who invented the bifurcated dagger invented what?

7. How would a symbolic mixture of these elements help a headache: arsenic, phosphorus, iridium and indium?

8. Can you explain the origin of the name Charing Cross in London?

9. Identify the "Mountain of Light," which is now in Great Britain but is claimed by Pakistan.

10. After George S. Kaufman's partner in a bridge game had made an utter mess of one hand, he asked Kaufman how he would have played the hand. What response did he get?

VARIETY SHOW

1. "God gives us our brothers, but we choose our friends."

2. They were dummy spines of books used by Dickens to hide some woodwork.

3. A shoulder strap for knapsacks or an infant's harness. What we call a brassiere is known in France as a *soutien-gorge,* or breast supporter.

4. "It's just like living above the store."

5. Marshal of the Royal Air Force Sir Arthur William Tedder, whose title was Deputy Supreme Commander and who, oddly enough, started out as a naval historian. (General Walter Bedell Smith was chief of staff to General Eisenhower.)

6. The fork.

7. Their chemical symbols spell aspirin: arsenic, As; phosphorus, P; iridium, Ir; Indium, In.

8. Charing Cross is named after the original Eleanor Cross, which marked the last resting place of the coffin of Eleanor of Castile, Queen Consort of Edward I, on its way to burial in Westminster Abbey in 1290. Later this area was associated with charcoal burning—hence Charing.

9. The Koh-i-noor Diamond, weighing 108.9 carats, which is set in the Queen Mother's crown.

10. "Under an assumed name."

WAR GAMES

1. The loss of which French city by the English in 1453 ended the Hundred Years War?

2. In 1757, the British, with only a few thousand men, conquered Bengal. In 1857 the Enfield rifle replaced the old musket, and because of it the British were faced with the Great Indian Mutiny. Why?

3. An aiguillette is an ornamental cord worn around the shoulder by naval or military aides. What connection does it have with a hangman's noose?

4. If he had been a naval commander today, and well versed in bureaucratic jargon, he might have said, "Area accessed in combat mode; mission finished." Instead he said, "We have met the enemy and they are ours." Who sent this message, and on what occasion?

5. Bull Run and Manassas, Antietam and Sharpsburg, Stones River and Murfreesboro—these are all famous Civil War battles. What is curious about each pair of names?

6. When a temperance committee asked President Lincoln to fire General Grant because he drank too much, what did the President reply?

7. "Russia has two generals in whom she can confide—Generals Janvier and Février" was whose observation?

8. Amid the early disasters of the Boer War, who sent this message to which future Prime Minister: "Please understand there is no depression in this house and we are not interested in the possibilities of defeat; they do not exist"?

9. The artist Frederick Remington was a war correspondent for the Hearst papers before the Spanish-American War. After a period of inactivity, Remington asked to be allowed to leave Cuba, as there was no war to cover. What did Hearst cable back?

10. The U.S. Army Rangers, similar to the British commando units, are soldiers specially trained to fight in small groups and undertake surprise raids in any terrain or weather. From what do they derive their name?

WAR GAMES

1. Bordeaux. Only Calais remained in English hands.

2. The English cartridge was coated with grease so it could pass easily down the barrel of a gun. The Indians believed that the grease was cow or pig fat. As the cow is sacred to the Hindu and the pig is an unclean animal to the Muslim, the Indian soldiers in the Bengal Army were outraged.

3. During the French Revolutionary Wars a Dutch regiment under Prince William of Orange panicked under fire and were ordered to wear a hangman's noose around their shoulders as an ominous warning. The next day the regiment performed bravely and was permitted to wear the rope permanently as a mark of honor.

4. Oliver Hazard Perry, in a dispatch from the U.S. brig *Niagara* to General William Henry Harrison, announcing his victory over the British at the Battle of Lake Erie in 1813.

5. Each pair refers to the same battle, the first name in each pair being the Union terminology. Union commanders tended to name the battles, if possible, from the nearest important river, while Confederate generals chose the name of the nearest railhead.

6. "If you tell me the brand of whiskey Grant drinks, I would like to send a barrel of it to the other generals."

7. Czar Nicholas I, referring to the frigid months of January and February. (When he died in February 1855, *Punch* magazine printed a cartoon of the Czar in bed and Death, in a military uniform, standing beside him with one bony hand on his chest. The caption read: "General Février turned traitor.")

8. Queen Victoria, in an 1899 letter to Arthur Balfour. Prime Minister Churchill was so impressed with the sentiment that he had it prominently displayed in his secret War Cabinet Room under Whitehall.

9. "PLEASE REMAIN. YOU FURNISH PICTURES AND I'LL FURNISH THE WAR."

10. Roger's Rangers, a group of expert woodsmen commanded by Major Robert Rogers in the French and Indian Wars.

WATER HAZARD

1. Which common verb derives from Maiandros, a river in the ancient region of Phrygia in what is now central Turkey?

2. The *Pontus Euxinus* (Hospitable Sea) is a bit of a misnomer. By which name do we now know it?

3. According to which fly-by-night hotel manager and Florida land salesman, what kind of water was discovered by Hernando de Soto?

4. What is wrong with the phrase "Still waters run deep"?

5. What prompted President Lincoln's poetic announcement to a still-divided country: "The Father of Waters again goes unvexed to the sea"?

6. In the words of whom, what comes "from haunts of coot and hern"?

7. Why is the Missouri River called the Big Muddy?

8.   The great seas number seven,
          And I've seen them in my day;
          But there's nowhere nearer heaven
          Than Tobermory Bay.

    Can you name the Seven Seas, and where is Tobermory Bay?

9. From the east coast of Florida you usually see large ships steaming south, but never north. How do you account for this?

10. A former gun-runner and soldier of fortune, now a saloon keeper, explains to the police that he "came to Casablanca for the waters." On being told that Casablanca borders on the desert, how does he laconically reply?

WATER HAZARD

1. Meander, which means to follow a winding and turning course.

2. The Black Sea, which has a climate that has been described as "four months cold and eight months winter." As George Gordon, Lord Byron observed in *Don Juan:*

   There's not a sea the passenger e'er pukes in,
   Turns up more dangerous breakers than the Euxine.

3. In *Cocoanuts* [sic] Groucho Marx says, "You've all heard of the water that they've named after him: de Soto water."

4. By their very definition, still waters do not run at all.

5. The surrender of Vicksburg in July 1863, which once again opened the Mississippi to trade.

6. The brook, in one of the refrains from Alfred, Lord Tennyson's poem of the same name:

   I come from haunts of coot and hern,
   I make a sudden sally,
   And sparkle out among the fern,
   To bicker down a valley.

7. "It's too thick to drink and too thin to plough."

8. The Seven Seas are the Arctic and Antarctic, North and South Pacific, North and South Atlantic and the Indian oceans. Tobermory Bay lies off the little port of Tobermory on the Scottish Island of Mull.

9. Northbound ships take advantage of the Gulf Stream, which flows north at about four miles per hour just over the horizon.

10. "I was misinformed," says Rick Blaine (Humphrey Bogart), dryly dodging the questions of Captain Louis Renault (Claude Rains) at the end of the film *Casablanca.*

WAY OUT WEST

1. "Git along, little dogie" is a popular Western refrain. What precisely is a dogie?

2. The 1848 Treaty of Guadalupe-Hidalgo with Mexico described the new U.S.–Mexico boundary vaguely, but what was the real reason that President Franklin Pierce arranged for the Gadsden Purchase in 1853, whereby the United States purchased about 30,000 square miles of land for $10 million along the Rio Grande in southern Arizona and New Mexico?

3. Owen Wister wrote *The Virginian,* whose success marked him as the founding father of the Western novel. What is the most famous line in the book, and who said it?

4. Which city lays claim to being the Gateway to the West, and what did it build to symbolize this?

5. James Wilson Marshall made a singular contribution to the opening up of the West. What did he do, and what happened to him as a result?

6. Of the many who went west in 1849, Levi Strauss hoped to make a fortune selling what for which specific purpose?

7. What did Robert Leroy Parker and Henry Longbaugh have to do with one of the biggest-grossing pictures of its day, and what happened to them?

8. Which Italian opera takes place in 19th-century California, where Minnie owned a bar called The Polka?

9. Everyone has heard of the Chisholm Trail and the Oregon Trail, but what was the Honeymoon Trail?

10. Which was the only Western film to win an Academy Award?

WAY OUT WEST

1. A dogie is a range term for a motherless or stray calf.

2. This area was the only practicable route for the southern railroad to the Pacific. The purchase was negotiated by James Gadsden, a railroad promoter and diplomat.

3. "When you call me that, smile," spoken by the Virginian, by which name alone he is known to the reader.

4. St. Louis, Missouri. The 630-foot-high Gateway Arch, designed by Eero Saarinen, dominates the city's skyline.

5. In 1848 Marshall discovered gold in the tailrace of the Swiss pioneer John A. Sutter's sawmill, of which he was a partner, on the American River at Coloma, California. By the end of the year, the word had spread and the Gold Rush of '49 followed. The claims of Sutter and Marshall were ignored, the mill failed for want of lumber and the two men were financially ruined.

6. Denim cloth to make tents for the 80,000 prospectors and miners. Because of the mild climate, however, Strauss found that the miners did not need tents, but did require tough pants that would withstand hard wear. A tailor by profession, he used his denim material for pants and his fortune was made.

7. They were the real names of the subjects of the film *Butch Cassidy and the Sundance Kid,* starring Paul Newman and Robert Redford.

8. *La Fanciulla del West (The Girl of the Golden West)* by Giacomo Puccini, who adapted it from a play produced on Broadway by David Belasco.

9. In the mid-1800s most Mormons settled in Utah, but a large number went to Arizona and New Mexico. If the latter wanted to marry, however, they had to use the temple in Utah, and so a seventy-mile trail was blazed from Palm Spring, Arizona, to St. George, Utah.

10. The only Western to win an Academy Award was the 1931 film *Cimarron,* starring Richard Dix and Irene Dunne.

WINE LIST

1. When Marie Antoinette served champagne, she used glasses made from wax molds that were exact replicas of her breasts. This evolved into the shallow, wide bottom coupe glass that has what three disadvantages?

2. There are two other shapes of champagne glasses in common use. What are they, and which is preferable? And how should the glass be held?

3. Of these six wines, name the odd man out: Château Belgrave, Château de Bellevue, Château Kirwan, Château Talbot, Château de Tertre, Château Clarke-Rothschild.

4. What is wrong with serving a superb sauterne such as Château d'Yquem with the dessert?

5. To whom are these lines addressed, by whom?

   > Drink to me only with thine eyes;
   > And I will pledge with mine;
   > Or leave a kiss but in the cup
   > And I'll not look for wine.

6. Wine has legs, which the Germans called *Kirchenfenster*, or church windows. What are they?

7.   Have some Madeira m'dear; you really have
         nothing to fear.
      I'm not trying to tempt you—that wouldn't be
         right.
      You shouldn't drink spirits at this time of night.
      Have some Madeira m'dear. It's really much nicer
         than beer.

   So went the English music hall ballad. Can you name the four basic variations of Madeira?

8. Explain the connection between the number of this question and Methuselah.

9. What dubious distinction is held by two wines named Bosca and Omar Khayyam?

10. Boots Poffenberger, a one-time pitcher for the Detroit Tigers, had a fondness for wine. When he had to have an appendectomy, how did a Detroit sports writer report the news?

WINE LIST

1. The bubbles disappear quickly, there is no aroma and the wine gets warm.

2. The tulip and the flute. The tulip is the preferred shape, as the bowl curves in at the mouth to retain the bouquet and the glass is tapered to a point where it joins the stem, so that the bubbles rise from a single point. The flute, shaped like a narrow elongated V, does not retain the bouquet, nor does it hold very much. A champagne glass should always be held by the stem or base, never by the bowl.

3. Château de Bellevue is a red Beaujolais; the others are Bordeaux.

4. Nothing except the spelling of the wine, which is always Sauternes, after the region of the Medoc where it is produced, and not sauterne.

5. Celia, by Ben Jonson in his poem "To Celia."

6. Legs are the lines of a colorless glycerin that make their way down the inside of the glass. As these lines descend they form nearly perfect Gothic arches.

7. Madeira, named for a Portuguese island off the west coast of Africa, is produced as sercial, verdelho, bual and malmsey. Sercial and verdelho are the drier of the four and should be drunk chilled as an aperitif. Bual and malmsey are sweeter and should be drunk after a meal. A fifth variety, called rainwater, is a blend that resembles sercial.

8. A Methuselah is a bottle containing the equivalent of eight normal-sized bottles of champagne.

9. According to Alexis Lichine, author of the definitive *Encyclopedia of Wines and Spirits,* these are the worst wines in the world. Bosca is produced south of Bombay and Omar Khayyam emanates from Egypt.

10. "Boots Poffenberger, the wandering right-hander, who is also known as a wine taster, was operated on the other day for appendicitis. I'm no doctor, but I do hope the surgeon opened Boots up at room temperature."

WOMEN

1. *Lucy, The Beginnings of Mankind,* by Johanson and Edey, was a bestseller about the discovery in northern Ethiopia of "Lucy," the oldest, most complete and best-preserved skeleton of an erect-walking human ancestor ever found. Why was she named Lucy?

2. Who invoked the goddess Mirth to let him live with her, first amid the delights of rustic beauty, then in the "towered cities" amongst the "busy hum of men" in a poem that contains this quartet?

    > Haste thee Nymph, and bring with thee
    > Jest and youthful jollity
    > Quips and cranks, and wanton wiles
    > Nods, and becks, and wreathéd smiles.

3. Can you name the first woman to earn her living by the pen?

4. A madam is a brothel keeper, but who or what was popularly known as "The Madame"?

5. Who was "the lady with the lamp," and what is the meaning of the phrase?

6. How did the young Graham Greene, as a film critic, describe the carriage of Jean Harlow?

7. Which two-time Olympic gold medal winner was voted by the Associated Press in 1950 Woman Athlete of the Half-Century for the variety of sports she excelled in?

8. Poontang is a southern vulgarism for a "piece of ass." How did the term arise?

9. Name the first three women to be portrayed on a stamp for the Great Americans series.

10. According to the old limerick, what was the chief pleasure of "naughty old Sappho of Greece"?

WOMEN

1. When the paleontologists were celebrating in camp on the night of their discovery, a tape of the Beatles' song "Lucy in the Sky with Diamonds" was playing. (The capital letters in this title, incidentally, spell LSD.)

2. John Milton, in "L'Allegro" (the cheerful man, in Italian).

3. Aphra Behn, the 17th-century poet, playwright and novelist. She was witty, gifted and prolific: for 17 years no London season went by without a play from her, which drove dramatists like William Wycherley, whose total output was four plays, wild with envy.

4. The guillotine, which was extensively used during the French Revolution. From the time it went into operation until its retirement, "The Madame" had lopped off over 8,000 heads.

5. Florence Nightingale, the Englishwoman who is considered the founder of modern nursing. By the end of the Crimean War she had become a legend for her services in the field. She was called "the lady with the lamp" because she believed that a nurse's care was never-ceasing, night or day.

6. "She toted a breast as a man totes a gun."

7. Mildred "Babe" Didrikson Zaharias. The Babe won gold medals in the javelin throw and the 80-meter hurdles in the 1932 Olympics. Later she gained far greater fame as a champion golfer, winning 17 consecutive tournaments in the 1946–7 season.

8. Poontang is a corruption of the French *putain*, prostitute.

9. Pearl Buck, the only woman to win both a Nobel and a Pulitzer Prize for Literature; Rachel Carson, the scientist and environmentalist; and Dorothea Dix, the humanitarian and crusader for the poor and the mentally handicapped.

10.	Naughty old Sappho of Greece,
	Said, "What I prefer to a piece
		Is to have my pudenda
		Rubbed by the enda
	This little pink nose of my niece."

1. What astonishing feat did Lieutenant Gunther Prien, in command of the German submarine U-47, accomplish in October 1939?

2. Bill Mauldin drew a memorable cartoon of two battle-weary GIs, Joe and Willy, crouching in the rubble while enemy shells screamed overhead. What comment did Joe make to Willy?

3. Which branch of what service had as its motto "We build for the fighters, and we fight for what we build"?

4. How did it happen that, in only three minutes during the morning of May 4, 1942, American aircraft ensured that Japan would not win World War II?

5. To what use was something with the code name of "window" put during the war?

6. After the Japanese claimed in 1944 that most of the U.S. Third Fleet had either been sunk or had retired, what signal did Admiral William F. Halsey, Jr., make to Pearl Harbor?

7. In June 1944, it came to pass that Jupiter's wife, a metal blade, two more or less western states and a precious metal lay in close proximity. Can you clarify this matter?

8. They were considered expendable, a word popularized in the title of a book by W. L. White, *They Were Expendable*. Who or what were they, and which of them became the most famous "expendable" of the lot?

9. The German rocket bombs against England towards the end of the war were called buzzbombs or doodlebugs by the English, and V-1s or V-2s by the Germans. What does the V stand for? And where does Operation Crossbow come in?

10. Referring to his difficulties in dealing with General Charles de Gaulle, who said, "Of all the crosses I ever had to bear, the heaviest was the Cross of Lorraine"?

WORLD WAR II

1. Prien penetrated the defenses of Scapa Flow, the main anchorage of the Royal Navy in the Orkneys, and sank the battleship *Ark Royal*, the flagship of the 2nd Battle Squadron of the Home Fleet.

2. "I feel like a fugitive from the law of averages." Mauldin's war cartoons appeared chiefly in the *Stars and Stripes* and later were collected in his book *Up Front*. In 1945 he won the Pulitzer Prize for Journalism.

3. The Construction Battalions of the U.S. Navy, who were known as CBs or Seabees.

4. Dive bombers from the carriers *Enterprise* and *Yorktown* sank three Japanese carriers during the Battle of Midway. It was a strategic turning point in the war and a blow from which the Japanese Navy never recovered.

5. "Window" was the name given for strips of metal foil dropped from airplanes as a radar countermeasure.

6. "OUR SHIPS HAVE BEEN SALVAGED AND ARE RETIRING AT HIGH SPEED TOWARD THE JAPANESE FLEET."

7. Juno, Sword, Utah, Omaha and Gold were the code names given to the five Normandy beaches where the Allied forces landed on D-Day, June 6th, 1944.

8. The PT boats, including their officers and men. The film made from it starred Robert Montgomery as Lieutenant (now Rear Admiral) John D. Bulkeley, who brought General Douglas MacArthur out of Bataan in March 1942. The most famous "expendable" was John F. Kennedy, who was unique in the annals of PTs in that he was the only officer to get his boat, PT 109, which lay dead in the water, sunk by collision with an enemy ship, the Japanese destroyer *Amigiri*. Naval men still wonder at this feat of seamanship.

9. The V stands for *Vergeltungswaffe,* meaning retribution weapon. Operation Crossbow was the name given to the Allied air attacks on the German rocket sites.

10. No one knows. When asked about it after the war, Churchill grunted, "No, I didn't say it; but I'm sorry I didn't, because it is quite witty . . . and so true."

"AND THE END"

1. Fill in the blank spaces and explain the meaning of the words: "I am ——— ——— ———, the beginning and the end, the first and the last."

2. The word taps—the bugle call—derives from what final act by Dutch barkeeps?

3. Who would only rest content if his heart was buried at Wounded Knee?

4. What was the concise last order of the (British) Indian Army?

5. In *Algiers,* starring Charles Boyer and Hedy Lamarr, Boyer was dying in the arms of the detective, who said, "I'm sorry, Pepe. He thought you were going to escape." What did Boyer say as he died?

6. He was known as the Master to his friends, and thinking of them, he wrote this last poem.

> When I have fears, as Keats had fears,
> Of the moment I'll cease to be,
> I console myself with vanished years
> Remembered laughter, remembered tears,
> And the peace of the changing sea.

7. What are the last words of these animals?

   a) the weasel
   b) the walrus
   c) the hare
   d) the skunk
   e) the camel

   f) the dragon
   g) the snail
   h) the pig
   i) the cat
   j) the dog

8. Which St. Louis–born poet penned these lines?

> What we call the beginning is often the end.
> And to make an end is to make a beginning.

9. In what felicitous manner did Will Durant end *The Life of Greece*?

10. Near the end of which famous novel, who decides the following—a sentiment with which the author of this book thoroughly concurs: ". . . and so there ain't nothing more to write about, and I am rotten glad of it, because if I'd 'a' knowed what a trouble it was to make a book I wouldn't 'a' tackled it, and ain't a-going to no more"?

"AND THE END"

1. "Alpha and Omega," the first and last letters of the Greek alphabet. The line, spoken by the Lord, may be found in Revelation 22:13. (It is an expansion of Revelation 1:8, with which it is often confused.)

2. When the time came for soldiers to return to camp, the barkeeps would call *tap toe*, meaning turn off the taps. The actual melody of taps that we know today was composed during the Civil War.

3. Stephen Vincent Benét, who wrote in his poem "American Names":

   > I shall not rest quiet in Montparnasse.
   > I shall not lie easy at Winchelsea.
   > You may bury my body in Sussex grass,
   > You may bury my tongue at Champmédy.
   > I shall not be there. I shall rise and pass.
   > Bury my heart at Wounded Knee.

4. "This is the last Indian Army Order."

5. "And so I have, my friend." (The famous line "Come with me to the Casbah" was never said by Charles Boyer to Hedy Lamarr, for the simple reason that he never left the Casbah—until, of course, the end of the film.)

6. Noël Coward, who died in 1973 at his beloved hilltop home Firefly about Port Maria in Jamaica, where he wrote these lines.

7. a) "Pop!"
   b) "The time has come."
   c) "Over to you, tortoise."
   d) "Strew on me, roses, roses."
   e) "I feel the penultimate straw."
   f) "Where's St. George?"
   g) "This house to let."
   h) "I hope to save my bacon."
   i) "I am going to look at a king."
   j) "I have passed the last lamppost."

8. T.S. Eliot in "Little Gidding," one of his *Four Quartets*.

9. "For those of you who have come this far: Thank you for your unseen but ever-felt companionship."

10. Huckleberry Finn, in Mark Twain's best-known work.

ABOUT THE AUTHOR

Norman G. Hickman, an executive in the mining and investment business, is a graduate of the Hotchkiss School and Yale University and is a Churchill Fellow of Westminster College.

During World War II he served as a PT boat commander in both the Mediterranean and the Pacific, and was awarded the British Distinguished Service Cross and the U.S. Bronze Star.

He was associate producer of two films, which were nominated for Academy Awards, *The Finest Hours* and *A King's Story,* and is the author of *The Quintessential Quiz Book* and, with his wife Minnie, of *The Quintessential Quiz Book 2* and *Quizzes for Whizzes.*

Minnie and Norman Hickman live in New York City, Southampton and London.

PERMISSIONS

Grateful acknowledgment is made to the following for permission to reprint previously published material:

A.D. Peters & Co., London, for *Sonnets and Verse,* by Hilaire Belloc.

Bruce L. Felknor for his article "Intelligencewise."

Dodd, Mead & Co. for *The Collected Poems of Rupert Brooke.*

Doubleday & Co. for *Fractured French* © 1950 by Fred S. Pearson.

Faber & Faber Ltd. and Harcourt Brace Jovanovich Inc. for *Collected Poems 1909–1962* and *Old Possum's Book of Practical Cats,* © 1939, 1943, 1963, 1964 by T.S. Eliot and renewed by Esmé Valerie Eliot.

G.P. Putman's Sons for *Spilt Milk* © 1942, 1969 by Morris Bishop.

Weidenfeld & Nicolson for *Noël Coward and His Friends* by Cole Lesley, Graham Payne and Sheridan Morley.

Little, Brown & Co. for *The Face Is Familiar* © 1940 by Ogden Nash. First appeared in *The Saturday Evening Post* (Curtis Publishing Co.).

New Directions Publishing for *A Child's Christmas in Wales* and *Under Milk Wood* © 1954 by Dylan Thomas.

Norma Millay Ellis for *Collected Poems,* Harper & Row, © 1921, 1948 by Edna St. Vincent Millay.

Oliver Jensen for *The Gettysburg Address in Eisenhower.*

Random House for *Academic Graffiti* © 1971 by W. H. Auden and *Cautionary Verse* by Hilaire Belloc and published by Alfred A. Knopf, Inc.

Simon & Schuster for *Earthly Powers* © 1980 by Anthony Burgess and *The Most of S.J. Perelman* © 1930–58 by S.J. Perelman.

Workman Publishing Co. for *Sailing* © 1981 by Henry Beard and Rod McKie.